THE STEWARDSHIP OF COMMAND

MANAGING IN TURBULENT TIMES

For the Manager Who Manages Managers

A Primer for the Newly Appointed Executive

A Refresher for the Veteran

Book two of the Stewardship of Management Series

Like a ship at sea, an organization will accomplish its mission or founder, depending on how it is managed.

Lawrence Wade Johnson

1407070707

THE STEWARDSHIP OF COMMAND

MANAGING IN TURBULENT TIMES

For the Manager Who Manages Managers

A Primer for the New Executive, a Refresher for the Veteran

The world of top-level management belongs to the bold. As every successful manager knows, rewards are granted for results, not for effort.

Executive Managers are the stewards of the organization's resources, the natural custodians of its stability, its reputation, its methods, and its future. The chief executive is the chief steward.

ISBN-13: 978-1456557324

ISBN-10: 1456557327

©2011 Lawrence Wade Johnson
©2013 Lawrence Wade Johnson

All rights reserved

Raven Publications
PO Box 1486
Clinton, Tennessee 37717

Acknowledgements

I am indebted to those who read the manuscript and provided me with the benefit of their thinking regarding the delivery method, the believability of the case study, the connection of the case study to the management assessments and the value of the management philosophy I used in the executive assessments.

Captain Ron Eslinger, MS., USN retired
Captain Harold D. Oshucha, MA. USN retired
Colonel Gary Goff Ph.D., US Army Special Forces retired
        President Roane State Community College
Paul Phillips, Ed.D. Former Assistant Superintendent Dade County Florida Schools

Thanks to these sailors who provided me with some sea stories to add to the adventure:

Robert Howard
Raymond Cadwallader
Gene Stockdale
Ed Osborne

My very special thanks to:

Commander Bruce Bevard, USNR-R Nuclear Submarine Officer
Leon G. Jaquet, Veteran's Service Officer & Retired Senior Chief.

I also want to thank these fine folks.
Cindy Van Sandt
Ken Swiger
David Truan
Paul Goldberg
Bruce Horne, Ph.D.
Jutta Bangs
Wayne Berry

Cover design by Steve Sharp (steve_sharp@comcast.net)

THE STEWARDSHIP OF COMMAND
Managing in Turbulent Times for the Manager Who Manages Managers

Preface	9
Chapter 1 – History and Fitness	11
The Ship	14
The Ship's Company	16
Managing culture, tradition and structure in Turbulent Times	17
Chapter 2 – The Shake Down Cruise	21
Executive Assessment: Strengthening The Team with Replacements	30
Chapter 3 – Planning for Turbulent Times	35
Executive Assessment: Plans for Crises Management	37
Risk Management	38
Crises Management	39
Command Axioms	
Chapter 4 – Battle Plans	42
Executive Assessment Assessing the Probability of Success (Using SWOT)	60
Strategic Planning	61
Command Axioms	62
Chapter 5 – Assembling the Team	63
Executive Assessment Testing The Crew and the plan	68
Empowering the crew to test, tweak and implement	69
Creating an Atmosphere for Success Expectation	69
Command Axioms	70
Chapter 6 – Trouble begins	71
Executive Assessment Crises Management Plans Activated	82
Command Axioms	84
Chapter 7 – The Storm Before the Turbulence	85
Executive Assessment Weathering The Storm	106
Command Axioms	108
Chapter 8 – After the Storm Reinstating Normal Operations	109
Reinstating Normal Operations	116
Command Axioms	117
Chapter 9 – Situation Normal	
Executive Assessment Dealing with Minor Crises During the Crises	126
Command Axioms	126
Chapter 10 – Anticipating the Onslaught	127
Executive Assessment – Employing the Team – When the Plan is Threatened	135
Command Axioms	136
Chapter 11 – The Fun (If you can call it that) Begins	137
Executive Assessment Functioning as a Team in the Midst of the Crises	145
Command Axioms	146

Chapter 12 Fear and Faith During times of Crises	147
Executive Assessment Fear and Faith in the Crises	151
Command Axioms	152
Chapter 13 When Bad Things Happen in Clusters During the Crises	153
Executive Assessment – Cluster Headaches	102
Command Axioms	160
Chapter 14 Finally a Break!	161
Executive Assessment – Awareness Learning Under Pressure	172
The Right Person in the Right Job	172
Command Axioms	173
Chapter 15 The Hits Just Keep on Coming	174
Executive Assessment Staying Abreast of Trends	182
Chapter 16 - Facing the Unexpected Threat	183
Executive Assessment Taking risks –	187
Making what could be irrevocable choices under conditions of uncertainty	187
Chapter 17 – When things go very, very, very wrong	192
Executive Assessment When things go very, very, very wrong	205
The Burden of the One in Command	134
Command Axioms	206
Chapter 18 - The Aftermath - Recovery Management	135
Executive Assessment After action Assessment	209
Assessing the situation	210
Assess the risk:	210
Evaluate alternatives	211
Evaluate Progress	211
Dealing with outcomes	212
After Action review	212
Chapter 19 Weathering the Consequences	213
Executive Assessment After Action Learning	222
Command Axioms	223
Chapter 20 The return voyage home	224
Executive Assessment When Sabotage Caused the Turbulence	231
After Action learning -2	232
Chapter 21 They sailed out with shame they returned with fame	233
Command Axiom:	236
The Captain	237
Glossary of Naval Terms	238
The Navy Hymn	245
Anchors Aweigh	246

Preface

The Stewardship of Command – Managing in Turbulent Times is the second book in two book executive management series by Lawrence Wade Johnson. The first book ***The Stewardship of Executive Management – for the Manager who Manages Managers*** introduced the USS WARREN LYNN CARD (DE 383) as the vehicle for illustrating the executive principles covered in the book. In this first book the case study began when Robert Mills was appointed to command a very dysfunctional organization and how he brought it up to combat readiness.

This second book continues where the first book ended. The crew of the *Card* takes the ship to the U.S. Naval base in Guantanamo Bay Cuba to participate in combat readiness exercises. During this cruise the ship and the crew experience not only the rigors of a very realistic combat training exercise, they also experience an onslaught of dangerous do or die situations that test their mettle as managers and maritime professionals. The experiences of the crew are compared with the turbulent times faced by commercial and industrial organizations in the private sector. Like the first book, the author provides expert advice and management axioms for handling those difficult situations drawn from his 40 plus years serving in the executive function and as a professional consultant to management.

The *U.S.S. Card* is a fictitious ship. The model for the ship itself was taken from two ships on which the author served; *USS Mills (DE-383)* was an *Edsall*-class destroyer escort built for the U.S. Navy during World War II, and the *USS Roberts* (DE 749) a *Cannon*-class destroyer escort also built for the United States Navy during World War II. The officers and crew are also fictitious.

Why a ship? A ship is an excellent composite organization. Like a self-contained ship at sea, organizations reach their objective, or fail, depending on how the combined technical and interpersonal skills of its people are utilized. The story of the ship is simply the framework around which the principles of management are exposited.

Why a U.S. Naval Reserve Force Ship? The military provides a clearly defined operational organization and unity of command. The members of such an organization could be less homogeneous; a wider variety of motives, intensity and involvement can be ascribed to them for the purposes of analysis and discussion.

Quite some time back, the Department of Defense decided that reserve units should be able to join the active duty forces without delays for extensive upgrading and training; consequently both the Captain and the Executive Officer are now on full-time active duty rather than participating in the management of the ship only on weekends or other occasions. This arrangement did not work as well, for the purposes of this book, so the former arrangement was retained.

The factors examined in this work are timeless. Human nature does not change as the centuries go by, thus the management of human beings does not change as well. The story takes place in the early 1970's. Women were not assigned to ships until the 1990's. Women were included in the story since the management of human beings in the work place has included women since the late 1920's.

Chapter 1

History and Fitness

USS WARREN LYNN CARD (DE 383) is a fully commissioned US Navy warship, permanently assigned to the Naval Reserve Force for almost 7 years. As a Naval Reserve Force vessel the *Card* has performed in a number of roles as task group escort and anti-submarine warfare over her lifetime. While she was never involved in actual hostile action, she and others of reserve destroyer squadron 34 has set sail with less than 12 hours notice to embark on secret missions involving submarine detection and control off the eastern coast of the United States.

One weekend a month the reserve crew comes on board and takes the ship out to sea for a training drill. The *Card's* major sea-going activities are an annual exercise in which the *Card* rendezvous with the rest of the destroyer squadron in Mayport, Florida. From there they sail into Guantanamo Bay, Cuba, for a four-day intensive combat exercise followed by two days in a Caribbean liberty port, and a five day voyage back to the home port.

When Commander Mills took command of the *Card* in February, the *Card* had suffered from neglect more than most reserve ships. The never-ending battle against rust, equipment failure, and general deterioration had only been approached in a half-hearted manner. As a result, the Card had been unable to join the squadron for the annual combat readiness exercise for the past two years.

Moreover, an accumulation of equipment problems primarily in the engine room have prevented her from leaving the pier for over nine months. In that condition, the ship did not warrant a space at the D & S piers (Destroyer & Submarine) at the Navy Yard, so ComResDesRon (commander Reserve Destroyer Squadron) had it towed to a special pier near the Coast Guard Yard, where it has been for the past six months. Having the worst record on station for "getting under way", the name "*CARD*" has been corrupted to "CARP" by the *Card's* own ship's company and other ships' crews -- the implication being that she's only fit to wallow in the mud.

The *Card* had the worst advancement record in the Navy. This held true for both officers and enlisted, for regular Navy and reservists. A major obstacle had been the ship's limited amount of underway time. The officers and enlisted alike were unable to perform operations which were required for advancement that could only be gotten at sea.

While three of the officers had experience "conning" the ship, only two had ever performed the task of "conning the ship" alongside a refueling tanker. None of the enlisted helmsmen or throttle men advanced, as they should.

Additionally, the lack of a concerted on-the-job training program meant that only the most dedicated and motivated of the enlisted were able to pass the examinations required for their advancement.

Advancement tests for sailors E-5 and above required testing while the ship was at sea. In short, the *USS Card* was a career dead-end for all who were assigned to it and they knew it well. The Navy's target for re-enlistment for reserve sailors was above 60%. Most ships were above 50%, but the re-enlistment rate on the *Card* hovered at around 13%.

The Captain identified part of the problem as a bad attitude on the ship. Job performance, job behavior and military bearing of the officers and the crew were unacceptable. It is easy to understand why there was no commitment to discipline, no commitment to the mission, no commitment to the organization, and the only cooperation between departments is to maintain the status quo. There is no real job involvement.

A ship of the *Card's* class would normally carry a crew of 8 officers and 201 enlisted personnel; manpower shortages and the Card's dismal record combined to have her complement cut to 22 regular navy full time enlisted who form the "Nucleus Crew" who man her everyday and 98 Reserve enlisted men and 31 reserve enlisted women (151) and 9 officers. When the reserves come aboard they are integrated into the operations of the ship alongside the others.

Of that complement, six of the officers are full-time active duty and the other four, Commander Mills included, are reservists. One of the regular officers serves as the Officer in Charge (OIC) and has custody of the ship when the Captain and Executive Officer are not on board, and assumes most of the day-to-day operations.

The reserve Captain must authorize all major events, purchases and movements. When the Captain assumes command, and he doesn't have to be physically on board to do so, OIC assumes duties as Operations Officer and Navigator. The former Commanding officer, Captain William Footsellers Gallagher had only nominally been in command of the ship almost managing by abdication. When Lieutenant John Winthrop, a regular navy officer, was assigned to the Card as Officer in Charge both Captain Gallagher and the Executive Officer Lieutenant Commander McCormick allowed him to manage not only the daily operations but also the operations of the drill weekend. In reality it was Mister Winthrop who was actually in command.

Three months after Lieutenant Winthrop reported aboard, Captain Gallagher officially retired; why, the sudden decision to leave now, no one knows for sure. The ship had been without a legitimate commanding officer since 01 July of the previous year.

We know that Captain Gallagher was at one time competent chief executive and was responsible for the successful careers of many young naval officers under his mentorship.

After captain Gallagher's departure, Reserve Lieutenant Commander McCormick, the ship's executive officer, assumed the role of acting captain, but he continued to allow the officer in charge to call the shots even when the reserves were aboard.

The daily routine of the ship is slow and easy. Only routine work is done. Although the officers and men follow the regulation plan of the day, no major work is performed. During the drill weekend, the reservists would spend most of their time doing assessments in classrooms or performing training tasks on the ship's equipment. No major repairs are undertaken except when the reserves were aboard. The crew was permitted liberty every night including drill weekends, although normally the drill weekend requires the crew to stay on board throughout the full 72-hour period.

Captain Buck Sorenson, the Commander of Reserve Destroyer Squadron 34 (ComResDesRon) decided the *Card* was in too poor a condition to assign just any senior officer to captain the ship. He needed a turn-around expert, one who knew how to save lost causes, and the one person for that task was Commander Robert Mills. Captain Sorenson's boss Admiral Pulaski, Commander Reserve Destroyer Division 5 (ComResDesDiv 5) (ComResDesDiv 5)

Commander Mills has sixteen years of sea duty experience on several Destroyers and Destroyer Escorts but has not had actual command of a naval vessel, of any size. His father and uncle were killed when their corporate plane went down leaving a thriving three generation "turn-around" consulting firm, The Benchmark Group, without leadership. Robert Mills transferred from the regular navy to the ready reserves to take up the family business. Commander Mills has a Master of Science degree in Industrial & Organizational Psychology, from the University of Wisconsin in Madison.

His first assignment with the Benchmark Group was for the Navy. He was contracted to several squadron and battle group commanders, to implement a new operational protocol directed toward a more cooperative battle management procedure. The project required a great resource of finesse coupled with hard-nosed persistence. This assignment was followed by other organizational development activities on board several regular navy ships.

Captain Sorenson asked Commander Mills to meet him for lunch, and presented the offer to assume command of the *U.S.S. Card.*

The Captain briefed him on the ship's history and its current operational status. The project intrigued Commander Mills, but before he took the assignment he did a project analysis of the situation.

Date: 14 January
To: Robert Mills CMDR USNR-R
From: Commander Reserve Destroyer Squadron 34
Unclassified: Orders to command

You will assume command of USS WARREN LYNN CARD (DE 383) on 2 February. The ship and its officers and crew are to be brought up to combat readiness and join Reserve Destroyer Squadron 34 for combat readiness-evaluation exercises at Guantanamo Bay during the period 21 July through 3 August.

Bernard "Buck" Sorenson
Captain USN
Commander Reserve Destroyer Squadron 34

Captain Mills discovered the ship and the crew were so steeped in a status-quo, *don't rock the boat* mentality that only a major test of skill, material and equipment would wake them out of their stupor, and that is exactly what Captain

Mills did. He took them out and allowed them to fail. They learned from their failure and they took advantage of the opportunity he provided that would prepare them to meet their combat expectations. This time they succeeded, in spite of the unforeseen problem of getting out of channel. Overcoming that obstacle was another test they passed and it added to their self respect.

Getting the ship in combat shape is only one of the Captain's objectives. The other is developing a management team that can undertake all of the rigorous activities and responsibilities necessary to achieve the ship's mission.

Captain Mills began by giving the officers an assignment requiring them to make a detailed assessment of the departments under their command and develop a plan for correcting the identified problems that were keeping them from operating according to their assigned mission.

Another tactic employed in this recovery operation was to change the mindset of the ship's company. He changed their look by insisting on dress uniform for the quarter deck watches and the evening meal. He ordered the ship's company to wear clean pressed uniforms of the day with shirts tucked in and appropriate rank displayed.

Commander Mills could easily see the crew was ashamed to identify with the ship. If they were to be proud of her they needed to identify with her and bring her up to Navy standards. His first action toward that endeavor was to issue orders to have the ship's logo patch, with its motto; *seek – strike – prevail,* issued to every member of the crew including officers. They were to sew them onto their working jackets. He provided two more for their personal use. He had two large banners made each with the ship's logo and displayed it in the mess decks and in the officer's wardroom to assist in focusing their attention on the organization and what it stood for. He knew the *Card's* motto; *seek – strike - prevail* would encourage them to be the organization that is prepared to meet the motto's challenge.

To further ingrain identity he required them to wear the ship's identity patch on the left shoulder of their white and blue uniforms. To make sure they did, he ordered a sea bag inspection.

The Captain realized he had to get the crew's mind off the past and the current state of affairs and give them a vision of what can be, and the belief that they can make it happen. They needed to buy into his vision and actively participate in making it a reality. He took action that would allow them to identify with the ship, its motto and strive to bring that vision to fruition. The plan provided methods for focusing on being successful and not dwelling on failure. To dwell on failure will result in failure. To dwell on success will almost always result in success.

Next the Captain began a campaign to remove clutter from the ship and from minds of the managers and crew. He ordered a thorough clean up fore and aft, stem to stern. He wanted everything that was not required or unusable to be discarded; He ordered a paint job for the entire ship. It is amazing how clutter and neglect gets in the way of effective thinking, and the free flow of operational business activities. The clean-up operation was a big deal. He wanted them to change their point of view from what they thought they were to what they could be.

Once the entire ship's company accomplished something worthwhile it was a small step to the next method of renewal. The C.O. ordered each department head to use the department assessment as a means of comparison with their department's status with combat exercise requirements. This activity was followed by working with the captain to develop a plan to meet those requirements.

When the department heads realistically examined the status of their assigned areas of responsibility they recognized its deplorable condition and allowed the captain to help them take action to correct it. He told them he would visit with them and help them with their clean-up and "get-well" programs. His intention was to spend one-on-one time to encourage them, keep them from being overwhelmed with the task in front of them.

Captain Mills established deadlines for certain events to occur in the rebuilding of each department. He required an assessment report and a get well plan, ready for his attention at a specific time. To ensure their compliance he required weekly progress reports.

He continually stressed the importance of the plan, and the Guantanamo exercises and maintaining a steady and continuous fogbank persistence which eventually got the ship out to sea where they crew was able to see for themselves where their problems lie. He was assertive and persistent in getting his subordinate executives to get involved and take the action necessary to bring the ship up to combat readiness.

When his subordinate managers failed to act, he did! And did it without hesitation rendering that subordinate irrelevant, a situation no self respecting administrator would tolerate for long.

But it was the captain's desire for the subordinate executives to take charge of their own departments, using their own methods and leadership styles and with his assistance, deliver the means to accomplish that objective.

Once the crew experienced the actual accomplishment of the task of being part of the team that could perform the duties of military maritime professionals on board a ship at sea, they took on a serious attitude and renewed enthusiasm toward their job in particular and the ship in general.

The captain insisted on a higher level of training, not just training but training and professional development. Their fervor for competence training had given them a new level of confidence and they could now see themselves making personal and organizational progress and feel the exhilaration of possible success.

They, once again, were willing to identify with their ship, to wear its name on their uniforms and the coat of arms on their work jackets and civilian clothing. They were ready, willing and becoming able to make a substantial contribution toward making the *Card* a dependable, sea-going American defensive weapon again. They were looking forward to fulfilling their mission to "Seek – Strike and Prevail".

The officer corps of the ships company:

Nucleus Crew Officers

John Winthrop Lieutenant, USN, was assigned to the *Card* in March of last year to serve as officer-in-charge (OIC) of the ship. Lt. Winthrop is one of a long line of Naval Winthrops. His great Grandfather and his Grandfather retired as Navy Admirals, his father and uncle, hold the rank of Admiral and are currently serving in the Navy. Many other family members hold high positions in the Navy Department. He graduated from the U.S. Naval Academy where he did not excel in any subject except ship navigation.

After graduation he spent the next 19 months in Surface Warfare School, Navigation school and Anti-Submarine Warfare School. He then served an 18 month tour of duty on the *U.S.S. Pennington* DE 747 as Assistant Operations Officer. He was then transferred to *The U.S.S. Bristol* DE 218 where he served as the Navigator and Assistant Operations Officer for 22 months.

Mr. Winthrop's assignment to the *Card* came from on high, very high. Someone in the Winthrop family secured his assignment to the *Card* in order to be mentored by Captain (Full Bird-four striper) William Footsellers Gallagher, a long time friend of the Naval Winthrops. It is well known that John Winthrop was assigned to this reserve ship to be Officer in Charge as part of a "fast track" program to prepare him for command. After a few years under Captain Gallagher he was to be assigned to a deep draft ship. Mr. Winthrop became the center of attention the moment he set foot on the *Card*. He has exerted a great deal of influence since then.

Donald Faulk, Lieutenant, USN serves as Engineering Officer. He replaced Bill Fridel, who was "fired" for non performance before the *Card* set out on its shakedown cruise. Mister Faulk is a *Tin Can* sailor, who has made a name for himself as the one who knows more about Edsel, Buckley and Canon class destroyer escort engine rooms than any other officer currently serving. He entered fifteen years ago after graduating from Tennessee Technical College with a degree in engineering emphasis on diesel power systems. He went directly to ship board duty and has served on 3 ships in the fleet and has been sent for temporary duty to several DE's experiencing engine room problems.

Phyllis Grubaugh Lieutenant, USN, was assigned to the *Card* in February last year. She serves as the weapons officer. She is rated as a good officer and is now serving her third active duty assignment. She was born and raised in a little town in Iowa. She took an academic scholarship to the University of Maryland. After entering NROTC she became obsessed with the notion of being a career naval officer serving on a ship at sea. She decided the Navy was to be her career. After receiving her degree she took the first sea billet available, and has remained in a sea-going capacity ever since. When the reserve crew is not on board, Lt. Grubaugh serves as assistant to the officer-in-charge, Lt. Winthrop.

NOTE: Naval officers under the rank of commander are addressed as Mister or Ms. (sometimes Miss)

Marshall Goldsmith, Ensign, USN was assigned to the *Card* in April of last year. Mister Goldsmith was appointed as the Supply Officer. That job has a myriad of responsibilities beyond just supplies and spare parts. It includes all financial matters, food storage and preparation, and the medical division. In addition, Ensign Goldsmith handles the ship's personnel functions. This is his first duty assignment, having graduated from Ohio State two years ago with a degree in Human Resources Development. He went into the Navy as a personnel officer but was assigned supplies and stores when he reported aboard the *Card*, since that billet was vacant.

Lance Alexander (ensign LDO), USN. After conferring with Commander McCormick, the ship's executive officer, the captain decided he needed to replace Mister Cavatini the ship's communications officer. Mister Alexander was recruited during his last month at Limited Duty Officers School by Mister Goldsmith the Ship's Personnel officer. Mister Alexander was invited to participate in the *Card's* dependence cruise and arrived on board officially on 01 June, as communications officer replacing Ensign Cavatini who was reassigned to the Pentagon to assist in retrofitting the crypto system, using a new digital process he introduced over a year ago. While Mister Cavatini was a reserve officer, Mister Alexander is regular Navy. He is in charge of radio, the crypto unit and the signal bridge. He received his commission through the Navy's Limited Duty Officer Program after securing a Communications Electronics degree with a minor in Business Administration from the University of Maryland. His college program was an accelerated three year Bachelor of Science Program.

Important Regular Navy Enlisted Petty Officers (Non-Commissioned Officers)

O'Neal Williams YN1 – Yeoman First Class (E-6) His name is Orenthal Neal Williams, but he goes by O'neal. Williams handles the Administrative office. He does the personnel work, and other Yeoman duties. He has 12 years of exemplary service. He was handpicked by ComResDesRon Capitan Sorenson himself. Williams was one of those guys with a special set of skills. He knows everyone on the ship and apparently everyone in the Navy who can make anything happen, or knows someone who knows someone. He was one of those rare individuals one wants to get to know as he can get things done. The more people who get in his rolodex, the more effective he becomes. How he keeps up with all his contacts is a mystery. There have been times when he had multiple projects going just to get one item he needed. He is one of those guys the Navy calls a 'Rumpelstilskin' a person who, they say can spin gold out of straw.

Chief Gruber ENCS. Engineman Senior Chief Petty Officer: Chief Gruber is an old salt who knows the engine room of destroyers in general and after three years on the *Card,* He is the primary element in keeping the Card on station. His efforts have been thwarted over the past two years because of the change in the organization's officer corps.

Radarman First Class (RD1) Rex Jaworski. was recruited on the suggestion of Yeoman Williams who knew him from an earlier duty station. Jaworski is a very savvy combat exercise professional who has spent the last three years on the adversary force in Guantanamo Bay. Wanting to get out of Guantanamo Bay he contacted his friend Williams who convinced captain Mills he would be a big help in the combat exercises since he knows the program. He was a good find in that he was familiar with the way the Gitmo exercises worked particularly with destroyers and submarines. The captain set orders in place and Jaworski joined the Card's ASW (Anti-Submarine Warfare) team.

Chief Leon Jaquet, Chief Jaquet is the ship's master chef in charge of all galley and mess deck operations,

Reserve Officers

Mike McCormick, Lieutenant Commander, USNR-R, Commander McCormick is the Executive Officer. He has a B.S. degree in Marketing and Real Estate Management from Texas A&M. He is the official second-in-command and answers to the Captain during periods when the reserve crew is in possession of the ship. In the U.S. Navy the executive officer is the chief operating officer the official manager responsible for the day to day operations. All department heads report to the X.O. He has served on the *Card* for five years and has been in charge of every department of the ship at one time or another. In civilian life, he is a partner in a very successful commercial real estate firm.

Georgia Sterling, Lieutenant USNR-R. Ms. Sterling is a highly skilled electronics engineer. After graduating from MIT with a master's degree in cyber electronics, she served six years on active duty aboard a large destroyer tender. While at her last duty assignment in the Regular Navy, she assisted a team of civilian engineers to install a complicated "combat seek and control system" in a new class of destroyers. She so impressed the civilian team they made her an employment offer she could not refuse. She joined the firm on the condition she could serve in the Navy Ready-Reserves. Since her job took her to the ComResDesRon area, she was assigned to *Card* as the Combat Information Center (CIC) and ASWO (Anti-Submarine Warfare) Officer where she has been for the past 13 months.

Frank Hooper, Lieutenant junior grade (j.g.) USNR-R. He is in the eighteenth month of his mandatory two year reserve active duty requirement. Mister Hooper is the Deck Officer. In civilian life, he is a sales representative for a multi-national ship supply company. Mr. Hooper's father is a third generation commercial fisherman on the coast of Maine and Mr. Hooper spent his youth working as a general repair hand on one of his father's boats.. His He applied for an appointment to the Coast Guard Academy but when the appointment did not come through he attended the University of Maine. He received his commission through NROTC after graduating from with a degree in Naval Engineering. Except for a surface warfare school he has had only his two-year mandatory active duty experience.

Nick Winchester Ensign, USNR-R, was assigned to the *Card* as its Damage Control officer in July of last year, after completing surface warfare officer school. He earned a degree in mechanical engineering from a small college in Oklahoma and was accepted into Officers Candidate School where he attended sixteen weeks of concentrated courses before receiving his commission. His many requests for transfer have been denied. Mr. Winchester has the demanding job of training the ship's crew in damage control procedures. In addition, he is Assistant to the Deck Officer, Lt (jg) Hooper during drill weekends.

Note: Lieutenant Junior Grade is equal to a first lieutenant in the Army.

Lieutenant (j.g.) Foster Gilliam. Deck Officer with the reserve force at the Philadelphia Navy Yard. He is assigned to the *USS Granger*. The Granger has a full billet for the Guantanamo combat exercises so ComResDesDiv assigned him to the USS Card for the reserve drill assignment. While visiting the Card in March He was teased about being stuck on the carp for the summer cruise. His response to that tease was this statement. "The reputation of any organization is created by the crew that mans her. If you want a ship with a good reputation, then you must provide the level of commitment and competence that will result in that level of honor. I am proud to have the opportunity to serve on the *Card*. I can tell you ladies and gentlemen, I will give this ole girl my best efforts in an attempt to give her a proud reputation. If you will do the same, we may go to Gitmo in disgrace, but we will return in Glory."

Boatswain's Mate First Class (BM1) Ezra Furman: He is a crusty old salt who for some reason, had left the regular Navy, took a civilian job and joined the Ready Reserves. He volunteered for duty on the *Card*. In an accidental early morning with Captain Mills asked him why he left the regular navy. Furman answered this way: "I made a deal with my wife. She said she would stay married to me if I got out. As much as I love being at sea I decided I loved her more, and I did and she did. But I didn't get out entirely. I'm here."

Managing culture, tradition and structure in Turbulent Times

On the *U.S.S. Card,* as in any other organization, culture is not constant. Values and norms change as events affect the population involved. These shifts in values may precede or accompany political shifts, such as a significant change at the senior management level, as they will bring in their own values and visions, or a major change in the status or position of an organization in the market place.

The officers and crew of the *Card* did not realize they were experiencing turbulent times. They did not realize the organization's culture had devolved to what Clayton Christiansen and Thomas Davenport *(Harvard Business Review)* calls accidental culture. Accidental Culture, they say, is caused by the inaction or incorrect actions consequential to poor decisions by the organization's leaders.

While they were dissatisfied with the way things were the officers and crew were comfortable with the existing culture, which made very few demands on them, dissuading them from examining their status which would indicate a need for change.

While Commander Mills had extensive experience in saving lost causes, changing this accidental culture to a deliberate culture would be a daunting task. After doing his "Homework" he knew going in it would be the most difficult project he would ever take on.

The *U.S.S. Card's* organizational culture did not change with Captain Gallagher it began before he took command. It began to change when the conditions required them to miss week end drills at sea and the annual combat readiness exercise. Training took a big hit also since they were not able to do simulations in underway conditions with any semblance of fidelity. The *Card's* organizational structure was adjusted to accommodate its pier-bound condition when certain officer billets and enlisted billets were discontinued.

Organizational structure greatly influences the culture because behavior is not random and is directed by some degree of formalization toward a goal, and the decisions made concerning structure contributed to the change in culture.

Captain Gallagher's decision to allow Mr. Winthrop to exercise his discretion with regard to the *Card's* condition, and Lieutenant Commander McCormick's acquiescence simply contributed to the change in culture. The culture deteriorated into lethargy after a while, and the executive team contributed to its downward spiral by not holding itself and the crew to proper naval discipline and competence. What was worse, he had a reputation for being a "king maker," consequently the Winthrop naval dynasty relied on Footsellers Gallagher to do for the next generation of Winthrops what he had done for so many other Naval Academy protégés. But instead of passing on his great wisdom, leadership and command philosophies he allowed Mr. Winthrop to develop his own based on what he observed at the feet of the legendary naval guru. Combine that with the serpent advice from Lieutenant Fridel, absence of any demonstrated experience from Lieutenant Commander McCormick, and the entire Officer-in-charge program had been detrimental to the *U.S.S. Card* as an entity and to the officers and crew that manned her.

In book one, we witnessed that Navigator Lieutenant John Winthrop had been a thorn in the Captain's side from the time he came on board. He was belligerent, independent and bordered on being disrespectful but at least he had the good sense to refrain from being insubordinate.

He had an unrealistic perception of leadership, management and command that was handed down from his previous commander who had abdicated the command mantel and given it to one whom he knew would make his few remaining years comfortable without any real challenges.

Mister Winthrop's influence over the officers and crew of the *Card* was extinguished when he challenged the Captain's decision to take the auxiliary channel out to sea, instead of waiting for the main channel to be cleared. His argument was that the auxiliary channel was too shallow and the *Card* would run aground. The captain had discovered the auxiliary channel had been dredged earlier in the year and Mister Winthrop was not aware of it. Realizing his career could be in the toilet, he subordinated himself to the captain and the captain chose not to relieve him.

Captain Mills recognized the importance of changing the culture on the *Card*. It is the current culture that is hampering effective operations. Changing norms, roles and values that are deeply entrenched in an organizational culture is a difficult and in many cases impossible venture.

Captain Mills must bring the entity, and the ship's company back to the traditions and norms it enjoyed before it was allowed to deteriorate. He began that process at his first visit when he changed the uniform of the quarterdeck watch.

Getting the ship in combat shape is only one of the Captain's many objectives. He determined this project would need five phases; 1- An organizational assessment, conducted by the officers in their own areas of responsibility, comparing the current status to the navy expectations. 2- Developing a program to correct the discrepancies, 3- Developing a management team capable of undertaking the activities necessary to bring the ship up to combat readiness and test that readiness in combat readiness exercises in Guantanamo Bay Cuba. 4- Develop a comprehensive set of plans for handling contingencies for what captain Mills called turbulent times. 5- Develop a strategy and tactics for the Gitmo exercise. All this in six months.

In tandem with all that it was imperative that he get the ship underway. He must get production out. The ship had lain idle too long. He must direct their attention to the task at hand. A lethargic organization does not usually realize the condition they are in until they are called on to produce to a higher standard. When the crew attempts to get the ship underway they will discover the deplorable state they are in. Only then can the captain begin to make corrections that will bring them to combat readiness. The crew on the *Card* may need to experience failure, before they can begin to move toward success.

For the *Card*, or any other organization to be effective, to grow, or to survive at all, it must fulfill some useful function. The common goals set by the founders of the organization must result in some product or service which is useful, and holds a certain sense of pride to those in the organization and is desired by others outside the organization.

Captain Mills was more of a father to them in the beginning. He was their captain not just their chief executive. He constantly reminded them of his vision for the ship, its officers and crew. He continually reaffirmed it and asserted it until each officer and enlisted bought into it and committed to it. They had to accept and implement the plans that would crystallize the vision and make it their own whole heartedly.

He brought them to a point of no return. They had come to grips with their own weaknesses. Like a personal athletic trainer, he provided the means to strengthen themselves for greater tasks, tasks that provided evidence of *Can-Do*. Once they gained that confidence in themselves, in their shipmates and the ship itself, they were ready to make the decision and take the action necessary for performance.

Now they are ready for the ultimate test. The combat readiness exercises in Guantanamo Bay Cuba. Turbulence of any kind can disrupt the organization's culture and interfere with its ability to meet its obligations, not to mention the adverse affects on those who are employed by it.

Some single mind must be master else there will be no agreement in anything. *(Abraham Lincoln, Feb 17, 1864)*

A genuine desire for the success of one's subordinates inspires their desire to perform at a level that will please the boss and removes fear that hampers innovation. In turbulent times it is that desire to use one's competence that will sustain the organization through these times.

Chapter 2 Shakedown & Dependant's Cruise

Friday 22 May – Sunday, 24 May 1970
USS Card
US Coast Guard Yard, Curtis Bay, Maryland

Time was now the adversary. If they were to meet the 10 July deadline for being in Guantanamo Bay in time for the exercise they had to activate as many of the ship's company reserves as possible. They had to do a three day shake-down cruise, to ensure the *Card* was ship-shape and could survive the long trip to Guantanamo Bay for the combat exercises. ComResDesRon required the *Card* to report to Little Creek firing range for a one day test of the ships gun batteries and assess the gun crews. The Captain planned a one day cruise for the dependents of the ship's company.

The *Card* made a successful shake-down cruise during the three day May reserve drill. The balance of the week was spent in preparing the ship for the dependent's cruise scheduled for Sunday, 24 May.

The Sunday dependent's cruise was a rousing success. Regular Navy and Ready Reserves of the ship's company enjoyed time with their invited guests. Shipboard watches were cut to two hours instead of the customary four so that sailors with guests could spend more time with them. It was a remarkable exercise in morale. The ship's company was privileged to show off their ship to their loved ones and brag about being a part of America's sea defense system. A few months prior to this time there was no bragging about this ship or any pretense of being part of its crew.

Among the special invited guests were ComResDesRon Buck Sorenson, The newly acquired Communications Officer LDO Candidate Lance Alexander, his fiancé and Lieutenant (jg) Foster Gilliam and his wife. Mister Gilliam is assigned to the USS Granger out of Philadelphia but his assignment came after the ship had a full complement of officers for the annual summer cruise to Guantanamo Bay Cuba for combat exercises. Consequently he was assigned to the only available ship in ComResDesRon 34, the *USS Card* for the summer cruise. Mister Gilliam was invited to the dependent's cruise out of courtesy.

The Galley crew served up steaks, hamburgers, hot dogs and chicken cooked on outdoor grills on the fantail. Along the weather decks were deck chairs, rented from one of the catering services in town. There were signs attached to each chair identifying it as being rented from the catering service, which served to show guests that chairs could be rented from this service, but more to let them know deck chairs are not standard fare on board a U.S. Navy Destroyer Escort. There were barrels of iced down water and soft drinks. Each member of the ship's company was authorized to take their guests on a tour of the ship with certain restrictions noted by signage on the areas where guests could not enter.

The highlight of the cruise was a hedgehog demonstration when a dozen blank hedgehogs were fired. Two depth charge demonstrations were scheduled. There was also a forward gun and torpedo display. Scheduled tours of the guns and torpedo tubes were demonstration only, explaining how they were prepared and fired. The ordinance specialists explained how to set the depth and one dummy depth charge was shot off into the water and retrieved by a recovery crew.

Monday, 25 May 1970
Conference Room
Benchmark Consulting Group
Silver Spring, Maryland

0900: RD1 (Radarman First Class) Rex Jaworski and ASW, CIC Officer Lieutenant Sterling arrived at Captain Mill's office in a semi-clandestine meeting to go over some tactics when faced with submarine drills at Guantanamo.

You will recall it was 12 January when Commander Mills agreed to take the job to restore the *Card* to combat readiness that he requested assistance from Captain Sorenson for a crash course in Anti-Submarine Warfare, only three of his officers were ASW qualified, but he had no experience in ASW. Captain Sorenson set him up with some experience attack team officers from SUBLANT (Submarine Atlantic Fleet) in Norfolk. Realizing he needed some hunter killer experience from the destroyer perspective and that kind of information is not always easy to obtain, Captain Sorenson made arrangements for a training session from Boise Haggerty the ASW officer on the *Rodgers*, an officer Mills had the pleasure to assist with a major problem some years back. Boyce agreed to share with him some *tricks of the trade* which one only acquires by trial and error and cognitive investment.

Captain Sorenson identified Lieutenant Sterling, as being one of those clever hunter killer people. To the question would you mind getting instruction from a subordinate Mills responded; "I don't mind picking the brain of competent subordinates, and from what I have deduced from her file, she is not only competent but brilliant and discreet."

Getting a crack submariner to give up some secrets of clever attack team tactics will be a tough cove to steer. But Sorenson did not get where he was without ingenuity and political networking. And of course one does not make friends in high places without being a competent contributor to the network.

He had called in a favor from Dunhill Winthrop, Commander Submarine Forces Atlantic, who had a stake in the *Card's* rescue what with his arrogant, ring knocker nephew on in what was to be a fast track to command program going bad. *(A ring knocker is an officer who graduated from a prestigious school like the Naval Academy and reminds everyone by knocking with his/her ring every chance they get every chance they get on some surface, such as a desk or door when they want to make a point.).*

This special training session was held on 14 April at the destroyer submarine Atlantic Fleet headquarters in Norfolk, Virginia. Three officers representing the hunter killer team from the destroyer perspective and four officers, secured by Admiral Dunhill Winthrop, were there to provide inside information about attack team tactics from the submarine perspective. The instructors brought overhead projections, written instructions and 35 mm film to facilitate stories and anecdotes regarding Destroyer, Submarine combat encounters. Several more session occurred after that with one, 2-day session on a submarine and another three days on an active destroyer escort off the coast of North Carolina.

The meeting with his ASW attack team began with the captain sharing what he knew about combat operations with a submarine, though he chose not to tell them of the meeting in Norfolk, or his sessions on the submarine and the DE. Jawarski was a treasure cove of information and suggestions as was Lieutenant Sterling. The Captain was pleased that she and Lieutenant Grubaugh had discussed tactics between themselves and Jawarski. The meeting broke for lunch. Captain Mills treated them to his favorite restaurant, the *Amble Inn*, not two blocks from his office. They reconvened at 1300 and finally secured at 1600. There would be more of these sessions before they shoved off for the exercises in Gitmo.

Tuesday, 26 May 1970
Sea farer room, Warf Restaurant
Outside US Coast Guard Yard, Curtis Bay, Maryland

As Captain Mills ordered, Lieutenant's Sterling and Grubaugh held a briefing with Lieutenant Winthrop and Lieutenant Commander McCormick. The topic was to explore tactics to use during submarine hunter killer exercises against the adversary foe at Guantanamo.

Wednesday, 27 May 1970
USS Card
Pier Side
US Coast Guard Yard, Curtis Bay, Maryland

Lieutenant Commander McCormick called the officers and chiefs together in the wardroom to discuss the Underway Replenishment Training Exercise. Those present were the CO; Lieutenant Commander McCormick was there both as XO and Operations Officer, Mister Hooper who will be the Conning Officer, Mister Goldsmith the Supply Officer, BM1 Furman (Rig Captain), Chief Gunnersmate, Ed Osborne and Lt Winthrop, who will be supervising the exercise.

He handed each of them a file folder. As they opened the files, the CO sat back in his chair and waited. When he thought they were ready to listen he began; "This is the exercise information you will need. In here you will find the Key items such as rendezvous location, date and time, course, speed and proposed length of evolution. The Steps and the need for replenishment are laid out, request for a transfer of movies, provisions, fresh water and fuel needs are identified."

He smiled. "Things are beginning to happen now, progressive things, good things," he thought to himself. He continued: "This will be the one and only opportunity to get the training and ship qualified with the skills needed throughout to perform the task. We must do this before we can go to Gitmo. The ship is scheduled to rendezvous with the *USS San Jose,* a Fleet Auxiliary Supply Ship working with the Battle Group 9 in the Mid-East Coast AOR (Area of Operations)."

Mister Goldsmith looked up from the file with an inquisitive look. "According to this, lunch will need to be adjusted and possibly extended. I think we all know

Chief Jaquet, well enough to know he is quite capable of making adjustments to accommodate any situation that affects our meals. I am satisfied we can handle it." Every one nodded in agreement.

The XO stated; "The *Card* will approach the supply ship from the west on course 095 at a speed of 10 knots. Once permission to approach is given by the *San Jose,* we will increase speed to 12 knots and move alongside at a distance of 125 yards. Once alongside, the speed will be 10 knots and maintain course of 095 until finished." He looked up from the reading.

"Now this is where the training for the Conning Officers comes in. Each of you will take turns bringing the ship alongside and holding it in the proper position. We will do this until we each have accomplished this. The last person to do this will be Mister Hooper who will hold the ship steady in place while the deck crew trains for the actual connection and replenishment activity."

Mister Hooper interrupted. "Commander McCormick, since Mister Gilliam will be on the OOD roster, perhaps we should include him in the training."

"Excellent idea Mister Hooper. In fact set up a meeting with him and share all this information. And get a commitment from him for this training."

The Executive Officer paused and looked around.

"Now for the replenishment training; The *San Jose* will shoot shot lines across to us once we are three quarters of the way alongside. The replenishment rig will be set mid-ships with the distance line on the bow." The XO paused and addressed Furman.

"Boats, I know you have done this before so I know you will assign two squared away seaman to the Distance Line forward, one on Sound Powered phones with the *San Jose,* and one on the Line."

They read and discussed each step of the exercise in detail to ensure everyone involved knew what needed to be done and how.

"The *San Jose* will tension the cable," the XO continued, "and send over the riding block rig to commence the transfer of requested items. We need all available hands on deck to ensure we get the lines over quickly and safely. Once all items have been transferred and we are ready to break-away the supply ship will de-tension the cable and the pelican hook will be released and then the cable will be let over the side carefully, so as not to cause any damage. Once the cable is clear and the leader line is off the ship, Conn will increase speed to 15 knots and bare a heading of 1-2-5 to move away from the *San Jose.*"

With that done the Commander concluded the meeting and the participants headed out to brief all the players.

Thursday, 28 May 1970
USS Card
Little Creek Firing Range - back waters of the Chesapeake Bay in Virginia

The gunnery crew participated in the mandatory testing exercise at the range. They were graded on the time required to respond to the GQ alarm, prepare for battle, radio check in and prepare the guns for action. Grading also included the time required to bring shells to the gun, load it, determine the target, set the trajectory and range and fire, unload and set again. Accuracy and effectiveness of the shoot, level of activity involved in intermittent and concentrated fire were also graded.

They did not fare as well as Lieutenant Phyllis Grubaugh and Chief Ed Osborne had hoped. When the exercise was completed the *Card* shoved off and headed back to its home port in Baltimore with twenty three items they needed to improve on before arriving at Gitmo.

Lieutenant Grubaugh called an after action meeting with the officers and certain senior enlisted and the entire gunnery crews. They reviewed the events and their response to them. They discussed the methods for improving the *gigs* received during the exercise. They wrote necessary *What-If* actions and set out a training program that would be conducted between now and the time they arrive in Gitmo. (*Gigs are documented errors and mistakes),*

"That was a tough grader they sent to evaluate us," said Forrest a Gunner's Mate Striker. "She showed no mercy to us on the mid ships antiaircraft guns. For a while there I thought she was mad at us."

Morgan Stokes chimed in: "Boy she came down hard on us on the after gun mount too. She gigged us and then told us what we were supposed to do, using the most un-lady like language and terms. She told us to keep a training manual on the mount and read it every day before we got to Gitmo. Boy she raised our anxiety level big-time!"

"She started out that way with us on the number one forward gun," said GM2 Rodgers, "then she pushed Mertz out of the way and showed us exactly how the exercise was supposed to go cussing up a blue streak in the meantime. Then she made us do it three times, and then graded us. We barely scored enough to pass."

"She paid dearly for the help," said Chief Osborne. "Her division officer read her the riot act after all that. He said she was not there as a trainer, she was there as a testing evaluator. She got into some big time trouble for helping us."

"She had us all scared. Even the guys on the deck force said they stayed out of her way," said another member of the gun crew.

Chief Osborne continued. "She was a real stickler for accuracy. We could use a person like that on our crew."

"If you mean that Chief," said Lt Grubaugh, "let's see about recruiting her. We need someone that will not settle for good enough. What do you say Williams? Can we get her?"

"What you saw out there is who she is," said Yeoman Williams. "Her name is Brenda Phelps, and that name strikes fear in the heart of every Gunnersmate on the east coast. From what I hear she knows her stuff but no one can get along with her. In fact she was transferred off four ships in the past three years. Finally they sent her to Little Creek as an evaluator. I am pretty sure I can get her C.O. to cut her loose. I'll make some phone calls and see what I can do."

"She may not want to join us," said Lieutenant Grubaugh "our reputation is not good and very well known in the fleet."

"Her reputation is not that good and she is well known in the fleet," said Chief Osborne.

"Well you got me there Chief."

Tuesday, 02 June 1970
USS Card
Pier Side
US Coast Guard Yard, Curtis Bay, Maryland

The officer opened the trunk of his Navy Blue 1969 Mercedes coupe and reached in to remove his luggage. He was proud of that olive drab canvas bag. "It's sea worn and salty," he thought. He noted the handle had been broken and repaired several times. He admired the black leather tag stitched near the handle with its gold embossed letters; *Faulk, Donald, N.* His name was Don Faulk, just Don Faulk, not Donald Faulk and no middle name. He thought Donald was more *official* so he used that instead of Don. The Navy insisted on some middle initial so he chose "N". Just after the letter "N" was; "Ens" with a black mark across it, followed by a LT (jg). The (jg) was crossed out leaving the initials LT. He could have replaced the tag each time he was promoted but somehow this charted his achievements. On one side of the bag, written in black ink, were the names of the ships he had been on. *USS Card (DE 383)* was already entered. On the other side were the names of the ports he had visited. He pulled the bag out, closed the trunk, lifted the bag and walked toward the pier where his new duty station was tied up.

He took in the salty smell from the harbor and the industrial smells from the plants across the bay. Reaching the pier's end, he stopped, dropped his luggage and took in the sight he loved so well; a US Navy Destroyer Escort riding her moorings. He was facing the stern of the ship and he smiled at her name painted in white letters against the navy gray background; *CARD*. This was the fourth ship in his long list of duty stations and each ship presented opportunities for new experiences, new adventures and the different challenges he was wanting.

All the memories of past shipboard assignments and the familiar smells and sounds came crowding back. In his mind he heard those old familiar noises of a teeming community engrossed in activity seeing to the welfare of the ship and their shipmates. He allowed himself to recall the revelry the first time he reported aboard a D.E. He thought he would not enjoy a ship this small, as he stood on the

0-1 weather deck overwhelmed by the stench of steel, paint, seawater and diesel fuel. Now it was no longer a stench it was a sweet savor to his nostrils.

He heard a car door close, somewhere in the parking lot just off the pier followed by the sound of a high powered engine fading away in the distance. After a few seconds he instinctively turned his head at the sound of footsteps coming up behind him. There was something very likeable and reassuring about the man who approached with a new Val Pack bag. He seemed a bit old for an Ensign. He had the look and sea-legs swagger of an experienced sailor about him. The ensign stopped beside the Lieutenant and dropped his bag on the pier.

"This must be the ship," he said. "Since there is no other ship around the ship, this must be the ship." He threw up a right hand salute to the senior officer. Mister Faulk returned the salute.

"Lance Alexander, Ensign, USN, fresh out of LDO School - My first assignment as Communications Officer."

"Don Faulk, Engineering Officer."

"Well," said the Ensign. "She has a bad reputation now, but I hear she was once a proud vessel. It appears as though this new Captain has been recruiting a crew to take her to Gitmo. I think he has plans to bring her back to life."

The Lieutenant moved slightly to the left to get a good look at the ship's numbers. Apart from her name, the ships numbers are the second most important item in the memory of those who claim her. Without taking his eyes off those numbers, he said;

"This Captain manages as nature does; he shows neither malice nor pity. Time and weather helps or hurts depending on how one is positioned. I have known this officer for years. He has brought many a ship back to life, but this is his first command. He has wrestled the officers and crew into believing in themselves and the ship. Those who want to be part of her glory are still on board. Those who could not or would not, have been replaced. All a ship needs to be good is a crew who is willing to serve her and be loyal to her and what she stands for."

He turned to face the new officer. "You were handpicked Mister Alexander. There are high expectations for you. Don't disappoint him."

"I intend to be part of the ship Mister Faulk."

"Well said, Mister Alexander. Captain Mills once said you can't be part of the crew unless you are part of the ship. Not just on the ship, Mister Alexander, you must be part of her life, her soul, her being. It is your service that keeps her alive."

"I will remember that Sir. I have served on many ships and I have always felt kin to them."

The officers hoisted their luggage and headed to the gang way.

Lieutenant Don Faulk replaced Bill Fridel, who was "fired" for non-performance before the *Card* set out on its shakedown cruise. Mister Faulk is a *Tin Can* sailor who has made a name for himself as the one who knows more about Edsel,

Buckley and Canon Class Destroyer Escort engine rooms than any other officer currently serving. He entered eleven years ago after graduating from Tennessee Technical University with a degree in engineering with emphasis on diesel power systems He went directly to shipboard duty and has served on 3 ships in the fleet and has been sent for temporary duty to several DE's experiencing engine room problems.

Friday, 05 June 1970
USS Card
At Sea

0900 The morning arrives with a beautiful sunrise and calm seas. The *USS Card* was underway at 0700 on its way to the rendezvous area. Everyone is prepping for the upcoming task. The UN-Rep activities are reviewed over and over to ensure everyone understands their assignments. Mister Hooper is reviewing the equipment on station with BM1 Furman to ensure all required equipment is readily at hand if needed.

The *Card* entered the area where the underway replenishment (Un-Rep) will take place.

"Looks as though we have a good day for a Un-Rep," said Mister Hooper as he peered over the side toward the direction *the San Jose* will be approaching. "I feel a lot more confident now that I know you have experience in this sort of thing", he says to Furman as they work to get ready.

"I have participated in and supervised many of these events, Mister Hooper. I feel we will be ready and perform without a hitch."

The preparations were continuing on the bridge with the OOD and Conning Officer and the other officers who will be participating, reviewing course, speed and maneuvering plans with the Quartermasters.

The Forward Lookout calls the bridge "Bridge, Forward Lookout, ship on the horizon, bearing 150 about three miles"

"Bridge, aye, have them in sight"

"Bos'n of the Watch, notify the Captain we are nearing the Un-Rep AOR and the Supply Ship is in view," Mister Winthrop orders.

Lt Winthrop peered over the bulwark with binoculars to his eyes, "OOD, I have the Conn and will take it from here, Helm bring us around to course 095 and maintain speed of 12 knots"

"Course 095, speed 12 Knots, aye" repeats Helmsman.

Captain Mills arrives on the Bridge. The Bos'n of the Watch announces his arrival

"The Captain is on the Bridge"

"Very Well" responds Lt Winthrop.

Captain Mills moves to his seat and settles in. He is the observer on this exercise.

Mister Winthrop turned toward the captain. "Captain, we have arrived on station, a few minutes early, but ready. I have contact with the *San Jose* and they are ready when we are. Seas are calm, we are on Un-Rep heading 095 and current speed is 12 knots, recommend we station the Un-Rep detail and begin final preps"

"Very well, Mister Winthrop you have the Conn commence Un-Rep operations"

Mister Winthrop again focused his attention toward the oncoming supply ship. While still looking ahead he shouts orders to the Boatswain, Mister Hooper, who is standing ready for the word.

"Bos'n, call away the Un-Rep Detail"

"Bos'n aye" He signals the boatswain mate of the watch who pipes "Attention" and passes the word;

"Now station the Underway Replenishment detail, ship will come along side the USS *San Jose*, Post side Mid-ships station, now station the underway replenishment detail, all station report manning to the bridge"

The line handlers don their life jackets and hardhats. Final checks are conducted by Furman and LTGJ Hooper to ensure all personnel are ready and where they need to be. Station phone talker notifies the bridge that all hands are on station and ready to begin. Word is passed to Lt Winthrop who notifies the Captain.

"Let's get the show started LT, have Signalman raise the Romeo Flag to the 'Ready to approach' position."

The underway replenishment training exercise lasted from 1000 to 1600. The ship made several advances until the captain was satisfied all the Conning officers had sufficient introduction to the event. The deck crew and line handlers performed expertly, with few glitches, since many of the deck hands had prior experience with UnRep.

The galley crew provided the usual excellent food. The Mess Decks served a continuous meal from the morning Breakfast until after the evening meal at 1700.

Monday, 08 June 1970
USS Card
Pier Side
US Coast Guard Yard, Curtis Bay, Maryland

0800: GM1 Brenda Phelps reported aboard the *Card*. She was assigned to the forward gun with additional responsibility for training. She immediately checked out the guns. She then began writing a training program based on her previous experience with the *Card's* gun crews.

Executive Assessment:
Strengthening the team with acquisitions & replacements - Establishing a team you can depend on

You can't trust the market, the industry, the financial institutions, customers, suppliers or the government for operational stability and continuity. You must be able to trust your senior executive staff and their immediate subordinates.

In book one *The Stewardship of Executive Management* we read where the captain relieved Lieutenant Fridel, the Engineering officer. There was good reason as he was a hostile element in the management team, constantly stirring up doubt and suspicion within the officer corps as well as the enlisted ranks. He took credit for the work his chief did. If that was not enough, he had not kept pace with technology. The captain replaced him with Lieutenant Donald Faulk. As we take up the story in this book, the captain transferred Mister Cavatini to the Pentagon and replaced him with an officer who had the skills the organization needed at the time.

Team building means transferring team members when their skills are no longer needed or no longer effective. It is important to keep in mind the organization does not exist so that teams will have something to do. The teams exist for the benefit of the organization's mission, and that may mean redesigning teams to meet specific needs.

Having a competent Human Resources team is vital to getting experienced or trainable personnel. Your HR professional should be a recruiter as well as a placement agent. That means having the skill and patience and contacts to know where talent is located and go after it. It means staying in touch with people in other organizations working trade shows, staying in touch with transition agencies and outside recruiters.

When you have a loyal dedicated technician in a manager's position and you need a manager in there your HR director needs to serve as a recruiter. Find the one you need, even if you have to pirate that person away from another organization. But don't dump the loyal technician. Find another place for that tech in a job where they can make a substantial contribution to some other organization. This may mean selling that technician to another organization.

When an organization falls into difficult times every person who draws a paycheck must be worth more than they are paid.

Loyal, long term employees who are no longer effective must be removed, but all out effort must be made to find another place either inside or outside the organization where they can make a contribution. But if another place cannot be found within an appropriate amount of time the ineffective employee must be released to find their own place in another organization.

Dumping a loyal employee will create distrust among every remaining employee, and in turbulent times you need everyone dedicated to the organization's health.

Employees may be replaceable, but they are not disposable.

The *Card* made a successful shake-down cruise during the three day May reserve drill. And a successful dependence cruise. Regular Navy and Ready Reserves of the ship's company enjoyed time with their invited guests. Shipboard watches were cut to two hours instead of the customary four so that sailors with guests could spend more time with them. It was a remarkable exercise in morale. The ship's company was privileged to show off their ship to their loved ones and brag about being a part of America's sea defense system. A few months prior to this time there was no bragging about this ship or any pretense of being part of its crew.

The shakedown cruise and the dependents cruise strengthened moral, and enhance the training of the crew for preparation for the Gitmo exercise. The crew was able to see themselves actually performing at a competency they had not experienced in over two years.

Organization will benefit in numerous ways when they plan and promote family activities on company money. Parties, picnics, catering a party at an amusement park can be a morale booster and, as strange as it may seem, activities such as these can be a real competence developer. When employees feel pride in their organization and its managers they approach their assigned tasks with a greater willingness to improve their productivity and professional competence.

When your organization is experiencing turbulent times, the relationship you have established with your employees and their families will be very beneficial in seeing you through it.

The *Card's* managers talked through the underway replenishment exercise, and then they did a dry practice run. Senior managers would do well to require subordinate managers and lead persons to talk through, and walk through the start-up of a new project before you actually "flip the switch."

I recommend "dry runs" using simulation to prepare for the start up. A national candy company began producing their Christmas candy in July. It was customary for them to lose a considerable amount of product during the first week. We wrote a training program for each segment of the process and set aside a team, some were temps, to begin the production. The company set aside a portion of the warehouse as a training area and set up the machines needed for those particular items. We first talked through the process then did a dry run. When we felt they were ready we cranked up the machines and began production from the cookers, to the make-up through the packaging and storing. With production at a slow pace all the production went into the final product with very little waste. We systematically increased the speed of the units until they were operating at maximum speed, with maximum quality and waste was at lower than expected levels.

With any talk through and walk through, those hourly personnel who will be involved in the start-up need to be present. Fortunately there was one on the CARD who had experience with UNReps. If an experienced person is not on staff with a new critical start up you may need to hire an outside expert to ensure the project was done correctly.

The gun crew did not fare so well at Little Creek. They complained that Brenda Phelps GM1, the Firing range umpire was a tough grader and yelled at them unmercifully. She had them all intimidated, including the officers, and yet, even though she had a reputation as a loner and difficult person to work with they wanted her to join the *Card's* gunnery crew. You may wonder what was it that made them think she would be an asset and not a trouble maker. She did not just grade, she went outside the program and conducted training even personally demonstrating what was to be done.

Just because a competent or highly trained person is difficult to work with does not mean they are not worth the effort. Some people are just characters and enjoy exploiting their know-how. They usually, but not always, come with temperament and expectations of independence equal to their talent. What is your standard philosophy with regard to adding these people to your roster?

Handling a person with this obvious "I Know I'm right" behavior can be a daunting task but your best approach is to put them in a position to prove it. When they are right management adjusts tradition or practice to accommodate the new way of doing things. As long as they are substantial contributors to productivity by doing the job they are capable of doing and bring others along with guidance and training. The highly skilled employee should understand your expectations when they agree to come to work for you. Their performance appraisal should include these expectations.

We can see by the description in the book that Donald Faulk was a seasoned naval engineering officer who was brought in to replace Lieutenant Fridel even though this was only a reserve vessel. Why do you suppose ComResDesDiv and ComResDesRon permitted such a skilled replacement? Wouldn't you think he could be of more use on a USN regular navy ship? We could take a cue from ComResDesRon and ComResDesDiv. When you need a special skill you find it and hire it. If your organization's position in the market place is important then make the investment. It is axiomatic that along with placing skilled personnel on the job, you make an investment in the equipment they need to be effective. Skilled personnel are usually more expensive and more difficult to obtain. You give them them leeway to be creative. Supervision of these people is practically free-reign. They can be considered as the technical expert and work with the supervisor to make things happen. They have the technical improvement responsibility and you have the management responsibility.

What is it about Don Faulk (from the entry description) that causes you to believe he will be a good addition and will be easy to work with? He has pride in his accomplishments and has shown loyalty to the field and contribution to his former employers.

Ensign Lance Alexander was recruited and hand-picked for the job in the signal department.

Why did the *Card's* management think they needed to replace Ensign Cavatini? It was obvious Mister Cavatini did not know how to plan, organize, direct, coordinate and control the flow of work in the department. There are those items that only the executive can address, and apparently the Lieutenant (jg) could not grasp it.

How do you know exactly what skills and temperament is needed for open subordinate management positions? The department manager must be familiar with the operation under their command, the nature of the work, and the skills needed. Every operation has a unique personality and culture. That familiarity is must be considered when placing people into that environment.

We know there were no communication officers available in the reserve force for the trip to Gitmo, but why did captain insist on bringing in a Limited Duty Officer, with the skills they needed, in a full time position instead of making it a part-time – Temporary duty assignment from early June to the end of the Gitmo Cruise? The success of the *Card's* engagement in Gitmo was a critical factor in the ship's mission. There was talent in most departments capable of making a successful engagement in Gitmo, so to ensure the ship's successful performance those elements that were lacking had to be *beefed up*. Your organization should have all the talent it needs in order to stay competitive in the marketplace so where ever there is lack of performers, that talent must be found and placed.

It is important to note that organizations lose talented skilled people to other companies when the organization does not have a policy of hiring and retaining the best producers. It is also a fact that in an atmosphere of competence appreciation and training, others who may not grow in skill and confidence in other organizations will strive to be as effective as the best employees in our operation.

Most of the reserves coming aboard were experienced seamen who had obtained rank because of their competence and time in grade. Some were coming aboard an actual naval ship for the first time and know little about the job they will be assigned to do or how they will cope with the never ending movement of sea and the pitch of the ship.

Mister McCormick made it plain that executive staff and their subordinate leaders were to take note that since the crew is supplemented with sailors who are not familiar with our equipment, there will need to be some serious indoctrination and testing on the equipment and see to it that the new people are brought up to speed with the plan.

When orienting new personnel to the organization, and the department there are some important items to consider in order to ensure a smooth transition from outside person to member of the crew. The most important item is a structured step by step training system implemented by skilled trainers who are as much mentors and guides as competence development instructors.

What are some methods your organization uses for training new employees for the jobs they were hired to do? Do you have systems for measuring the effectiveness of the training? Is it possible for a new hire to flunk out of the training? Each segment of the training system should end in a knowledge test and a performance test. The knowledge test is a written or oral test and the performance test is a check off instrument where the trainee actually performs the job to a standard. Once they pass the tests they go on to the next segment. And where possible an increase in pay should be awarded.

The captain made a point of reminding the officers how important it is that each department works together in a seamless coordinated effort, not only in war operations but also in the daily routine and how important team work is to the success of the mission.

And certainly the orientation of new employees must include stressing the importance of working with other departments in a seamless coordinated way. The training program should include actually working with peers (customers and suppliers) from other departments.

Chapter 3 Planning for turbulent times

Friday, 12, June 1970
USS Card
Pier Side
US Coast Guard Yard, Curtis Bay, Maryland

Now that each department head had developed and successfully implemented their department get well plan, morale had improved to the extent that compliance had given way to cooperation ensuring the acceleration in the overall improvement of the organization's culture.

0900: Captain Mills called a meeting of the officers in the wardroom. When they were all assembled Captain Mills began.

"I guess by now you are aware that I work under the motto of *plan your work and work your plan*. We should all be used to that by now, as the Navy has publications with plans for almost all matter of situations, and you have all developed several plans since I have been in command. Well . . . here we are with another."

Everyone chuckled and playfully rolled their eyes as if they were saying *here we go again*. But they had seen the effectiveness of those plans and determined that yet another plan would also be helpful in the Gitmo situation. After all, navy planning tools were helpful, but the most helpful of all plans are the ones made by those who are responsible for carrying them out since one understands their own plan and how to implement it.

"I want us to develop a set of plans for managing in turbulent times. I know, I know, we have publications on handling crises situations. The Navy has contingency plans for almost every conceivable circumstance based on over 200 years of after action reports, but I don't want to know what John Paul Jones would do, I want to know what you will do under a certain set of unfortunate circumstances. We are expected to meet and exceed all naval expectations in the Gitmo experience."

The department heads all nodded in agreement and understanding.

"I want each of you to imagine what could go wrong in your department. I want you to identify any potential threat or crises situation that could possibly or probably go wrong. Example; Mister Faulk, what if we lost all power in the open sea, Ms. Grubaugh, what if we were in a combat situation and we took casualties that prevented you from manning some of the guns or other ordinance, Ms. Sterling what if we were in the open sea, or worse yet in combat and we lost our fire control computers or sonar or radar. You can see how any situation that occurs in your department that disrupts your normal operations will have a profound effect on all of us. Do you see where I am going with this?"

Everyone nodded. Of course they all thought about these things, and had a general idea as to what to do, but now they realized there needs to be an orchestrated plan they could immediately implement.

"OK, after you have identified the threat write a prevention plan and plan for dealing with it if the prevention plan fails. I recommend you consult with your senior enlisted."

The officers nodded their heads in agreement. They had been advised of this before and after some difficulty addressing the questions presented by the captain found it very helpful to get input from those on the *firing line.*

"I want to meet with each of you during this next week and go over your horror stories. Be sure to include a plan of action for dealing with each of those items. Please consult your publications for ideas. Then, Mister McCormick will call a meeting next Friday. At this meeting you will share them with the rest of the management team. Each department head will have a comprehensive plan for how their department will handle turbulence faced by other departments. If we lost all power in the open sea, what would the deck force do? What would the Communications department do? What would any of you do? To answer that you have to assess how that will affect your department, and what is your department's responsibility to the ship in this case? Mister Alexander, in any scenario you would be sending some urgent messages don't you think?"

Mister McCormick decided to secure some clarification. "So, you want individual plans, and an orchestrated overall plan? Does that mean we will form a crises management team and the one with the problem will be the head of that team?"

"Exactly, I think any crises situation must be dealt with at the lowest organizational level, but I want you, Mister McCormick, to supervise the events that occur during turbulent times. The next phase of this project is to test those plans to see how well they work and make adjustments as necessary. So we will conduct actual drills to test the system. After each drill each of you will conduct an after action report that will be shared in a general after action meeting. Mister McCormick will conduct the meeting, I will sit in."

Executive Assessment

Plans for Crises Management

A plan is a programmed course of action, made for a programmed decision. Plans made during times where favorable conditions allow for more careful planning will almost always be more effective than plans made under hostile or turbulent times.

As far as possible management must be prepared for interruptions in normal operation and not allow fate to dictate the response.

> *Fate makes demands on flesh and blood and what is most often the demand is flesh and blood.*

We know the *Card* was in turbulent times when Captain Mills took command. It was because of this condition that he was appointed to command the *Card*. There are two situations in play here that need to be addressed; Turbulent Times and Crises Times.

Turbulent times: A period of unrest and disturbance; when conditions vary erratically in magnitude and direction characterized by interference sufficient to disrupt the organization's culture and its ability to meet its obligations or maintaining the vision, mission and purpose of the organization.

Crises times: A significant event bringing a radical change in status creating an unstable or crucial state of affairs in which decisive change is impending; one with a distinct possibility of a highly undesirable outcome.

Usually it is crises, an event, or a series of events that bring an organization into turbulent times. The organization's management must prepare for such situations.

Organizations must take serious steps to ensure the continuity of the operation. Identifying possible crises situations is second only to planning for basic operations. There is a two phased approach to ensuring continuity; *Risk Management* and *Crises Management*. Most executives, particularly Risk Managers, are familiar with the term; *Crises Management* is a process by which an organization deals with a major event that threatens to harm the organization in some way. *Risk Management* involves assessing potential threats and finding the best ways to avoid them. Risk Management systems have a significant influence on the organization's insurance policies.

The Management in Turbulent Times process takes on four elements.

1. Risk management
2. Crises management (or management in turbulent times)
3. Recovery management
4. After action learning

1. Risk Management: Develop a plan to identify possible crises situations that could disrupt or threaten the very existence of the organization

Among other responsibilities, risk management also includes providing insurance to cover major losses when injuries or damage occurs. In order to secure the best possible coverage for the best possible rate, the risk manager takes an inventory of all organizational assets, and develops a plan for securing those assets, as well as specific actions taken during and after the event responsible incurring the loss. Other items are also included such as; management misfeasance or malfeasance, malpractice, errors and omissions and any other misbehavior that would cause loss to property, personal injury and anything injurious to organizational health and reputation. If the plans are approved by the insurer, a contract is made and a policy issued.

Of course the job does not end here. Policies and procedures are enforced, training for employees regarding safety and asset protection is conducted.

Organizations that have a poor loss record or a poor safety record may find themselves in an insurance pool, where the state requires an insurer to cover the operation, but usually at a greatly inflated rate.

Every organization should have "*What IF*" plans to assist in making critical decisions when terrible, challenging situations threaten the well being of the organization and its employees.

Begin with clear direction: You will notice the officers of the *Card* included all Chiefs in their briefing. They also included those petty officers of lower rank but who had critical responsibilities for the success of normal and crises operations. When an organization is in turbulent times, planning sessions and status meetings are important. Since everyone on the payroll now has a stake in the organization's continued existence it is wise to engage those managers, supervisors, foremen, and sometimes lower level hourly employees who will actually employ the strategies and tactical plans the management team has approved. These folks can help identify that only those on the line know about.

An additional benefit is the total dedication to the success of an operation these people will give you, because they understand how those ideas came to fruition and more importantly what the expected outcome is. Upper management would be amazed at the *tweaking* these people can do to make an expected outcome happen.

Each department head was required to have a basic operation and a plan for turbulent times. That included *WHAT IF* plans that covered possible or probable contingencies. For those organizations who did not have *WHAT IF* plans, and find themselves in a situation where IF has happened a *GET OUT* of *IF* or a *GET WELL* plan needs to be formulated and implemented immediately. I have worked with organizations under such conditions, and many have spent days and nights in a sequestered conference room until a proper program had been worked out.

One such contingency faced by a 24 hour manufacturing plant was *WHAT IF* we lost power. Even a 2 minute outage would cost $35,000 to put back on line, considering the energy required and the materials lost and customer orders will be delayed. Another organization in the finance business explore What IF a national financial crises occurred, how would they respond to protect and serve their clients as well as stay afloat themselves.

Provide a basic operation strategy for preventing identified inevitable or potential crises

1. Captain Mills assigned each officer to identify key issues or potential threats in their area of responsibility that require pre-emptive attention.
2. Once they had their list the captain looked it over and made recommendations and suggestions.
3. He then assembled the officers forming a crises management team to address each department head's list. They took each executive's list seriously, since any happenstance in one area affected them all.

Some key issues that could disrupt operations and threaten its very existence are:

- Natural disasters such as storm, wind, and flood damage.
- Technological disasters such as loss of critical computers, stolen data or human error.
- Confrontation issues when disgruntled workers, suppliers, customers or special interests groups issue public challenges.
- Malevolence when someone sabotages equipment, or products in order to publicly embarrass the organization or cause their ultimate removal.
- Misfeasance of office or management misconduct when executives take unfair advantage of their position or access to resources at the expense of the health of the organization or harm to customers, suppliers or others.
- Workplace violence when someone enters the workplace for the purpose of causing harm to members of the organization.

Prepare a contingency plan for handling events when they occur.

You cannot depend on a pre-emptive approach to keep you from experiencing identified crises, in spite of all you do to prevent it. A contingency plan is developed the same way the crises identification process was done.

1. The *Card's* Crises Management team then wrote specific actions that would be taken by their department in containing and managing the crises. Each department will have a part to play in another's turbulent times.
2. Once the managers had their plans together, they assembled into a working crises management document.
3. The plan calls for the securing of resources for handling the crises as well as maintaining the continuity of production. People, financial and technological resources must be provided for. In some cases outside experts need to be consulted or called in to help.

2. Crises Management Phase

Develop or appoint a crises management team to handle the event and the recovery

When the crises occurs the one in charge of the crises management team is the executive in charge of department affected. Everyone else assists.

If the situation goes public, a spokesperson should be designated to speak for the organization. This person is the only one to make public statements to the press. Anyone other than the designated spokesperson will be counterproductive to the recovery process. Everyone involved in the process should keep the PR person informed. While full disclosure is normally a good idea, questions with the potential for being destructive should be cleared by the chief executive. Each message should be crafted as truthfully and succinctly as possible.

Those who should be on the team are; the executive in charge of the department in crises, all the department heads that will be directly affected by the problems being addressed in the department with the crises. Others who should be involved are: The department head most affected, the chief executive or executive VP, Risk Manager, Public Relations Professional, and an attorney. It is a good idea to include the staff professionals in this meeting as well. Some professionals to consider are; Organizational Development Professional, Training Professional, the Risk Manager and an attorney.

Unless the crises has taken out your entire operation it is necessary to carry on in as near normalcy as possible.

Keep the structure intact. People need to have the structure that will create and maintain a feeling of comfort, knowing those responsible for acting are doing so and they can depend on the certain return to normalcy.

You will notice the *USS Card* faced some horrendous events yet the daily plan of the day, as punctuated by the timely 1-MC (*Public address system heard in all spaces of the ship*) announcements maintaining the feeling of normalcy.

Empower the authorized individuals and teams with authority to take action when conditions warrant:

It is imperative that the organization's managers are capable of making the correct decisions under crises and or uncertain conditions with a scant amount of information. A combat condition is a classic example of crises that brings on turbulence in which the officer must make critical decisions that will impact the safety of the ship and its crew.

Teams trained to comprehend the purpose of the operation and the intended outcome and authorized to make decisions are more capable of responding to the changing conditions without the delay that comes with having to get approval for taking action. The operative word in this section is TRAINING! Everyone needs to know how to comprehend what is going on and what they are required to do about it. There must be a realistic method for identification of expected outcomes and methods for measuring the effectiveness of those outcomes.

3. The Recovery Management Phase

Plans for managing in turbulent times, or in times of crises should not determine the basic culture of the operation. The organization's leaders (both formal and informal) need to operate in an atmosphere of optimism and innovation, with no fear of taking risks for the benefit of the organization and its people. Abraham Lincoln once said; *"We live in the midst of alarms, anxiety beclouds the future; we expect some new disaster with each newspaper we read."*

Given the Card's history, one bad situation after another will take some great faith in the ship's executive team to keep a positive attitude, especially at sea.

4. After Action Learning Phase

After or near the end of the crises situation all involved should write up an after action report stating how they become aware of the situation, how it was assessed at the beginning and what actions were taken and by whom, and as far as possible the thinking behind the decisions that were made.

What were the decisions and what was the outcome of those decisions. The report should conclude with statements under the heading: *What did we learn from this experience* followed by *actions taken to correct the situation.*

Again those reports are submitted to the chief executive who reads them and offers suggestions and recommendations for the final document.

Each participant's final document is placed in a first draft document for all participants to see. There will need to be a call for understanding as each participant will assess the situation in their own way. *We don't see things the way they are, we see things the way we are.*

A meeting is conducted in which the individual participants review the document and agree on or at least reach a consensus as to the how the event unfolded and what should be done in the future to avoid the situation, and to better manage it if it occurs again.

We will revisit the subject of taking risks in the later chapters.

The Dudley Axiom:

- **Give a man a job**
- **Get his input**
- **Assign the job to him**
- **He will do everything in his power to make it work because it is his job.**

Chapter 04 Battle Plans

Friday, 19 June 1970
The Gitmo Crew
USS Card Pier Side
US Coast Guard Yard, Curtis Bay, Maryland

0800: The plans for identifying and managing in turbulent times were complete and drills were scheduled to test them. Next on the agenda was the Gitmo exercise cruise schedule that specifically detailed each day's movements, moorings and activities.

The Captain had ordered the XO to activate all officers to report Friday, 19 June to go over the Gitmo schedule. The officers were assembled in the wardroom, each in their assigned places. The table was covered with a white linen cloth with the ship's seal embroidered in the center. At the aft end of the wardroom was a counter where fresh hot coffee, cold drinks and snacks were always present. Some of the senior enlisted, those whose jobs were critical to the operation were invited. They sat in chairs along the bulkheads. The attendees opened their binders as the XO went through each section.

When all was settled the captain entered.

"Attention on Deck." Cried the XO

Everyone sprang to their feet.

"Be seated." The captain said "Now," He said with a smile. Commander McCormick will tell us about the crew we will pick up in Norfolk and Mayport."

Lieutenant Commander McCormick turned his attention to a stack of papers in front of him. He handed a pile to his left and another to his right. "Here are the additional crew we will pick up in Norfolk and Mayport."

Yeoman Williams was sitting just behind him on his right. He turned to him. "Ok Yeoman Williams who are we getting from the other reserve units for the Gitmo cruise?"

Yeoman Petty Officer First Class Williams had the files. He opened the folder. "The reserves of our own ships company that did not sail with us to Norfolk will join us there. We will also take on eight enlisted and the doctor in Norfolk and five enlisted in Mayport."

He consulted his list from the binder and identified each person who was coming aboard and their duty assignments.

"Lieutenant Junior Grade Foster Gilliam will be joining us in Baltimore on 10 July. You may remember he visited us back in March. He is in the ready reserves out of the Philadelphia Naval Ship Yard. He shipped over from inactive reserve to Ready Reserves just last February so he does not yet have a billet there. He is presently teaching 10th grade world history in New Jersey, but will join us for his annual active duty requirement. He served two years active duty on board the *USS John R. Pierce* (DD 751). He was the Deck and Weapons Officer. Mister

Gilliam will serve as our First Lieutenant (*in charge of repair and deck tools*) and will assist Mister Hooper with deck assignments. He was a qualified driver and all he needs is some reorientation and he will be good as a Conning officer on the *Card.*"

"Great, we could use another officer to Conn the ship," said XO McCormick. "Mister Goldsmith, put him on the CONN and OOD schedule."

"Wasn't he the guy that gave that gung-ho speech about the crew being responsible for the reputation of the ship?" asked Lieutenant Grubaugh.

"The very one," Mister Hooper answered.

Everyone nodded approval. Since no further comments seemed to be in evidence Yeoman Williams continued. "We will also get Engineman Second Class Mike Brewer. He spent his two years reserve duty on the *Orion*, a submarine tender. He's from Wheeling, West Virginia. In civilian life he is a machinist and owns a job shop. This guy can make anything or fix anything or retrofit anything."

"Nice going Williams," said Chief Gruber.

"I wish I could take the credit for this one, but he applied late for the 2 week cruise and all the other ships in the reserve division had all the machinists they needed, so we got him." He consulted the next page and continued.

"Gunner's Mate Second Phil Northwood. This will be his second trip with *ResDesRon34*. Lieutenant Grubaugh has him assigned to the after gun mount. That was his GQ station on the *Lansing*. ComDesRon Sorenson himself assigned him here."

"We have GM1 Phelps from the regular ship's company on the forward gun mount. We needed another experienced hand on the after gun," the Weapons Officer interjected.

Lieutenant Grubaugh offered the roster for the rest of the big gun crew. "The midships guns (*two anti-aircraft guns located on either side of the 02 level*) will be manned by GM2 Rodgers and GMSN Forrest from our ready reserve crew. Phelps said they did very well in the drills we set up the last two months. The Number 3 gun, the three-incher, had no gunner, so we assigned Guido, a fire control technician to that one. She does alright, and with someone from the deck force to load, we think we will be OK there. We have Mertz and Stokes as well. We will have a Gunners Mate Striker joining us from middle Tennessee. Actually he has no "A" school experience." She searched the paper for more information. "Ah here . . . Seaman Apprentice Buford Thurmond."

She turned her attention back to Williams and he continued. "We are scheduled to get Charles Sandlin, First Class Photographer's Mate. He served eight years active duty out of Cheltenham, Maryland traveling the world on air planes photographing Navy ventures of every sort. He has been in the ready reserves for three years. This is his first two week training assignment on board a ship."

He paused and scanned the roster to see if he had missed anyone. "Did I mention Lieutenant Commander Mark Johnson? He will be our doctor and will come aboard in Norfolk."

Williams consulted his notes again. "We will also take on a hospital corpsman. He is HM1 Christopher Harris. He is a paramedic, a guy with combat experience. This guy is a real hero. He served with a Marine detachment in Nam. He was awarded several medals for bravery."

"You are amazing Williams, how did you get such outstanding people?" Hooper asked.

"Come, now Mister Hooper, if I told you my secrets all the magic will be gone from the mystery surrounding my job here."
"I am led to believe the less I know about your magic the better we all are," said Mister Hooper.

Williams continued; "Robert Benson Third Class Personnel-man will come aboard in Norfolk."

"He works part time for Commander Richardson, the Navy Liaison Officer at McGuire Air force Base. He is a desk jockey, goes to a community college at night. It seems the Commander was not happy that he put in for his two weeks required active duty training somewhere other than his office, so from what I get from my contacts, he pulled strings to get himself assigned to a small ship headed for Gitmo."

Williams shook his head and frowned. "Yeah the unofficial orders were for BuPers to put him somewhere where he will be glad to get back to McGuire. In spite of all we could do, the brass decided the worst they could do for him was to give him to us."

"What are we going to do with him?"

"Well . . . Sir . . . we have only one billet open and he *don't* even qualify for it, but unless something can be done, we will need to put him in the forward gun mount."

"Now wait a minute!" said Chief Gunner's Mate Osborne. "Phelps will have my head! She put in for a qualified, seasoned E-4 or E-5 Gunners Mate. You know her. She's a stickler for correctness, accuracy and detail. If you try to stick her with a desk jokey with no gunnery experience and no sea experience, she will make all our lives miserable."

"The chief's right. We don't want to make her angry, she is our ace gunner. We are lucky to have her," added Lieutenant Grubaugh.

Mister Goldsmith spoke up; "I was under the impression she was transferred here after being fired from three, no, four other ships because of her bad attitude."

Lieutenant Grubaugh spoke up in Phelps' defense. "She made First Class (E-6) in record time. She really knows guns. She has never been insubordinate. You know how it is with dedicated people like her. There is the right way, the wrong way, the Navy way and her way. Her bosses on the other ships wanted her to do things the Navy way. Her problem is she has had a lot of bosses but none of them were her master. On this ship, that competence and independent attitude is needed . . . and rewarded."

"I would worry more about Benson working for Phelps. I hear she can be a real bear," said Mister Winthrop.

"I know this guy Commander Richards," said Williams. "If he can work for him he can work for anybody."

"What else?" asked Lieutenant Commander McCormick.

"There will be about ten other reserves just out of *boots* (boot camp) that will be sent to the mess decks and the deck force." The Yeoman closed his binder.

The XO closed his binder and turned his attention to the Captain. "Well Captain that is our team."

"Good. See to it that the new people are brought up to speed with the plan. Deliver the necessary training. It is imperative that each department works together in a seamless coordinated effort, not only in war operations but also in the daily routine. We will be graded on every aspect of the ship's activities."

The Executive Officer scanned the officers and chiefs. His facial expression was signaling he had more to say, something they needed to hear. "And since the crew is supplemented with sailors who are not familiar with our equipment, there will need to be some serious indoctrination and testing on the equipment."

"You are correct Commander," said the Captain, "and we need exerted coordination between departments. I can't express enough how important teamwork is to the success of this Mission."

The Commander called an end to the meeting.

Friday, 19 June 1970
The Gitmo Crew
USS Card
Pier Side
US Coast Guard Yard, Curtis Bay, Maryland

Each officer received a black loose leaf binder that contained a copy of the battle events schedule. These plans outlined in great detail the battle drill and qualifying operations for each department. He passed them around.

"First, let's look at section one; Norfolk. Here we will join the other ships in ResDesRon34. The first week of the cruise is taking the ship to Norfolk where we are to take on stores and fit out for the Gitmo experience. We will need to take at least one third of the reserves to Norfolk. Do we have a sufficient crew from the reserves Williams?"

"We have a little better than a third Commander."

"Excellent. The other reserves of the ship's company will meet us there and we will take on some other reserves from various other reserve units. We will be there for three days then it's on to Mayport where ResDesRon34 will join up with ResDesRon35 and ResSubRon5. This will be the complete ResDesDiv5 compliment. The entire division of 8 ships will convoy to Gitmo. Both ResDesDiv5 and ResDesRon34 will have their flag on the *Lancing*. While in Mayport we will take on some more stores and some more reserves."

He turned the page, the others followed suit. He thumped the page with his pencil. "Next, we will look at section 2, entitled, Gitmo Cruise Itinerary." He waited until all personnel present had turned to that section. "I know you can all read, but I want you all to hear the same thing at the same time. OK?"

He began to read. "Well, we shove off at zero five thirty Sunday, 12 July heading south to Norfolk. We will be in normal cruising condition with all ship's work in standard sea going plan of the day schedule. The schedule will include the regular chow schedule with the exception of breakfast which will begin at the usual time, at zero seven hundred, but it will be extended until ten hundred."

He rearranged himself on his chair, and continued.

"Just after clearing the channel, approximately zero seven hundred; we will run four hours at flank speed to see how the *Card* is running." He turned his attention to Chief Commissaryman, Leon Jaquet. "Sorry about the extended time, but you know how it is, some of the crew will need to work through."

"Been there, done that XO, we will have plenty and will be staffed accordingly."

"Excellent. The lunch and evening meal schedule will be at the normal times." He again looked at Chief Jaquet. "I know, I know you just get one meal done and you start serving another. Can you cook one meal while still serving another and at full speed?"

"Commander McCormick, please."

"Sorry Chief, I was just trying to let you know it could not be helped."

"We can handle it Sir, no complaints, no glitches."

"I knew as much. Thank you." He then turned toward the binder and began reading again.

"At eleven hundred we will reduce speed to twelve knots and remain at that speed en route to Norfolk."

He looked up at everyone to see if he could sense some faces with question expressions. He saw none.

"We are expected to arrive at the Navy Base at zero eight hundred on Monday, 13 July. We will anchor out, just outside the D&S piers (Destroyer Submarine) and wait for the *USS Lancing* and the other ResDesRon34 ships. We will all berth on pier 4. Once the other ships are in their assigned positions in the nest we will then weigh anchor and birth in pier four on the end of the nest. We will pick up the doctor, a corpsman and six enlisted of various ranks who are scheduled to serve their two week active duty requirements, and of course the rest of our reserve ship's company. We will also take on some stores and some movies for the crew's entertainment."

He peered over the attending officers and chiefs, turned the page, waited for them to do likewise and read again.

"We will depart Norfolk on Wednesday, 15 July at zero six hundred and arrive in Mayport by 1100 on Thursday, 16 July. We will pick up some more enlisted and perhaps another officer. We will join of *ResDesRon35* and *ResSubRon5* in Mayport. Once in the convoy we are expected to keep up and enter Gitmo in formation. There will be no excuses. If something goes wrong, and we can't keep up, the *Card* will be dropped from the exercise."

He cleared his throat and continued. "We will depart Mayport at 0600 Friday, 17 July. Our ETA (*Estimated Time of Arrival*) in Gitmo is ten hundred (1000) Saturday, 18 July. We are required to be at our berth at eleven hundred."

"Do you know where we will be in the nest?" asked Lieutenant Hooper.

"Probably on the end," he said, directing his eyes toward the questioner.

"We will spend the remainder of the day preparing for the drills which begin on Sunday, 19 July. The drills will run, Monday, Tuesday and Wednesday, July 20, 21 and 22. Thursday, 23 July, will be spent evaluating our after action reports and those from the exercise team. We will make provision for making the necessary corrections and send that report to ComResDesRon. We will take on live ammo for the Firing Range Exercise off Dominica and we will leave Gitmo at 0600 on Friday, 24 July and make way to Ocho Rios arriving approximately 1200 on Saturday, 25 July. We will need to anchor out and take liberty launches to the beach. Liberty will be port and starboard. The port watch will begin liberty at 1300 ending at 2259 on Saturday. Sunday, 26 July we will call liberty for the starboard liberty party at 0800 Sunday 26 July ending at 1800. We will make preparations to get underway on Monday 27 July at 0600."

"Will we need line handlers?" asked Mister Hooper.

"We have made arrangements to anchor at the Reynolds Mine Harbor. It is just a short distance from there to the city, said Mr. Goldsmith. We also have several rooms at the Ocho Rios Resort and they have given us access to their beach area and the swimming pools. We have two rooms reserved for the enlisted and two for officers who want to hang out there a while and change into swim wear."

"One for men and one for women." Lieutenant Sterling added.

"Ah yes."

Every one chuckled.

"We leave at zero six hundred", the XO continued, "and proceed to the live fire target area a hundred miles west of Dominica. Tuesday and Wednesday, 28 and 29 July will be spent at sea. Our ETA at the range is 1800 on Thursday, 30 July. We will commence live fire drills beginning at zero eight hundred on Friday, 31 July. Once we reach our target range, we will send over some hedgehogs, depth charges, and conduct surface to surface gunnery exercise with targets we brought with us, also scheduled are torpedo runs using a different set of targets. We only have a limited amount of live ammo so we will need to make them count."

"Sir, will this be a General Quarters operation or is this just for the weapons crew?" Lieutenant Grubaugh asked.

"Good question. We will consider this a weapons exercise, so no General Quarters. I think CIC and Damage Control have scheduled some departmental exercises for this time, is that correct?"

Mister Hooper and Lieutenant Sterling nodded their heads in the affirmative. They all turned the page and Mister McCormick began reading on that page.

"We are expected to secure the live fire practice session at twenty one hundred on Friday, 31 July and immediately head back to Gitmo." He turned the page.

"Saturday, 01 August will be at sea. Our ETA at NAVBASE Gitmo is Sunday, 02 August at 0800. We will make our reports, unload any ammo we may have, take on more stores and fuel, then head out to Mayport on Monday, 03 August."

He paused in order for his listeners to digest the information then continued; "Our ETA in Mayport is eighteen hundred on Tuesday, 04 August where we will drop off the sailors who came aboard in Mayport at pier 4. It is a designated drop off and delivery pier. There will be line handlers available at the pier. We will drop the brow and allow our Mayport people to go ashore. We have one hour there, then we will proceed immediately to Norfolk."

He paused, took a deep breath, turned the page and directed his attention to the next schedule sheet.

"In Norfolk line handlers will be there for us at eighteen hundred on Wednesday, 05 August at pier four to drop off those who came aboard there. The drop off and pick up pier is similar to the one in Mayport. Again we have one hour. We will set sail as near nineteen hundred as possible."

The XO paused as everyone turned the page. He looked around then continued.

"We are scheduled to arrive back at our home port at zero nine hundred on Thursday, 06 August. We will spend Friday, 07 August squaring the ship; examining *lessons learned* training for each department. Drills will secure after lunch approximately thirteen hundred on Saturday, 08 August. Officers and Chiefs will meet to discuss the cruise and prepare agenda for the September drill based on lessons learned from Gitmo. Officers and Chiefs will be dismissed after evening meal at approximately seventeen hundred. Questions? Comments? Anything?"

There were none.

Friday, 19 June 1970
Gitmo Combat Exercise Schedule Meeting
USS Card
Pier Side
US Coast Guard Yard, Curtis Bay, Maryland

1000: "Now we turn our attention to the Guantanamo drill schedule binder." He removed the binders from a box at his fee and handed them to the officer on his right who then passed them around the table as each officer took one. There were enough for the invited senior enlisted.

"This binder outlines the events the *Card* and the other ships of ResDesDiv5 will engage. As you see this information is provided by the Combat Exercise Planning Unit at Gitmo, the Executive Offers said. "Now once in Gitmo we will undertake the morning of the first day of the drill with the *Amberjack*."

"That should be a morning to remember," said Mister Hooper. "I hear that is the foxiest submarine in the US Navy."

"May be the foxiest in any Navy," added Mills. "In any case, it will surely be an experience."

Lieutenant Commander McCormick continued. "Few ships have ever found the *Jack* in the first day and no ship ever gets away from it the first day. Expect to be sunk within the first few hours of the drill. Combat you will have a real job on your hands."

"With the help of Jawarski, our local Gitmo expert, we have been practicing some pretty difficult scenarios," said the CIC officer. "I just hope one of them will be a tactic the *Amberja*ck uses."

"Very good! I also know that you are working on some offensive tactics as well. Just keep in mind Lieutenant Sterling," the executive officer interjected, "this crew does this every day and they know all the tricks. It is not a failure or a disgrace to get sunk at least once during the exercise. But I know you and your crew want to find it, and help the torpedo crew and depth charge ordinance get her. I know you will do your best and I believe your best will prevail, in spite of this Fox."

"I have heard the word *Fox* and *Jack*, when speaking of the *Amberjack* and its crew but I think a better word would be Owl," said Lieutenant Sterling. "The Owl is a wise bird to say the least. But in the case of the Amberjack it applies in a different way."

She had everyone's attention.

"The owl is credited with having wisdom; but the Owl is just an efficient killing machine. It can fly nearly silent, due to its tattered fringe feathers, and can exert 400 pounds of pressure at the tips of each talon. And like the Owl, the *Jack* does not exhibit wisdom so much as instinct and training from day by day year by year combat operations. In spite of the *Card's* dubious reputation, we have the talent on board this ship to outwit the *Jack*. They are used to their prey following a set pattern of defense, and they know what to do with predictable behavior. I think we can defeat the *Jack* with unpredictable behavior."

The officers and chiefs who had been there all nodded in agreement.

Mister McCormick continued. "Well said. I hope you are right. Now, as you can see, this drill begins at zero nine hundred, so we will pipe reveille at 0500; 0600 breakfast. We will muster at zero seven thirty. The umpires are expected at zero six hundred. We will be prepared for GQ after muster and we will go to GQ on the first sighting."

"So the morning is mostly games with the *Amberjack*?" Mister Hooper asked.

"Correct." He turned the page.

"On day two the morning will be again ASW (*Anti-Submarine Warfare*) but the afternoon will begin with a series of air attacks from adversary aircraft. We can expect strafing by fighters and several bombing runs . . . Should be interesting Lieutenant Grubaugh. This will be a real test of your AA (*Anti-Aircraft*) batteries."

"No doubt they will attack simultaneously," said Lieutenant Grubaugh, "to split our defensive fire, not allowing us to concentrate. All aircraft will, no doubt, come at us at once from every direction. It will be a real test. We have practiced for this event, but this will be the first time we get a chance to do it for real."

"You and Lieutenants Sterling will have your hands full. Along with the tactics used to combat the submarine your gunners and torpedo crew will be graded on how well they handle the routine portion of their jobs. You will find a complete agenda packet for the torpedo crew, the gun crews and the depth charge crew. For the sake of clarification, notice the section on torpedoes."

The ladies fingered through the files in their briefcases to make sure they were there.

"You will be graded on methods of firing. The straight fire, particularly how accurately and quickly the team can set the torpedo gyro mechanism and the curved fire method, again how accurately and quickly the team can set the offset angle of the gyro. You will be graded on when to use the straight and offset methods. There are other items here, but be sure the crew is well trained in plotting the basic speed or vector triangle of torpedo fire. They will be very tight on grading the representation of the intercept problem in which the torpedo is directed along the correct course to hit the target. "

"We will take the time to practice these items on the way to Norfolk and Mayport," said Lieutenant Grubaugh.

The XO directed his attention to the page he was referring to. Without looking up he read: "Fire Control will be highly scrutinized. It is important the umpires see us solve the fire control problems correctly and deliver our weapons before the enemy can solve the problem and deliver his. I don't have to tell you that failure to do so might result in loss of the ship, and of the life of everyone aboard which means we will lose that particular drill. They will send us back to Gitmo if we are sunk, and we spend the day in dockside drills."

The Captain spoke up; "The adversary force will use the best tactics they have to put us in real trouble, you can count on that Lieutenant." He turned to his XO.

"Mack you will be OOD, I will have the Conn. We will need some very close coordination on this one. Mister Hooper we can expect the umpires to give us plenty of damage scenarios."

"Something a bit different this time," said the Commander, looking at his papers. "It says they will be dropping spring loaded yellow paint filled balloon bombs that open on impact and spread color all around. It will look real, and I don't have to tell you all this is a dangerous drill, and it will last for three hours, three steady hours, and you will have to keep reminding yourself this is not real."

"That will mean a cleanup job for the deck force," Mister Hooper interjected.

"I'm glad you mentioned that Mister Hooper, actually regular deck detergent will lift the paint and hose it right over the side. Not as difficult as it would appear."

"Thank Navy Drill facility for small favors." said Hooper

Lieutenant Commander McCormick turned the page of the report. "The second and third days of the exercise will be 48 hours of coordinated attacks on us, from below, above and surface-to-surface. We will be dealing with planes, subs and ships all day from zero eight hundred to sixteen thirty hours."

"Is this a constant hour by hour attack?" Mr. Hooper asked.

"We may have some time periods of relative quiet but we will be at GQ the entire time beginning at the first sighting until after the drill. The galley will prepare sandwiches, coffee and bug juice and deliver them to our battle stations. As far as sleeping arrangements, every department will be responsible for how that is to be handled, but my guess would be most all will sleep when they can at their battle stations."

The XO turned the page and continued his briefing.

"We will get more information once we get there. Just keep in mind the entire time we are in the war zone our every action is being graded by the umpires."

"Does that include normal ship board operations that have nothing to do with the battle drills?" Chief Osborne asked.

"Yes. Everything that takes place in the war zone is battle drill related."

"Except maybe head calls," Mister Goldsmith said laughingly.

"Including head calls." The XO said.

"Ohhhh."

"Then we break off the drill and head toward Ocho Rios, Jamaica where the crew will take liberty. The rest you know."

"Excuse me Sir," Mister Hooper inserted, "I didn't see smoke screens in the battle plan. You expect to see smoke screens on a ship to ship exercise. I got a feeling it was up to us to determine whether to use the smoke screen. If we do it at the wrong time we lose points or if we don't when we are supposed to, we lose points."

"I agree Mister Hooper, but that is the flag's call, not ours." He raised his left hand to check the time. "OKAY, ladies and gentlemen it is not eleven thirty. Lets adjourn for the new meal and we will commence again at fourteen hundred."

1300: The Captain found Mister Goldsmith standing on the after part of the 0-2 level engrossed in thought as he stood facing the Curtis Bay Channel. "Mister Goldsmith, you got a minute?"

"I got all the minutes you need Captain."

"What is the story on this guy Benson? I find William's explanation a bit suspicious."

"Well Captain, I don't know from firsthand experience, you understand. But I can tell you what I have observed."

"I have learned that some of the miracles Williams does, would best be left unquestioned or off the record. I am not asking for an official report," Mills assured him, "I just think there is more to this story than Williams was willing to divulge. It's not like Williams to get us someone that just does not seem to fit."
"Ok here is what I gathered . . . gathered off the record unofficially." The Personnel officers said, prepared to give full disclosure.

The Captain nodded in agreement.

"Robert Benson works part time for Commander Richardson, the Navy liaison officer at McGuire Air Force Base. He is a desk jockey - goes to a community college at night. It seems Benson served his first two weeks reserve duty at McGuire. Commander Richardson liked the kid and offered to give him third class and points toward retirement if he would work for him on weekends. As it turns out Benson was actually doing the commander's job, while the commander enjoyed the benefits of his position. When it came time to put in for his two weeks reserve active duty this year he put in for a ship. The Commander was not happy that he put in somewhere other than his office, so he contacted BuPers and tried to get his orders changed."

"He tried to change his orders?"

"Correct and that created a problem. The story is that Benson had contacted a Lieutenant at BuPers who owed him a favor and asked him to get him on a small ship headed for Gitmo."

"A Lieutenant at BuPers owed Benson a favor?" the Captain asked.

"The Commander bumped the Lieutenant when he and his wife needed a flight to Naples to see his mother in law who was dying from complications due to Parkinson's. The Commander put one of his four striper buddies on the manifest that was on annual leave. It was during the weekend and the Commander was not in the office so Benson switched the altered manifest with the original one allowing the Lieutenant and his wife to travel."

"You said asking for a ship created a problem for the Lieutenant?"

"Well, the Lieutenant felt he owed Benson and he had no love for the Commander, so he asked a Chief if he could fix him up. Well the Chief had come through for Williams so he called in some favors and Williams agreed to take him."

"As the Commanding Officer of the *Card*, I think it is the ship that owes the Chief at BuPers, not just Williams. I think it was a good trade. Pass that along to Williams, in case he is concerned." The Captain turned and headed toward his cabin. After a few paces he stopped and turned again to Goldsmith. "I find it hard to believe the Commander isn't still trying to change Benson's orders."

"The Lieutenant and the Chief and Williams are stonewalling him until it is too late to change them."

"And when was that?" he asked thinking the date must have already passed.

"Day after tomorrow."

"Sounds like a lot of good people are putting a lot on the line for this guy."

"To get ahead of the Commander's counter orders Williams drove to D.C. to hand-deliver the request. Well truth be known Sir, I'm doing what I can. Williams is a good man and he is taking a risk. This Commander is a snake and Benson is an alright guy. And well, the Lieutenant owes him. It was a dangerous thing to do; this Commander could have railroaded them right out of the Navy."

"What can I do to help?"

"Well . . . Sir . . . you could specifically request Benson. Coming from you that would cancel all counter requests."

"Get me the paperwork and have Williams hand-deliver it."

"Aye Aye Captain."

1330: GM1 Phelps, standing in the forward gun area was lost in thought as the afternoon sun stood hot and blistering over the Coast Guard Base. Chief Osborne was reticent to disturb her but he had to deliver the news.

"What!!" She was furious. "I ordered a first or second class GM with sea and Gitmo experience. Don't tell me there is not one of those somewhere on the east coast in the Ready Reserves that need a two week Gitmo cruise!"

"Now Phelps, Williams tried to get someone like that for you, but none of them wanted to take that cruise on the *Card!* You know the reputation this ship has. You know the connections Williams has. If he can't get someone they can't be got."

"Not only am I **not** getting a Gunner's Mate I'm getting a desk jockey that has no sea experience! He will probably spend the entire time hanging over the side feeding the fish (*Vomiting in the water*). I would be better off doing it by myself. Well, I hope this clown is a quick learner and likes fast hard work, because he is going to learn to be a Gunner's Mate in the time it takes us to get to Gitmo!"

Friday, 19 June 1970
S.W.O.T. & Strategies
USS Card Pier Side
US Coast Guard Yard, Curtis Bay, Maryland

1400: The management team assembled once again to continue the planning meeting. When all was settled the captain entered.

"Attention on Deck." Cried the XO

Everyone sprang to their feet.

"Be seated." The captain said "Now," He said with a smile. It appeared that he was about to segway into another topic. "We have acquainted ourselves with the Gitmo activities this is a good time to develop our strategy for the exercise."

He nodded to Mister McCormick giving him the sign to pull out a stack of yellow note pads inside a cordovan leather binder. They were passed around the table and to the invited senior enlisted.

"Most of you have industry management experience as well as military. Anyone want to share your definition of strategy?"

No one seemed inclined to take on the question.

The captain turned toward Mister Gilliam. "Mister Gilliam, were you involved in strategic planning at the Atlantic and Pacific Paper Company"?

"Yes captain but only as an onlooker. I provided the higher ups with the benefit of my thinking and assisted with setting objectives for satisfying the strategy set by top management."

"How one defines strategy is how one develops and implements it," the captain said. Did they provide a definition for your use?"

"Oh yes, they fixed it indelibility in our brain."

"Will you share it with us?"

"Strategy, as they defined it is a general plan directed toward a desired outcome, under conditions of uncertainty. The plan identifies several objectives that must be met at certain times against certain standards. The methods for accomplishing those objectives and the implementation of those methods are the responsibility of the department heads."

"Hmm," The captain stroked his chin. "That's a good one."

Mister Alexander decided to offer one. "In the LDO class on management we studied strategy by Doctor Vladimer Kving. His definition was; finding and formulating & developing a direction what will ensure long term success if followed forcibly."

"Yes, I am familiar with Doctor Kving," said the captain.

Mister Winthrop added his definition; "At the Academy we used; a consistent pattern of advance to ensure victory with a predetermined outcome."

"At the university," added Ms. Grubaugh, "they told us it was basic rules for normal operations established by an entity to ensure organizational consistency."

"These are all good definitions," the captain smiled.

Ms. Sterling raised her hand and spoke loudly and defiantly, "I'm going out on a limb here but I think we should want to sink the *Amberjack* and make fools of the *Hammerhead* and the *Redfin*. I think the major outcome of our strategic plan is to restore the *Card's* reputation and go back to Baltimore, as Mister Gilliam once said, in glory! There! How about that?" she said triumphantly.

Everyone smiled amused but hardly willing to accept her grandiose thoughts as achievable.

"Well said Lieutenant," the captain said smiling in her direction. He then set his attention to the group as a whole.

"I have been giving our Gitmo strategy a lot of thought." The captain began, "and I have decided our strategy will be a full court press. By that I mean we will take a proactive offensive action against the adversary forces from the start and maintain that offensive to the last shot is fired."

The officers looked at each other around the room. Their facial expressions betrayed their thoughts. Bewilderment at the very idea they could attempt such a strategy without making bigger fools of themselves than they already are. Ms. Sterling's expression showed her complete disbelief in what she heard. She thought they could do it, but did not think the captain, or anyone else would think so.

"I know," the captain said in a tone that addressed his crew's unspoken trepidation."I know that seems a bit unrealistic, considering the *Card's* poor reputation at present. But consider this we are no longer the *Carp*. We have come a long way since then. The adversary force is not expecting a real fight from us and a clever strategy is to attack the enemy where he feels safe."

"Sir I am with you," said Mister Winthrop, "but just how do you propose to maintain the aggression when they catch on to or strategy and unleash their vengeance on us for being so belligerent?" And you know they will. Just one clever move to thwart our audacious action and its Katy bar the door."

The captain raised his eyebrows and ever so slightly turned his head and his eyes toward his executive officer.

Commander McCormick turned his attention from the captain and addressed the officer corps. "We will expect each division to design tactics specific to their own area of responsibility for addressing the combat realities they expect to encounter and devise a plan for a proactive approach. The captain and I fully expect that there will be times when we will be on the defensive, but we want to see a tactic for recovery and advance. You are familiar with the phrase; *the best defense is a good offense,* and the phrase *you can't win with offense alone there must be a good defense that can recover the ball and advance it to the team's advantage.* Well that is what we will expect. It may very well be that the adversary force will begin the engagement with the ball, if I may continue in the analogy, believing we will be on the defensive from the start, but we will have a plan to steal the ball right away and put them on the defensive. They may be so steeped in *that's the way it always happens* that they may be in a quandary as to how to recover with retreating."

There were smiles all around but no one really expected they could pull it off.

"That is a good strategy," Mister Winthrop interjected, "but let's be realistic this is what they do."

"Mister Winthrop," the Executive officer was a bit perturbed by the navigator's comment but he showed almost no irritation. In a way he was pleased to have this objection in order to address it. "Two-thirds of this crew has Gitmo experience. More than two-thirds of this crew are seasoned sailors, Every officer on board and every senior enlisted is not unfamiliar with the Gitmo exercises and what is expected."

The management team realized the two top managers were serious.

"There may be some our shipmates who don't think we can pull that off. Let's take a look at what we have going for us and going against us and just see what kind of a chance we have during the exercises." He removed his foot from the bench. "Let's examine our strengths and compare those strengths to the task of taking on a submarine. Name one of the strengths."

"I can identify several," said Ms. Grubaugh, "For the past three months we have been drilled constantly in doing our job, in order to do what we need to do in a matter of seconds. We aren't there yet but by the time we get to Gitmo we will be able to do it in our sleep. Next we have the undisputed highest ranked gun battery instructor in the US Navy, and she has brought us all up to a level of proficiency that nearly exceeds Navy standards. Give us another two weeks and we will exceed Navy standards. We can set time and roll out depth charges in less than Five minutes and a few times we did it in three minutes. Our hedge hogs have never missed an application. I can only vouch for the weapons department, but we can put up a fight, a fight the adversary will not expect."

"Okay, Ms Sterling spoke up, I will give weapons their due, and we can boast of a CIC ASW attack team that can track and report without a miss. At least no misses in the past three weeks. And if that were not enough, we have Jawarski, the undisputed champion Sonarman direct from the Gitmo adversary force. I can almost guarantee neither of those subs will surprise us."

"We have a top notch Communications officer, CIC and weapons officer. We have an engineering officer who knows DEE EEEs better than any officer afloat. Our XO is experienced in Gitmo operations as is Mister Hooper, Mister Gilliam, Mister Alexander one third of our regular crew and two thirds of our senior enlisted reserves, the captain boasted."

"And if I may add", offered Chief Gruber, "Everything works. All our equipment and systems are operational."

You may add, Chief, said the captain. "Now let's look at our weaknesses, or the disadvantages we have concerning the events and our objective. Where are we not competitive with the adversarial force?"

"Sir, if I may," said Mister Alexander, "the adversarial force is actually forces, plural, and it includes at least two, sometimes three submarines, not the least of which is the *Amberjack*. It also includes two surface ships and a squadron of bomber jets and helicopters, a well-trained communication unit and other scenario coordinators, umpires and evaluators, all well trained, well-coordinated and, since they do this every week with a new group of ships, they rarely make a mistake. Their job is to win each event and evaluate how each ship and squadron in the test group fare against naval combat standards. That includes how they perform when sunk or damaged, a situation that is expected and provided for. No one escapes those three or four days without suffering humiliation. And if all that was not bad enough, those who score badly must go through it again. Usually when a ship goes through the exercise, they qualify in three or four days then they go to a liberty port. Sometimes if they don't qualify in that time period that liberty port time is spent in Gitmo correcting mistakes."

"To add to that, captain," said Commander McCormick, "There is no experience coordinating the movements and battle plans with ships in ComResDesRon and ComResDesDiv. Admiral Pulaski and Captain Sorenson may have experience with the other ships in the division but the *Card* is an unknown element and not highly regarded, so we aren't sure how much attention they will give to us in the heat of battle."

It was Mister Winthrop's turn, "While many of our ship's company have Gitmo experience, only a few have done it on the *Card*."

"Hmm. We *are* up against it. Now let's explore some, what I call, opportunities those elements we can exercise that will allow us to exploit to our advantage. In other words what Opportunities are available to us? What can you foresee that we have that may give us a fighting chance or . . . a competitive edge."

There was silence for the space of 30 seconds. Each person present trying to think of any unique advantage may be available in their department.

"Well I can think of one, a very important one, one I don't think anyone here is aware of, but I think it is time the ship's company was enlightened," said the captain's chief of staff.

The captain smiled in the direction of his executive officer. "Permission granted Commander."

"Ladies and gentlemen, our captain has had several weeks of on-the-job training in ASW warfare. I mean on destroyers hunting and engaging submarines and on submarines hunting and engaging with destroyers. We are all aware of the captain's learning abilities. He was trained by the best submariners and destroyer-men in the US Navy. He has been privy to some tricks of the trade picked up over the years and horded by those experts. There, shipmates, is one very strong advantage. We have the opportunity of witnessing those arrogant champions in the adversarial force having to deal with expertise they do not expect. We will have them on the ropes in no time, going back to the drawing board to figure out how to handle us."

This was good news to everyone. The captain took it all with humility. "Thank you for your vote of confidence Mister McCormick but you are too complimentary, you give me a great deal to live up to."

"I suppose our best opportunities lie in the fact that we have a reputation of being ner-do-well week end warriors on a rusty tin can known as the *Carp*," said Mister Winthrop.

"Let's identify any threats or elements in the event or the environment that could cause trouble for us in these exercises," said the captain.

"By environment, do you mean political elements or physical elements or unforeseen elements?" Mister Winchester asked.

"I would say yes to those two elements and yes to any other circumstance that may interfere with our achievement in the exercises." The captain said.

Mister Faulk took his turn. "Let's be realistic here. The opportunity Mister Winthrop has identified is an exact opportunity, but it is also a threat. I have been to several of these Navy games and I'll tell you the political climate is against us. The adversary forces will not sit still and let us win! The umpires and the evaluators will not permit any ship, but especially this ship to prevail in any pre-set event. You can bet once we score a few times, and especially if we score because of some clever offensive tactic they will begin to disallow depth settings, range and trajectory settings, and who knows what else. They will throw stuff at us that are not in the drill schedule. We should re-think our objective and just be satisfied with qualifying like any other ship. That is considered a win for any ship of the line and would be a remarkable win for the *Card*."

Everyone present, who was at one time fearful of the Gitmo exercise began to believe they could do what Lieutenant Sterling offered as an objective, only to be deflated by Mister Faulk's venture into political reality.

"You certainly have a point, there Mister Faulk," the captain agreed, "But let's just take a reading here of what we have discovered. Our strengths are well known to us and unknown to them. Our weaknesses are the same as any other warrior entering combat against an unknown foe with vague rules of combat. Our opportunities can also be our biggest threat. Ms. Sterling," he turned a smiling face to his CIC officer, "I like your attitude, and your suggested objective represents your general frame of mind. I think Mister Faulk's is being realistic but because we know that we can prepare for it." He turned back to face the audience at large. "Let's win with clever tactics, valor and the implementation of our strategy and the related objectives each department head develops employing knowledge, skills and abilities coordinated with all the departments of this magnificent vessel. I would be perfectly satisfied to lead this ship in battle and make a grand impression on our adversaries and our bosses on the *Lancing*.

Ms. Sterling provided her, now expected enthusiasm, "You have to admit it's a stretch but not out of the question. I think we can do it. My CIC group knows what to do they just need a lot of practice between now and then. And if anyone still doubts Lieutenant Grubaugh's gun and ordinance crew it's because they have not paid attention. Personally I can't wait to get started."

"Good. I will expect to see your tactics and drill plans before we shove off. We will spend the time between here and Gitmo refining the tactics as our practice drills indicate." said McCormick.

"OKAY, ladies and gentlemen, the commander continued it is late. Let's adjourn for today and meet here again at ten hundred tomorrow.

Executive Assessment
Assessing the probability of success in an organizational endeavor

Pay attention to the meeting the captain had with the officers and chiefs on the mess deck. His analysis was actually a system geared toward the assessment of the probability of the *Card's* success in the combat exercises.

The captain was unofficially conducting a SWOT analysis SWOT is a structured planning method used to evaluate the **S**trengths, **W**eaknesses, **O**pportunities, and **T**hreats when considering some new or unique business activity. The technique is credited to Albert Humphrey, of the Stanford Research Institute (now SRI International).

The SWOT system identifies the internal and external factors that are favorable and unfavorable to achieving that objective. SWOT analysis is a powerful model for many different situations. The SWOT tool is not just for business and marketing. It can be used to assess the possibilities or the probabilities of almost any unknown objective. To reiterate - SWOT analysis may be used in any decision-making situation when a desired end-state (objective) has been defined. SWOT analysis may also be used in pre-crisis planning and preventive crise3s management.

- **S**trengths: characteristics of the business or project that give it an advantage over others
- **W**eaknesses: are characteristics that place the team at a disadvantage relative to others
- **O**pportunities: elements that the project could exploit to its advantage
- **T**hreats: elements in the environment that could cause trouble for the business or project

The original SWOT analysis suggests we start with an objective, if the analysis shows the objective cannot be attained another objective is selected that can be attained according to the analysis.

Users of SWOT analysis need to ask and answer questions that generate meaningful information for each category (strengths, weaknesses, opportunities, and threats) to make the analysis useful and find their competitive advantage.

One way of utilizing SWOT is what Humphrey calls matching and converting. Matching is used to find competitive advantage by matching the strengths to opportunities. Converting, says Humphrey is to apply conversion strategies to convert weaknesses or threats into strengths or opportunities. If the threats or weaknesses cannot be converted, a company should try to minimize or avoid them]

Analysis may view certain factors as strengths or as weaknesses depending upon their effect on the organization's objectives. What may represent strengths with respect to one objective may be weaknesses (distractions, competition) for another objective.

Each identified weakness, opportunity or threat should be clearly defined so that planned strategies to overcome or to implement the identified circumstance can be developed.

In using the SWOT care must be made not to de-moralize those who are making the analysis in that they give up on a project because the weights are too heavy in the negative. On that same line of thought users should be careful the analysis does not allow for moving forward on a project that looks promising but cannot work due to insufficient evidence of negative factors. One way to ensure this does occur is to have clear strategies developed for each item in the SWOT process.

We were privy to only a small portion of their analysis but enough to get a fair understanding of how the system works. Consider each segment the captain asked about, and consider what you know about the ship and its crew so far and identify any other items within those segments that should be added to the analysis mix.

Strategic Planning
Normally you would expect the captain to have a strategic plan before now. And in fact he did have a strategy but it was not announced until now. One can see from the actions the captain took up to now, was to bring them to a point in their renewal activities where they could experience successful outcomes to their drill exercises. Every action taken up to now required them to develop plans that tested each crew member's competency and resolve and initiate drill exercises to sharpen those skills and instill confidence in themselves and their shipmates.

No organization can expect to operate without an overall strategy outlining the mission, or the reason they are in business how they will do business, with whom and where. Each department has an active role to play in seeing that their part of the strategic plan is carried out on a daily basis and that obtainable, measurable objectives are set that will ensure a successful outcome. With that tactics are in place that state specifically what action is to be taken in order to meet those objectives. Anyone, in management, that is not able to make this contribution must be trained or removed from this level of responsibility.

Effective organizations will devise plans for identifying possible competitive threats and devise a system for dealing with it. In the military there are S-2 officers in charge of intelligence. Many Organizations in the competitive market system will have such reconnaissance methods to detect what the public and their customers need or want in order to have plenty of time to gear up for it. This civilian organization S-2 will also provide discovery information on what the competition is up to in order to stay ahead of the competition. I do not necessarily recommend sending spies into competitive operations but there are ways in which pertinent information can be discovered in order to plan for engaging in R&D for developing needed new products or markets before the competition discovers or in order to produce a better product or market than the competition is planning.

Does your organization have an S-2? Should there be one? What are some ways a company's S-2 can make these discoveries? How bold is an acceptable method of securing this information?

Of course there will be political elements and unforeseen elements that will threaten any good strategy and support tactics. You can bet once you score a few times, and especially if you score because of some clever offensive tactic those with political clout will throw stuff at you that is not on the level. But if you have prepared, you have a good strategy and workable tactics designed to accomplish every aspect of the strategy and – get this – as far as possible secure your own political alliances.

One (whether an organization or as an individual executive defending against political adversary) must not just take a defensive stance but a pro-active offense in order to thwart the attack and to expose the other for what they are, hopefully destroying their credibility and thoughts of trying it again. It is amazing to me how self-important executives will attempt to dislodge effective executives for their own self-interest at the expense of the organization or the morale of the crew.

The officer corps had to admit it was a stretch but not out of the question. Anytime you are up against a formidable foe that has been here before you must be brave and have a good attitude.

Command Axiom:
- *"Ponder and deliberate before you make a move." (Sun Tsu – The Art of War)*
- *"Never begin a battle until you count the cost."*
- *"If you are ignorant of both the enemy and yourself you are destined to be in peril." . (Sun Tsu – The Art of War)*
- *The best defense is a good offense, but you can't win with offense alone there must be a good defense that can recover the ball and advance it to the team's advantage.*
- *A clever strategy is to attack the enemy where he feels safe."*
- *The belief that that's the way it always happens is the most effective approach to a battle that has been fought before will bring the operations in to a quandary with very little opportunity for escape.*

Chapter 5 – Assembling the Team

Sunday, 12 July 1970
USS Card Pier Side
Steaming from Home Port Baltimore to Norfolk

The *Card* was moored through the night. Each four hour watch coming on and going off as scheduled. Certain hands getting out of the rack to take care of the ship's business and others climbing into their rack after taking care of their watch obligations.

0400 Reveille was piped and all hands, except those coming off the 0400 watch hopped out of their racks and began taking care of the early morning personal preparations. Mister Winthrop assumed the OOD duties on the quarterdeck.

0415 The ship board intercom came to life; "Now turn to, scrub down weather decks, sweep down all compartments, Sweep down all lower decks, ladders and passageways, empty all trashcans, now sweepers."

0545 The Boatswain keyed the 1-MC (ship-wide address system) and made an announcement that sent chills up the spine of the entire ship's company. They had heard it before, but this time there was electricity in it.

"Now all hands make preparation for getting underway. Start all propulsion engines. The ship will shift from shore power to ship power in five minutes."

At the end of the five minute time period the quartermaster counted down the seconds. The shift was made without a glitch.

0600 "Now . . . The Officer of the Day has shifted the watch from the quarterdeck to the flying bridge. Now set the special sea and anchor detail. The maneuvering watch will lay to the bridge."

0655 The final getting underway order was given.

"Now . . . cast off all lines."

The lines were cast off from the pier and retrieved by the deck hands on the *Card*. They were promptly and properly coiled and placed in their proper storage space.

When the last mooring line was dropped and the Boatswain Mate of the Watch blew a long whistle blast and passed the word to shift colors. The jack and ensign were hauled down smartly and the *steaming* ensign was hoisted on the gaff and the ship's call sign was hoisted.

One of the sailors, standing on the forecastle, said to himself, "I thought I would never hear me say, we're on our way to Gitmo Bay"

The *Card* shoved off at zero seven hundred as scheduled but a cold rain that swept down from the north had brought unusually cold temperatures in the area.

While it was 70°, a cold day for July, the water was still warm. The rain that had been going on steadily all night threatened to dampen the first day at sea. The ship left the channel and entered the open sea at zero nine hundred. The rain ended at zero nine fifteen and the water temperature was slightly warmer that the air temperature.

The *Card* was to run the first four hours under a full power run to make sure she was truly sea worthy. They had been running along at a full 24 knots for about 40 minutes. The sea mist was thickening quickly, it was not unusual in these waters at this time of the year, but usually it burned off quickly.

Now as Mister Winthrop stared abeam he felt a sense of dread as the fog seemed to engulf the exposed elements of the ship and stick to it like pale weed. He looked aft and up toward the mast. He could barely see the base of the mast and it disappeared in the murk, looking over the side he could not see the ocean below.

He ordered the duty Boatswain's mate to set the low visibility detail. Sailors from supply and the deck force E-4 and below are assigned in four-man sections in two-hour shifts. The first crew took positions on the forecastle with binoculars.

They slowed to 10 knots traveling in the blind, using every conceivable method for keeping on course and not hitting anything. "Keep a sharp weather eye out." He said to the lookouts, as if such an order was necessary.

"I feel like we're floating in mid air." Said one of the lookouts.

The Duty Boatswains Mate sounded the ship's fog horn every sixty seconds. The horn only added to the mystery and the eeriness of their predicament.

The Conn officer slowed the ship to 8 knots, then, to 6 as the fog grew thicker.

Though the ship was in deep fog, normal sea going activities continued unimpeded. Those who had the various watches were trained in handling the fog.

0700 The ships bell, which normally sounded six bells at this time, was belayed as was the shrill whistle of the boatswain's pipe that called attention to breakfast because of the fog. The word was passed by supervisors.

0720 The 1-MC announced; "Now on deck section Bravo, lifeboat crew of the watch to muster."

0750 "Now officer's call

0800 "Now on Deck section Alpha. The officer of the Deck is Lieutenant Hooper". On deck also was Ms. Grubaugh serving as navigator. The captain sat in his chair on the port side of the bridge.

0955 The OOD made an entry into the Bridge Log; "The fog began to clear."

1016 Bridge Log entry: "The visibility had improved to almost 1 mile."

1030 Bridge Log entry: "The fog had dissipated to overcast. The low visibility detail was secured, and the ship assumed peace-time day time cruising."

1115 "Now knock off ship's work and prepare for the evening meal. Sweepers man your brooms. Make a clean sweep down fore and aft. Clean all lower decks ladders and passageways, empty all trash cans. Now sweepers."

1120 "Now mess call for on-coming watch."

Bridge log entry: "Fog dissipated. Overcast conditions. Increased speed to flank according to Plan of the Day."

1130 "Now the noon meal is served on the mess decks."

1245 The 1-MC announced the end of the evening meal schedule. "Now secure the mess line."

1300 The captain ordered all stations to undergo combat readiness drills from now until they arrived at the D&S piers in Norfolk Naval Shipyard. The purpose of the drills was to determine where the weaknesses were and correct those mistakes before joining the squadron. There were *man over board* drills, abandon ship drills, damage control drills in all parts of the ship, as well as battle station scenario drills.

"This will not be a pleasant experience but we must know what we need to know and do in order to be confident when we join the squadron. We must have faith in ourselves and our ship. There is only one way to do that and that is be so well trained and so good at what we do that we can have absolute faith in each other when we meet for the big one in Gitmo."

The ordinance men were to set depths on the ash cans (depth charges) then re-set them for speed. The captain had wanted depths changed on the cans in less than three minutes. They would do it for an hour on and an hour off until they could reset the cans on each side in less than three minutes.

The captain and several other officers and chiefs had been there before and they knew what to expect and what was needed to do to meet the enemy at the big show.

The captain made it very clear when he said "When we set sail for Gitmo we must be sure we were ready, we must test ourselves to be sure we are ready. We can't get ready when we get there we must be ready before we get there."

All that day the *Card* ran freely toward the horizon. The watches changed, the standard word was passed in due times, drills were carried out. The drills lasted all day.

1600 Finally the 1-MC made the announcement they were all waiting for; "Now on deck section Charlie. The OOD is Lieutenant Winchester. Now sweepers, sweepers man your brooms. Make a clean sweep down fore and aft. Clean all lower decks ladders and passageways, empty all trash cans now sweepers."

When the ship's day was done the word was piped to knock off ship's work the sailors who were not scheduled a watch for the evening could enjoy the luxury of being at sea with no pressing work to do.

The 1-MC blasted the announcement; "The ship's store is now open".

Each sailor basked in the delight of being on the high seas. For those who have been at sea it did not take long for them to get their *sea legs*. It took a little longer for those who were experiencing it for the first time. The ocean spreads out in every direction, huge blue-green swells lift the ship and surge it forward assisting the engines. One feels heavy in the feet when the swells lift, and light footed when the swells move past and drop the ship into its waiting trough.

The routine aboard such a small ship was regular and carefully planned. Standing underway watches or casually moving about the deck. There were some disadvantages for being at sea, however. Strict water discipline had to be maintained as the ship had to convert salt water to fresh water and the *Card* had only one evaporator. Showers were scheduled in a port and starboard arrangement depending on one's watch quarter and station billet. There was port and starboard for men and another time frame for women.

Then there was the gray steel, the smell of diesel fuel and salty ocean air, the constant vibration of the decks, as well as the up and down and rolling motion created by the relentless, movement of the sea, keeping one alert as to balance when walking. There was the panoramic view of endless water meeting endless sky at the horizon.

1615 "Now test running lights and emergency identification signals, report their readiness to the OOD"

1630 "Now early mess for mess-cooks MAA and on coming watch. (*MAA Master at Arms the duty police patrol)*

1655 "Now mess call, clear the mess-decks.

1700 "Now mess call – Evening Meal for all hands. Close watertight doors. Set material conditions throughout the ship."

1730 "Now security patrols make reports to the OOD. Coxswain of the life boat crew reports all boats ready for lowering and engines tested." "Now relieve the watch on deck section Alpha"

1800 "Now sweepers, sweepers man your brooms. Make a clean sweep down fore and aft. Clean all lower decks ladders and passageways, empty all trash cans. Now sweepers. The OOD is Lieutenant Sterling."

1955 "Now Eight O'clock reports. Permission to strike eight bells." The Quartermaster rings the ship's bell. ding ding, - ding ding,- ding ding, - ding ding - ding ding,- ding ding,- ding ding, - ding ding

The mornings and evenings were especially beautiful with the myriads of colors that streaked the sky and reflected on the ocean. All too beautiful and all too short lived as it was followed by what most often seemed to be a never ending daytime sky and sea day after day, never changing.

There are few things as beautiful and as inspiring as a sunrise that identifies the horizon by illuminating where sky meets the sea, unless, of course, it is the splendor of the sunset as a profusion of magnificent glowing colors slowly descend into the ocean streaking the sky and reflecting off the waters. There is no grandeur like the silent explosion of colors that quietly and slowly fade growing dimmer and dimmer until the sky and the sea become one to the awestruck eye of the beholder. The darkness settles in and the stars turn on, first dimly then grow brighter.

There are few places on this earth that can calm the soul like the gentle movements of the waves tenderly rocking the craft, and the sound of the splashes against its skin.

First class boatswain Mate Furman first met Captain Mills early one morning just a few days after the captain had reported on board. It was on the 0-2 level at 0400 one morning as it was their custom to walk the deck at that hour to be alone and reflect. During their brief encounter Furman explained that when he was on a destroyer assigned to the Caribbean how he would go out on the O-Three level next to the stack at (4:00 am) spread eagle on the deck and look up at the stars. He said "The deck was always warm against his back. He liked the feel of the vibration of the engines, the sound of the sea splashing against the sides, the gentle rocking of the vessel, a warm south-seas breeze wafting across the deck, the smell of saltwater and diesel fuel. He would just look up and watch the ship's mast move like a pendulum across the stars.

It was all part of the romance of being a sailor in the constant unchanging atmosphere of life aboard a naval vessel at sea. It was part of the experience that one grew to love and enjoy. Mariners call it having salt water in one's veins. It was an experience that true sea fearers never get enough of, and never forget. Those who cannot adjust don't last long in the *steaming* segment of the Navy.

Execuive Assessment Testing the Plan

The captain reminded the officers and crew they had planned and prepared carefully for this combat readiness exercise. They had a plan to revitalize the ship and the crew. They had plans for daily operations, and they made plans for handling contingencies (what ifs), and turbulent times. They had planned the route they would take to Gitmo with stops to replenish the crew and the ship. They had a basic combat plan for their adventure in the combat exercises. They had extensive plans for testing the plans and the testing the crew in handling the implementation of the plans and the crew's technical skills. Now they had a strategic plan in which all these other plans and activities were directed.

The captain made it very clear when he said "When we set sail for Gitmo we must be sure we were ready, we must test ourselves to be sure we are ready. We can't get ready when we get there we must be ready before we get there." He ordered all stations to undergo combat readiness drills from now until they arrived at the D&S piers in Norfolk Naval Shipyard. The drills would determine where the weaknesses were and correct those mistakes before joining the squadron. There were *man-over-board* drills, abandon ship drills, damage control drills in all parts of the ship, as well as battle station scenario drills.

The captain said it would not be a pleasant experience but we must know what we need to know and do in order to be confident when we join the squadron. We must have faith in ourselves and our ship. There is only one way to do that and that is be so well trained and so good at what we do that we can have absolute faith in each other when we meet for the big one in Gitmo."

Constant training and testing for a successful outcome can be monotonous when a continuous operation is required and or when they must train and test for contingencies that may or may not occur. However, those being trained and tested will appreciate it when they are called on to perform.

A plan is a programmed course of action, made to implement programmed decisions. Plans made during times where favorable conditions allow for more careful planning will almost always be more effective than plans made under hostile or turbulent times. A plan is only as good as its effect on a desired outcome. Plans are tested and tweaked under controlled conditions. When the plan works in trial we have more faith in it, and those implementing it when the time comes to employ it.

As far as possible management must be prepared for interruptions in normal operation and not allow Fate to dictate our response.

Fate makes demands on flesh and blood and what is most often the demand is flesh and blood.

Confidence in others is evidenced only through experience. The constant drills, ordered by the captain, provided that evidence.

Untested Character, faith and confidence cannot be trusted.

Empowering the Crew to Test, Tweak and Implement

Ms. Sterling said there was enough talent on the *Card* to defeat the Jack. The problem was they had not had a chance, in the past two years, to test that competence. We have evidence of the competence the Lieutenant referenced was the fact the time from beginning the tests to the point in which they could perform effectively was very short. With the assistance of the captain (because of his extensive training with the ASW and Submarine experts provided by ComResDesRon 34) The ASW crew, the gunnery crew and the deck ordinance crews (hedgehogs, depth charges) had their own tactics they believe would be effective because they do not follow the standard format of attach and defend. They have planned an aggressive offensive rather than a defensive escape plane.

The crew must be clear regarding their part in the plan, and the only way to endure a level of confidence is to implement the plan under, as near turbulent conditions as possible and repeat the activity time and again, until it is almost second nature.

Creating an Atmosphere for expectations of Success

There is a Navy recruiting poster hanging in my office showing a war ship on the high seas silhouetted in front of a late evening sky. In the foreground is dark blue-black ocean swell that seems to be rising up above the ocean surface creating a feeling of the restlessness across the open sea. Inside that dark wave are these words; *Navy. Not just a job, it's an adventure.*

In that terse statement lays the secret of organizational success. When members work and live in a climate that provides for innovation and discovery they find the work is not just a mundane task but a worthwhile experience that tests their skill and allows them to witness progress on the job and in their lives.

When work leads to personal achievement because they are empowered to have influence on what they do and how they do it and professional development is a way of life those employed by the organization will be in the proper frame of mind to handle the adversity that comes with turbulent times.

When the job is an adventure there will be a can-do attitude that will see them through. They would have experienced the confidence management had in the rank and file and therefore they will have confidence in each other and in the management team. They personally participated in making the good times good, and will understand that the good times can be made to return if they don't give up.

When the organization makes optimism possible, and the employees enjoy the self respect that comes from an innovative, vigorous operation they will be much more inclined to share in the sacrifice during times of turbulence.

Confidence in others is evidenced only through experience. The constant drills, ordered by the captain, provided that evidence.

You cannot depend on a pre-emptive approach to keep you from experiencing identified crises, in spite of all you do to prevent it. A contingency plan is developed the same way the crises identification process was done. Every organization should have a contingency plan for handling events when they occur and include crises situations that occur in spite of your basic operational pre-emptive plan.

Command Axioms:

- Effective response to crises, or prolonged turbulent times does not come without proper planning, training and <u>testing.</u>

- Prepare for what is difficult while it is easy to do what is great while it is small.

- Prepare to move and act as second nature. The worst calamities that befall an army arise from hesitation: (*Sun Tsu – The Art of War*).

- Confidence in others is evidenced only through experience.

Chapter 6 Trouble Begins

Monday, 13 July 1970
Destroyer & Submarine Piers
Norfolk Navy Base Virginia

1100: The *Card* entered the channel leading to the D&S Piers and was progressing toward their assigned anchorage area.

"Slow to four knots"

"Four knots Aye"

As the ship was slowing a loud graveling sound came from the starboard forward bow.

"Bridge, this is the after watch (fantail) we are dragging something astern."

"We aren't close to anything to ram, and the maps do not show any debris in the area" Added the Navigator.

"The anchor watch on the Pelican had tripped the release and the anchor deployed. He applied the break but it jammed. The chain continued to spill out. The yellow painted section appeared indicating the chain was nearing the end. Then the red paint appeared indicating the end of the chain. The pull of the ship ripped it lose from its moorings in the anchor bay with ear shattering sound of thick steel tearing lose from inside the forward hull forward. Then all was quiet.

"Forward watch, what was that noise?"

"The anchor watch must have tripped the release and the anchor deployed" Shouted the forward watch.

"All Stop" shouted the Conn officer.

"All stop" shouted the engine room.

"Have we lost our anchor?" the Conn officer asked the forward watch.

"Yes Sir, it sank."

Mister McCormick and Mister Winthrop came onto the bridge to inquire about the noise. "What do we do about this Commander?" Mister Goldsmith asked.

Commander McCormick gave a sigh of disbelief and disgust, slowly shook his head. Mister Goldsmith was noticeably agitated and fearful. "Notify the captain, Mister Winthrop. Mister Goldsmith you had the Conn so you contact ComResDesRon tell him we need authority to contact a Destroyer Tender in the yard for repairs." said McCormick. The radio message was sent to ComResRon34 and ComResDiv5 with info to Material and Repair Naval Base Norfolk. The message noted the problem. Material and Repair, anticipating approval assigned the *Card* to the *USS Yellowstone (AD18)* at the end of the D&S piers next to the *Orion (AS18)* a Submarine Tender.

The Tender assigned them to repair pier 18 a short distance from the *Yellowstone* and informed them they would send over a crane and look for an anchor. They would also send a team to look at the damage. They were none too happy when they were ordered to put the *Card* as priority one since it was to remain on schedule for joining the Division in Mayport to sail to Cuba.

If that was not enough, Furman, after clearing it with Mister Hooper informed them they will need a camel so the *card's* deck force could make some cosmetic repairs, a dent in the side and a coat of paint for their appearance in Mayport. Mister McCormick added the camel to the list.

"Material and Repair won't be none too happy about giving us a camel, so maybe me and Mister Hooper should go over to repair and do some one-on-one nah-go-she-eight-en." Said Furman.

1200: "Now pipe to the noon meal" came over the 1-MC as the ship moved to repair piers.

1230: The *Card* tied up at the repair pier. As soon as the first mooring line was made fast on the pier, the Boatswain Mate of the Watch passed the word to shift colors. The ship's call sign and steaming ensign were hauled down, and the jack and ensign were raised. The shift from ship power to shore power went without a glitch.

The deck force began preparing for fresh paint on the starboard side and on the numbers.

1220: The 1-MC shouted "Relieve the watch on deck section Bravo. Commence daily routine."

Waiting on the repair pier dock was Lieutenant Commander Doctor Mark Johnson a reserve who has made this cruise for the past five years. He requests a different ship each year and this year he was cautioned against accepting a billet on the *Card*, it was a jinx ship with a poor reputation. That was all the incentive he needed to put in for it. He even called his commanding officer to make sure he was assigned to the *Card*. Doctor Johnson had a lucrative family practice but his avocation was the Navy. He felt more like a Navy doctor than a doctor in the Navy. He drilled with a naval reserve unit on a Marine base in Pensacola Florida. He was forty, married with two children; a boy 11 and a girl 14.

Standing with him was his corpsman, navy Petty Officer First class (HM1) Christopher Harris. Harris and the doctor were assigned to the same duty station and had made three such trips together. They made an excellent team. Harris usually led some casualty drills on ships that had little training in such matters. Those casualty drills were not usually welcomed by the crew until those on the casualty team had to use those skills in a Gitmo drill scenario. Harris was more than a corpsman, he put in four years with the first Marine Corps Division and saw combat in the last war. Before going to boot camp he and his father took a thirty day vacation and walked across Europe.

After his four year hitch he reenlisted for another four years in the ready reserves and received certification as a paramedic. He has been with a major trauma helicopter search and rescue unit as well as an ambulance company. He was about 24 with a wife and one adopted three year old girl he rescued from a small aircraft crash in the forest that took the life of her parents.

The ship was secure and normal moored operations were underway and the officers were relaxing in the wardroom, when the captain entered.

"When the doctor comes aboard I want to talk to him about a mass casualty drill. I want these drills to commence on the way to Mayport after we clear the sea channel."

"The doctor is on board now sir. He was waiting for us when we pulled in. He has already stowed his gear and is now checking out our sickbay with his corpsman assistant" Said Mister McCormick.

The captain keyed the intercom. "Doctor, may I see you in the wardroom?"

"Certainly. I will be right there."

The doctor approached the wardroom door, checked himself, brushed the front of his uniform, to make sure he was presentable to the captain, uncovered (removed his hat), turned the door handle and pushing the door open he stepped inside. The captain was leaning against the coffee counter sipping from a cup.

"Lieutenant commander Johnson reporting as ordered captain." He said directing his presentation to the captain.

"Glad to have you aboard commander."

"How may I be of service Sir?" He asked

"As soon as we clear the sea channel I want some mass casualty simulations. I understand you and your corpsman have experience in such things."

"Indeed we do sir. We have been to Gitmo several times and we are pretty good at preparing the crew for what they will encounter."

"Good, so I can just leave that to you then?"

"Certainly I will inform the quartermaster when to call for damage control and casualty assistance."

"First we will talk them through a scenario. Then later, I will ask for volunteers to simulate actual casualties."

The captain turned to Mister McCormick. We will call general quarters and try to make it as real as we can."

"That is what I would suggest sir."

I want forward gun, mid ships and after gun mounts, depth charge racks, another by the stack, engine room and pilot house."

"Captain, may I suggest we also do one on the bridge?"

"Agreed."

"That would include lookouts. We can do it with limited interruption."

"That sounds excellent doctor, thank you." Now gentlemen and ladies let's sit for evening meal". The captain moved to the head of the table, the officers moved to their places. The captain sat down, followed by the XO followed by the other officers.

MM1 Mike Brewer reported aboard and went right to work making repairs on the items Chief Gruber had prepared for him.

Finding another anchor was not as easy as finding a camel that was not in use. But finally one was extracted from a destroyer that had come in for strip down and decommissioning. The *Yellowstone* scheduled a crane brought to the pier for use in hoisting the large anchor.

Photographer's mate Charles Sandlin reported aboard. The petty officer of the watch consulted his watch, station and quarters bill and directed Sandlin to stow his gear in the after berthing area near the port bulkhead, section A16. Upon completing that, and testing the mattress on his assigned rack, he went immediately to set up a photo shop in a small space just off the ship's store.

Monday, 13 July 1970
Somewhere on I-64 between Charlottesville and Richmond

1600: Orville Smidlap was pleased with himself as he sat in the front seat of the Greyhound bus rolling down I-64 toward the D&S piers in Norfolk and the beginning of phase four of his plan to become a quartermaster on a US Navy ship. Phase one began when he met with the Navy recruiter that visited his high school in hometown of Frace Virginia. He joined the Navy reserves and drilled with a reserve unit until he completed his senior year. Phase two was off to boot camp in Great Lakes, Illinois. After a 9 week basic training program, phase three of the plan took shape when he applied for and was accepted into Quartermaster "A" school. Now after a six month program he was a certified Quartermaster striker. He was authorized to wear the ship's wheel insignia on his uniform just above the two stripes on his left sleeve.

He was a Quartermaster like his recruiter. Now he was on his way to phase four, active duty, on a US Navy ship, heading for war games in Guantanamo Bay, Cuba. And not just any ship - a tin can just like his recruiter. After this cruise he will have two years of obligated duty. By then he planned to be a Third class or maybe even Second Class Quartermaster. That will trigger phase five of his plan – Re-enlisting in the regular Navy and staying until retirement. All his life he was Orville Smidlap. When he reports to the *USS Card* he will be Smiddy, with two ds. He was eighteen and headed toward being a man. Not just a man, a Navy man.

1600: The 1-MC, on the *USS Card* again came to life with the announcement to knock off ship's work, and shift into clean uniform of the day.

Robert Benson reported aboard. He was greeted by Chief Osborne who escorted him to his rack (bunk) and waited until he stowed his gear, then took him to meet his new boss. The chief wanted to introduce Benson personally hoping to belay any fireworks the top gunner may set off.

In the meantime Captain Mills visited Captain Sorenson on the flagship, *Lancing*. He was escorted to ComResDesRon's stateroom. Captain Sorenson greeted him with enthusiasm. "Hello Bob, I see you made it in."

"Not without some trouble I am sad to relate."

"Yes I suspected you would want to tell me about losing your anchor. Some reserve seaman let the Pelican go too soon, I take it."

"Your intel is right on Captain. I am well aware of the consequences of losing an anchor. I am yours to command sir."

"Ordinarily, there would be grave consequences, Captain Mills, but Pulaski and I don't see the *Card's* situation as ordinary or your assignment as ordinary. ResDesDiv fixed it with the navy base. You have lived up to our expectations and your reputation so far, and we expect, aside from this little incident you will succeed in bringing it through the Gitmo exercises in fine fashion. Now sit, let's eat."

1620 Chief Osborne found Phelps in the forward gun mount. The duty Quartermaster began ringing eight bells indicating the end of the afternoon and the beginning of the dog watch. Chief Osborne approached the forward gun mount to find GM1 Phelps.

"Phelps."

"Yes Chief."

"Here is your new loader Robert Benson."

GM1 Brenda Phelps was in a squat position tinkering with something that looked to Benson like some kind of firing mechanism. Benson took a mental note of his new boss. Phelps was an independent sort of woman in her mid-twenties about five foot nine with an athletic build. Her short cropped black hair was well groomed under her work hat. She was not a beautiful woman, and not what you might call pretty, but she was attractive and easy to look at. She had a confident look about her. There was no mistaking that she knew what she was there for and she knew she was good at that job.

Phelps looked up at Benson. She noticed his boyish face and crooked grin. She quickly calculated him to be in his early twenties, maybe 21 or 22, about five foot ten, maybe eleven or so, good build but that was to be expected of a boy of his age.

The chief expected some un-lady-like old sea dog language, but she just looked at Benson without expression.

"I'm looking forward to working with you Phelps."

"You may change your mind about that in a few hours, Benson. I am determined to make a good showing at Gitmo and that means you have a lot of learning and training to do between now and then. So let's get at it."

She stood up and turned toward a deck locker that was welded to the forward mount and the deck. She opened the metal box and took out a gunner's mate training manual. She tossed it to Benson who much to her pleasant surprise caught it.

"Well I'll leave you two to your work," the chief said and he moved out quickly.

"OK Benson, we haven't much time so let's get at it. First, I will show you how the fire control system works, then on to where and how the gun batteries are placed and then we will focus on the forward gun and its ammunition. It is not automatic so there is a lot for you to know before we reach Gitmo."

She took him below decks to the area where the fire control computer is mounted. "There are two main parts in the fire control system, the director and the computer. Both handle the fire control problem. The fire control problem is the entire series of measurements and computations used in the control of weapons, beginning with the designation of the target and the type of fire, and ending with the destruction of the target."

Without saying a word she moved to the ladder that took them topside. Benson dutifully followed her.

"The director is a box-like steel compartment mounted high in the ship's superstructure. It is large enough to hold a small number of people and a large amount of fire control gear." She pointed to the place where the director was located. "On top of the director is a radar antenna, and projecting out of either side are the ends of the optical rangefinder. So, the director *sees* both electronically and optically. When the target is picked up by the director, its range, bearing, and elevation are sent below decks to the computer."

She looked into Benson's eyes to see if any of what she was saying was registering but Benson expressionless face gave her no idea if in fact he was getting all this. She continued;

"The computer, you will remember is way down below decks. It receives information from the director, and combines that with the ship's course, speed, the ship's roll and pitch, the drift of the projectile and other factors fed into from people feeding information into it. The computer sends these answers to two places - back to the director for a check, and on to the gun. That is where we come in."

She paused, and looked again into his eyes to see how much of this, if any, he was digesting.

"You got that?"

"Ah, yeah, so far. . . I think."

"Well you better get it before we get to Gitmo." For the rest of the day Phelps oriented Benson to the forward gun business.

1715: "Now evening meal is being served on the mess decks," came the blasting word from the 1-MC.

"OK Benson it's chow time. Are you up for some after duty extra instruction?" Phelps asked.

"You bet. I have a lot to learn if I am going to make a contribution to this gun during the war. Why not have supper together and work through supper?"

"Negative. Take this manual and read as much as you can between now and 0800 tomorrow morning. They will pipe to the flick (movie call) at eighteen hundred. The crew will assemble by the BRT. Let's knock off and start again tomorrow.

"Ah Phelps."

"Yes."

"Where is the BRT?"

"You have never been on board ship before have you?"

"No. I guess I have to learn the ship board jargon."

"Well just go up to the oh-two and ask someone."

"What is the oh-two?"

She pointed toward the 0-2 weather deck. "That is the oh-two,"

"Got it."

"So I will find the BRT on the oh-two?"

"Right."

1750: "Now relieve the watch." Came the word from the duty Boatswain's mate over the 1-MC.

1800: The ship's intercom system blasted. "Now liberty call, liberty for all hands sections Bravo, Charlie and Delta, liberty to end at zero seven hundred tomorrow morning. Now, liberty."

1815: "Now sweepers, sweepers man your brooms. Make a clean sweep fore and aft. Sweep down all lower decks, ladders and passageways. Empty all trashcans. Lay below to the MAA office for muster, all restricted persons."

1920: "Now Rig for Movies."

2000: The eight O'clock reports were piped at twenty hundred followed by the 1-MC announcement; "Now movie call, movie call." When movie call was piped some of the crew assembled on the oh-two level around and in front of the stack looking aft while others sat on the fantail between the depth charge racks looking forward to the movie screen that was erected on the end of the oh-two.

As darkness fell the movie was about to start. Benson went up to the oh-two and asked a sailor where he could find the Bee Are Tee.

"The B-R-T?" asked the old salt boatswain mate. "Who told you to ask for the B-R-T?"

"Phelps, Gunner One."

"Figures. Look, the B-R-T is that thing." He pointed at a wide mouth short stack looking item that rose above the deck about four feet high. "That is the fresh air vent for the lower decks, he said. Sometimes sailors refer to the stack as the B-R-T; it stands for Big Round Thing."

"Ah ha."

"Sit here mate. The flick is the *Investigators*. I have seen it before, it stinks but it beats sitting below decks drinking coffee."

The screen came alive with the Warner Brothers cartoon target but the music was drowned out by the roar of two Navy fighter planes flying low coming in over the ocean on their trip from a carrier somewhere off the coast heading for NAS Oceana

Monday, 13 July 1970
Greyhound bus
Destroyer & Submarine Piers
US Naval Base, Norfolk, Virginia

2200: The hound, carrying Smiddy (with two-ds) pulled into the D&S piers. He was surprised the bus could just drive right through the gates into the base. The bus came to a stop in front of a line of ships. The driver called out the names of the ships and sailors stood up and moved down the aisle and out the door. Smiddy did not hear the *Card's* name called, but he got off anyway. The driver opened the luggage bin and pulled out the sea bags as the sailors called out their names. When everyone had their luggage the driver looked up. "Name?"

"I didn't hear you call out the *USS Card*."

"That one is in a nest down the pier aways. Hop on board and I'll get you there long before 2359, so don't worry."

"Apparently the driver was an ex-navy man," Thought Smiddy.

After two more stops the driver found the young QM in the rear view mirror. Hey Quartermaster, this is your stop. He slowed the big bus to a stop and opened the door. There were a few more sailors getting off here. Most had ship patches on their uniforms, but none were from the *Card*.

The driver opened the luggage bin and pulled out the sea bags as the sailors called out their names.

The driver hesitated about removing Smiddy's sea bag. "Wait a minute," he said. The *Card*; Let me check my master sheet." He climbed into the driver's compartment as Smiddy stood in the doorway. "Oh yes. We got word the *Card* was sent to the repair pier. That's about a mile down this road. Hop in."

A few minutes later they pulled up to the repair pier. There was a lone Ship standing stately in the water. The lights on the pier shown against the ship's hull, and from where they were sitting, they could see the full view of the stern of the ship. There was no mistaking the raised white letters against a navy gray hull; *CARD*.

The driver opened the baggage compartment and removed Smiddy's sea-bag. "Enjoy your cruise sailor," he said.

Smiddy hoisted his sea bag onto his shoulders and headed toward HIS tin can. When he reached the gangway he stopped and admired the *USS Card*. He wanted to take it all in. Finally he climbed the gangway and stepped onto the ship. He lowered his sea bag, opened it and removed a packet with his orders in it.

"Is this your first time boarding a Navy ship, lad?" asked the OOD.

"Yes Sir."

Turn aft and salute the Ensign. Then salute the OOD. That would be me, and request permission to come aboard. Then you present your orders."

Smiddy followed the OOD's orders.

"Granted."

He looked at his watch. 2232. "I will remember that time for the rest of my life. It was the first time I said permission to come aboard - My first ship."

The duty petty officer called the duty Quartermaster to come and take Smidlap to the after berthing compartment at the very rear of the ship. Haralson, QM3 of the *Card*'s regular navy ship's company met him on the quarterdeck and they walked aft down the non-skid walkway on the outer portion of the main deck toward the fantail.

On the fantail a hatch door was open between the depth charge racks that sat near the edge of the starboard and port sides. "Its lights out Smiddy," said Haralson, in a voice just above a whisper. "It's dark so watch your step."

There was some emergency lightening that allowed some visibility in the otherwise dark sleeping area. Smiddy smiled as he thought to himself "The most powerful navy in the history of man sleeps with a night light."

"This is your rack." he said in a low voice as he pointed to the top rack in a stack of three, in a row of 12. It was a single sized bed that connected to the bulkhead with hinges that allowed the bed to be folded down and out of the way. A single sized thin mattress laid on a canvas piece stretched across four tubes arranged in the shape of a bed.

Along the bulkhead, near a row of racks, was a row of lockers that opened from the top. "This is your locker." He raised the lid and propped it open. "Stow your gear here." He patted the new guy on the back. "Report to the Bridge at zero seven hundred in the morning after chow," said Haralson. With that he climbed back up the ladder and out of the hatch leaving Smiddy alone.

Smiddy decided to get out a working uniform for tomorrow and leave everything else to put away in the morning. He removed his dress whites, folded them neatly and placed them in the locker on top of his full sea bag. Standing there in his skivvies, he worked out in his mind how he was going to get into his rack without bothering his new shipmates on the bottom and middle rack. He noticed pipes hanging over his rack so he decided to use them to pull up. He jumped, caught the nearest pipe, and pulling himself up he swung his legs and feet into the rack and then positioned his shoulders so his head could rest on the small pillow.

"There. That worked out all right," he thought. He lay there and let his mind take in the ambiance, and the thrill of his first night on board a US Navy ship. He relished the gentle rocking motion of the ship, the sound of the water against the hull, the smell of diesel fuel and steel and fresh paint. He listened to the breathing of his shipmates as they slept peacefully completely at home, comfortable and waiting for the dawn, when again they could participate in the shipboard routine. He intended to spend more time enjoying this new experience, but sleep overtook him.

Most of the crew was back on board before midnight. Many of the first timers to Norfolk took the opportunity to shop at one of the local Seafarer stores to purchase some tailor made uniforms, or purchase some liberty cuffs to sew on the underside of the dress blue uniform cuffs. Although it was not regulation to turn the cuff sleeves up to display the various patterns available, few officers or senior enlisted objected. Some were very nice; dolphins, sharks, destroyer silhouettes or rebel flag designs.

Monday, 13 July 1970
Repair Pier
US Naval Base, Norfolk, Virginia

2300: The rain began at twenty three hundred and continued to grow stronger and the wind increased to about 20 knots. The water by the pier was getting restless. The storm picked up steam, and the ship was rocking hard.

The 0-2 level spanned an opening between the port side weather deck of the ship to the starboard side weather deck providing a large overhead covering served as a shielded for the deck officer and the petty officer of the watch. They moved from the uncovered quarterdeck near the brow to the cover of the 0-2 span.

The rain beat hard against the ship pushing it out from the pier and then thrusting it back into the pier. When Mister Winthrop took the deck officer duties at 2359 he ordered the engine room to start the port engine and run it in reverse to hold the ship to as close to the pier and camel as possible. The deck force had to let out the lines three times during the night. The storm was not predicted to blow all night. Mister Hooper took the deck officer watch at zero four hundred. The ship was still beating hard against the camel in spite of the port engine, but he maintained the port engine order and continued under the shelter of the port to starboard passageway. The storm blew out at about zero five hundred.

Mister Hooper discontinued the use of the port engine to maintain stability.

Tuesday, 14 July 1970
Repair Pier, U.S. Navy Base Norfolk, Virginia

0614: Slowly the eastern sky began to lighten. A brilliant red, yellow and pale blue appeared over the arc of the sea. Then a burst of sunshine sent sprays of color in every direction pushing the night sky into the west. The deck officer stepped out and peered over the starboard side at the camel. It was badly damaged caught between the ship and the concrete pier, the storm's wind and rage had caused massive damage. The deck officer was impressed. That camel was six feet by six feet made up of 6X6 railroad tie–like wood beams and here it was badly damaged.

0700: Mister Hooper sent the bridge messenger to the Captain's cabin informing him of the damaged camel.

The Captain came out on deck to see the damaged camel. The deck officer stood by his side, as his relief, Mister Goldsmith the eight o'clock deck watch came up. They stood there shaking their heads.

"If our relationship with the Navy base was not already in the can, this will surely do it!" opined Mr. Goldsmith.

"I am afraid you're right mister Goldsmith," sighed the Captain. "We came in with a bad reputation before the anchor incident. Notify the navy base and tell them about their camel and tell them we need another one," He said with a noticeable sigh.

Mister Hooper chimed in; "The anchor should arrive about ten hundred. The crane is already in place. I think we can consider the painting completed. There are some noticeable dents in the side of the ship, but they pose no threat to the integrity of the hull. So unless you think we need one perhaps we can do without it."

"Well Mister Hooper you are the one to know. If you say we don't need one, let's not give the navy base something else to shake their heads at. Just write up a damage report and submit it along with the other paperwork."

"Aye Sir."

Executive Assessment

Crises Management plans activated - Crises Management with Disruptive Surprises

The *USS Card* had a bad reputation coming into Norfolk. The problem with the anchor and the camel only added to the distrust of those in command positions. Perhaps some type of PR activity would have reduced further erosion of the organization's reputation, or maybe the reputation was too far gone. BM1 Furman knew some people on the Yellowstone and was willing to go talk to them in order to relieve some of the pressure after all this week end warrior ship with ner-do-well reserves was placed in front of regular navy ships in order to get it ready for Gitmo, even though it would probably flunk out on the first day.

There are times when an hourly employee makes a better P.R. person because they can communicate with those who are actually doing the job on the floor. A manufacturing firm was experiencing problems getting the color right on the product. As much as they tried technician and managers were not able to get the supplier to understand the problem they were experiencing. The company flew a team of hourly employees who worked with the product to meet with the hourly personnel who were actually making the color to resolve the issue.. They were successful. AGAIN: If hourly employees are well trained and authorized to do what is needed productivity is assured.

Did you notice there were those on board who knew what to do in the circumstance with the anchor? Responsible executives know their departments well enough to plan for contingencies and be ready to deal with them. Every manager is responsible for contingency plans for major accidents or other destructive events that damage important equipment and facilities.

Mister Winthrop exercised a critical SOP regarding holding the ship in place while tied up to a pier in a storm. There is evidence that others were aware of the SOP and what to do when energized. There are those "tricks of the trade" for dealing with situations that do not occur very often but has a critical impact on equipment and personnel. The boss and the boss' subordinates need to know what they are.

The captain ordered the doctor to run casualty drills, and even gave him carte blanch as to when and where and how eventful those drills would be. When assigning a person or a team with the responsibility for running some major drill, is it wise to let them disrupt operations? In many cases, yes, if there is a possibility such an event could occur there. Everyone in management and staff, professionals and hourly personnel, are required to participate in those drills. Even if those drills interrupt the standard flow of operations.

Notice GM1 Phelps' had a planned, structured indoctrination, orientation and training of this rookie, Benson, who had no idea what fire control and gunnery was all about. It was imperative that Benson's training would promise a *hit-the-pavement-running* competence.

MM1 Brewer blended with Chief Gruber in making repairs and retrofitting the *Card*. We have spend a considerable amount of time on the need for planning and setting procedures in place for dealing with day-to-day operations as well as out-of the-ordinary situations. Blending new managers and employees, especially temporary personnel, into the mainstream of the on-going operations is critical for operational continuity as well as for employee environment comfort. A well-planned and presented orientation program followed by a step-by-step training and inclusion program is the key. Notice that regardless of what was going on with the newly arriving personnel and the necessary repairs, the ship's business and routine was uninterrupted.

As if they did not have enough problems with Material and Repair and the navy base they failed to remove the camel before the storm and it was destroyed. The captain, on recommendation from his officers decided to put it into a report, where it may not be noticed until long after they were gone, shove off and leave it and send an official report to Material and Repair Division. Is it ever prudent to ignore or hide a glitch in the operations?

Situations like coming into port and losing an anchor would normally cost a captain his command even though it was not his fault. You probably heard of head football coaches and head baseball coaches losing their job when the team can't seem to win. More often than not executives in charge are the first to be fired when bad things happen because their job is to see that things like that do not happen.

Captain Sorenson and Admiral Pulaski didn't see the *Card's* situation as ordinary. ResDesDiv fixed it with Material and Repair and the navy base. From this you can see the importance of having friends in high places. Professional competence, bearing and an attitude of expectancy, along with maintaining pertinent political connections will be a big help in getting your job done. Just be careful that your behavior does not appear to be a *suck up*.

Command Axioms

There are times when an hourly employee makes a better P.R. person because they can communicate with those who are actually doing the job on the floor.

Responsible executives know their departments well enough to plan for contingencies and be ready to deal with them.

Every manager is responsible for contingency plans for major accidents or other destructive events that damage important equipment and facilities.

if there is a possibility an event could occur there. Everyone in management and staff, professionals and hourly personnel, are required to participate in those drills. Even if those drills interrupt the standard flow of operations.

Chapter 7 The Storm before the turbulence
Wednesday, 15 July 1970
USS Card Underway to Mayport

Reveille was piped at zero five hundred. Breakfast went down at zero six hundred. The maneuvering watch was posted at zero seven hundred at which time the ship shifted from shore power to ship power and the Officer of the Deck, Ensign Winchester, shifted the OOD watch from the quarterdeck to the flying bridge. The Captain, the XO, Lieutenant Commander McCormick and Mister Winthrop joined him there. The special sea and anchor detail was set at zero seven thirty.

The last mooring line was dropped and the Boatswain Mate of the Watch blew a long whistle blast and passed the word to shift colors. The Jack and Ensign were hauled down smartly and the *steaming* Ensign was hoisted on the gaff and the ship's call sign was hoisted on the Signal Bridge. The force of the engines driving powerful screws sent a steady tremble though the ship and into the legs of those who stood on her decks.

The *Card* steamed out of Norfolk at zero seven fifty. They cleared the sea channel and increased speed to join up with the squadron. Mister Winchester had the Conn. The Captain was in his seat on the port side of the Bridge. Mister Winthrop and Lieutenant Commander McCormick were by the bridge chart table. Mister Hooper was standing by as he was to relieve the Conn at 0800.

"Mister Winchester," the Captain called.

"Sir."

"Point her south and let her eat."

"Aye Aye," he keyed the wheel house toggle. "Helmsman, point her south. come to zero one zero.

"South, Zero, One, Zero Aye."

He toggled the engine room toggle. "Engine room all head full.

"All ahead full Sir."

0800: Mister Hooper relieved Mister Winchester from deck watch and assumed the Conn.

0830: Mister Alexander entered the wardroom, uncovered and placed his hat in its assigned position. Pouring a cup of coffee he turned toward the wardroom table to the officers who sat there.

"Say, Mister Winchester, you were on the Conn when my messenger came up for relative bearing grease. Where did you get it?"

"From the Doctor here."

"I carry a few vials with me on each yearly cruise. There is always someone who comes asking for it," said the doc.

"What was it?"

"Sunburn ointment. I put a label on the vial that says relative bearing grease, use sparingly."

"I had just come out of crypto when Murray came into Radio Central and gave a vial to Anderson and told him he got it from the Captain who said he would be down in 30 minutes to inspect how efficiently the grease was used. Sure enough about thirty minutes later the Captain came in."

"He gave Anderson and the radio crew thirty minutes to come up with a story?"

"Oh, I bet that was a revolting development," chimed Mister Goldsmith.

"Yeah, the Captain came in and told Anderson he wanted to inspect the use of the relative bearing grease. Anderson told him the TBL transmitter had relative bearings inside and he used some on them. The Captain said I don't suppose you could show me. Anderson told him he could but he would have to take the sides off the TBL and that would shut down communications. The Captain said I hope you have some for next time. Anderson assured him he did. The Captain said well then you will not be sending messengers to the bridge in search of it. Anderson told him Murray was not sent to the bridge, going to the bridge was his idea. Well it worked the Captain told him."

The officers laughed. Lieutenant Grubaugh entered just as Alexander was finishing his tale.

"You told him about the relative bearing grease?"

The officers, still enjoying the story nodded their heads.

"Yeah, one of the recruit reserves asked me where he could find five feet of slack line."

"One *boot* (referring to a recent boot camp graduate) asked Mister Hooper for six yards of shore line," said another officer.
"Rookie reserve hazing has always been a tradition on all the cruises I make each year," the doctor said. "I was suckered in to looking for relative bearing grease. That is what started me carrying it."

Lieutenant Grubaugh added her sea story; "They sent them for sky hooks, left-handed monkey wrenches, bulkhead stretchers and the like. It's all in fun and a lot safer than some of the hazing we had in college."

"The next thing you know they will catch the sea bat," said Mister Alexander.

"Or standing the mail buoy watch," the doctor added.

"One guy was told to go to the crow's nest and get some crow's eggs for the Captain's breakfast. Of course this guy was smart enough to realize it was a gag so he took the opportunity to tour the ship," added Mister Goldsmith.

The doctor took a sip from his coffee cup and said "Well, all this sending new people to various other workstations to find things that do not exist has a purpose greater than just fun for the old timers. After a few days of wild goose chases throughout the ship, being sent to every space and to every senior enlisted they learn their way around the ship and they get used to traveling through hatches and watertight doors."

Officers' call came at zero nine hundred. Mister Goldsmith reported Harold Hillman, Third Class Commissaryman, was not on board. Missing movement was a serious offence in the Navy.

"I thought Hillman had mellowed a bit since he was assigned to the *Card*," said Mister Winchester.

The XO turned to address Mister Goldsmith. "How is it we didn't know this before we left port?"

"Hillman is one of those guys who does not always come out of the galley for muster. Apparently he failed to sign out when he went ashore, so we didn't know he was not on board."

"Are we sure he did not come back after liberty and he did not fall over board?"

"We got a radio message from the shore patrol. I guess he was soused and needed some action," said Goldsmith. "He was in a bar in Norfolk drinking with some marines he knew from the last ship he was on. Some bikers came in and Hillman stood up and said; 'Who is the meanest SOB in here and why am I?' The bikers decided it was not him and started a fight. Of course the marines couldn't let their buddy get beat so they joined in. As it happened they were all arrested by civil authorities and thrown in a civilian jail. Hillman sustained a pretty bad beating. From what I get from the police he spent the night in the hospital and was arraigned this morning. The base police were notified but they can do nothing until the judge decides his fate, and the fate of the marines and bikers. Fortunately the bikers have a history of bar room fighting so the brunt of the charges was against them."

"So that means we will be without Hillman's great bread for a while."

"I have heard the ship's crew say that if they had a choice of a last meal before execution they would ask for one of Hillman's breakfasts."

"I can tell you first hand, no one makes bread like Hillman," Lieutenant Grubaugh added.

"I don't know what his secret is, but there is no finer meal than Hillman's special biscuits, his own recipe for gravy and steak and eggs. No one can explain it, but some of the crew had a contest once comparing Hillman's steak and eggs breakfast with four other Commissarymen. It was a blind test. Chief Jaquet was the officiating judge. Twenty out of twenty picked Hillman's steak, eggs, biscuits and gravy."

Mister Alexander looked up from his Navy Times newspaper and asked; "If this guy is such a great cook, why is he cooking for the enlisted and not for the officers?"

"The officers of the ships company thought the enlisted had it bad enough just being stationed on the *Card,* so at least they could enjoy great food." Lieutenant Grubaugh added. "And we get some benefits of his chow. The duty officer can always count on a treat during mid-rats. *(Midnight rations served from 10 pm to 1 am for night duty personnel)."*

"From what I understand, Hillman took very good care of the marines on his ships, and now I know why. Each time he got drunk on the beach it was the marines that saved his hide," said Grubaugh.

"Well he's in trouble now, missing movement, A-W-O-L." Said Mister Winchester, "I'm not so sure Captain Mills will be as lenient as his other Commanding Officers. This Captain doesn't have the day to day relationship with Hillman's food."

"What did the Captain say about Hillman missing movement?"

"He has asked the Navy Base to get him from the civvies and arrange transportation to Mayport. The Captain will hold Captain's Mast on the quarterdeck as soon as he steps foot on board."

Harold Hillman was a sailor's sailor. He loved his job and took great satisfaction in doing it. When on board, he was rarely adrift at his post, but ashore he is a - *has a girl in every port* -kind of sailor. He knew how to enjoy liberty. He was a ruggedly handsome man. The ladies will tell you he is good to look at, and even the men will say he is a good looking person. He is a likable chap and gets along well with everyone on board.

He has never married and does not speak of a family or home. That is one of the many mysteries about Harold Hillman that makes him an intriguing sort. He made First Class (E-6) twice, but has been reduced in rate several times when his exploits ashore were particularly disgraceful. He has a sense of humor that makes him appear almost dangerous in that he finds humor in everything and does not appear to take anything seriously, anything that is except when he is on duty. The Captain of the *USS Kearney* put him on permanent shore patrol whenever the ship pulled into port. He does not get into trouble when he is on duty.

"To give you an idea of how well liked he was on the *Samuel B. Roberts,"* said Mister Goldsmith, "his Division Officer put him on report for some inconsequential act and he had to face Captain's Mast. The Captain restricted him to the ship for 13 days."

"Instead of . . . ?" Mister Alexander inquired.

"Well it seems they were steaming at the time. They had been at sea for three days and had thirteen more days before they reached port."

"So he was restricted to the ship while they were underway?"

"That was his punishment." Said Mister Goldsmith,

"I'll bet that went over big with the Division Officer." said Mister Alexander with a smile.

1100: GM1 Phelps approached the wardroom door, knocked three raps, uncovered and opened the door. She stepped inside. Mister Gilliam was sitting in one of the side chairs looking over the First Lieutenant locker assignments. Lieutenant Grubaugh was at the wardroom table frowning over some Gitmo preparations. Both officers gave Phelps their attention.

"Lieutenant Grubaugh, I have a request from Seaman Apprentice Buford Thurmond. He came on board in Norfolk as part of the reserves from West Virginia"

"Yes?"

"He says he refuses to take orders from a woman and insisted on seeing the Captain. I told him he had to go to the chief first. The chief suggested I bring it directly to you. When I told Thurmond the chief suggested he talk to his Division Officer. Thurmond then, insisted I get an appointment to see *him*."

The Lieutenant smiled. "Well, send him in."

No more than ten minutes later Thurmond and Phelps were standing outside the wardroom door. "OK," said Phelps. "Knock three times, uncover and enter. Wait until the Division Officer addresses you then say what's on your mind."

Thurmond did as he was told.

Standing in the wardroom Thurmond and Phelps were facing Lieutenant (jg) Gilliam and Lieutenant Grubaugh. Both were sitting side-by-side at the wardroom table. LT(jg) Gilliam spoke first. "You wanted to speak to your Division Officer, Thurmond, so speak."

Thurmond faced the j.g. On the outside he stifled a smile, but on the inside he was laughing. "Now here was a real man, look at those muscles. This guy knows real men," he thought to himself. His courage was renewed and he spoke up.

"Sir, I don't take orders from no woman."

"Why not?" the j.g. asked.

"Real men don't take orders from women."

"From what I understand, real men don't do housework or wash dishes do you agree?"

"Yes sir. Real men don't cook or wash clothes either."

"Real men don't go grocery shopping either, do you agree?"

Thurmond thought he had found a comrade. "That's right sir. Real men do not do women's work and women don't do men's work."

"Now let me see if we understand each other," the j.g. continued. "According to your definition, a real man does not do housework, cleaning, mopping, waxing, dusting, dishes, laundry, cooking or grocery shopping."

"That's right you got it, you understand alright."

"Well . . . Thurmond, from your definition, it appears that a real man is quite helpless without a woman around. Wouldn't you agree?"

Thurmond was stumped. "Ah, no sir!"

"A real man can't feed himself if he won't buy groceries or can't cook. He would live in a filthy environment if he didn't clean or wash dishes or clothes. Thurmond a real man is self -sufficient, and self- reliant. He does what he has to do. OK enough of this. You wanted to speak to your Division Officer, there she is," he moved his head and eyes in the direction of Lieutenant Grubaugh.

Thurmond breathed in deeply. He had been hoodwinked.

Lieutenant Grubaugh took up the line. "Seaman Thurmond, you refused to take orders from Petty Officer Phelps because she was a woman. But she is also a non-commissioned officer in the US Navy. Well you will be pleased to know you may not have to take orders from a woman."

Thurmond breathed a little easier.

"You have two choices. You can be pleased with yourself knowing you kept the real man code and did not let a woman tell you what to do – while sitting in the brig waiting for Summary Captain's Mast on charges of refusing to obey a lawful order. Of course the Captain's Mast could lead to more brig time and an undesirable discharge from the Navy. Or . . . you can man-up and get with the program. You are not now where you come from, this is the United States Navy and you are on a US Navy Warship where we all depend on each other, and we take orders from those who have earned the right to be in charge."

She paused to see how he was taking all this. Apparently he realized he was in over his head.

"Thurmond, some men whose man-hood is not intact are threatened by women in positions of authority. Now I look at you and I find it hard to believe that you are one of those immature men who can allow his man-hood to be threatened by women."

Thurmond glanced at Lieutenant (j.g.) Gilliam. His thoughts begin to calculate the situation; "This woman outranked him. If he can go along with this set up, then I guess I can also." He shrugged, glanced at GM1 Phelps, then at Mister Gilliam then back to the lady Division Officer.

"My manhood is intact. I guess I can take orders from my supervisor, even if she is a woman."

"Good, then we will have no more of this kind of thinking, are we square on this?"

"Yes."

"Yes Mam," Mister Gilliam said.

"Yes Mam."

"OK," said the lady officer. "You will go to your duty station and do what needs to be done. After chow this evening you will be confined to your rack. At twenty hundred you will report to the duty officer for muster. You are on restriction until 0700 tomorrow. You may go now."

Phelps, who was standing next to him, discreetly tapped him on the forearm and leaned in closer and whispered; "About face." She and Thurmond did an about face and both headed toward the door.

1000: The bridge was notified of a Notice to Mariners hurricane alert, heavy seas and it gave the location and direction as coming up across Florida and hugging the coast line. It was forecasted to travel due North up the coast and die out before reaching the Chesapeake Bay.

1030: Mister Hooper had the Deck and noted that at ten thirty hours a lower than normal barometer reading but no sign of rough seas. Mister Gilliam entered the bridge. He approached the OOD. "There's a strange feeling in the air Frank, what is the barometer reading?"

"You are correct Foster. I have seen this a few times before, the barometer dropping and no sign of rough seas. Those times never turned out favorably. There's a storm brewing somewhere."

"I saw this same phenomenon off the Falklands. I had the Conn. Within two hours of a constant falling barometer we were up to our ears in swells."

"I spent my youth on my father's fishing fleet. Several times this happened and we rigged for heavy seas even though there was no indication of it at the time. I called for rigging for heavy seas. They all thought I was crazy, but they did it and after that no one questioned my decisions."

Frank Hooper sent the messenger to the Captain with a note that read: "DesRon WX Off (weather officer) wrong. Seen this before - Barometer indicates we are in the path of the storm. Recommend rig for heavy seas, wind and rain. Gilliam concurs."

At eleven hundred "Mess gear" was sounded. At eleven fifteen the word was passed to knock off ships work.

1120: The Captain retired to his cabin.

1140: The noon meal was piped down and the crew went to evening meal according to each department's schedule.

1200: Lieutenant Sterling took the Deck and the Conn relieving Mister Hooper.

"Keep a weather eye on the barometer George. I predict we are in for a major storm, with dangerous seas, wind and rain."

"The fleet weather service says it will stay well to the West of us, if we steer a steady course," she said.

"I put my predictions and recommendations in the log. I have seen this situation several times before, growing up in a deep sea fishing family."

1300: The order for "turn to continue ship's work," was piped. The seas were getting rougher and the skies began to take on an ominous color.

The new guy reserves had been at sea long enough to realize they had some work to do in getting their sea legs with the rolling motion of a ship at sea. Many would spend the first day in the head driving the *porcelain bus* (Actually the facilities were stainless steel). It was an ugly sight, but almost all sailors went through it at some point in their time at sea. For some it lasted several days and they ended up in sick bay. For the ones that did not make it to the head, they learned very quickly that real sailors clean up after themselves. If they did not do so on their own they did it under the intimidating supervision of every sailor in the area. Although there were a few who had compassion for these new reserves with no sea experience, they were far and few to be found.

1330: The Captain made rounds throughout the ship to ensure all was secure.

1400: The Captain's last stop was at the Radio Shack where he intended to catch up on the latest news and weather bulletins.

Radioman First Class Anderson, Radioman Striker Seaman Franklin and Third Class Radioman Matthews were busy with the rigors of the communication system on board a ship at sea. It was a routine, but complicated task bringing up the fleet broadcast system for ships in the southern sector of the U.S. receiving messages and passing them along.
"Is the coffee ready Anderson?" he asked as he entered the coded door way"

"It should be, Captain, it's been cooking since last Tuesday."

The Radio Shack coffee was one of the ongoing jokes on the *Card*. There is the story that a guy named Murphy is in charge of the coffee mess in the shack. No one has ever met Murphy. The Radiomen take turns making the coffee but they all claim it was Murphy that makes it, so that no one will be accused of making bad coffee.

The Captain remembered visiting the Radio Shack a few days before setting sail for Norfolk when a Radioman Striker, who apparently had just come from completing some dirty job, came into the shack and announced that he had just finished working aloft cleaning the antennae. "Half of the *yack* on those antennae is on my clothes and in my face, not to mention a few sea gulls made bombing runs on my head. Is there any other disgusting task you want me to do chief?"

RM1 Anderson said; "Have a cup of Murphy's coffee Pellington, and take a load off."

"Now Anderson," he said, "I will do just about anything you want me to do, but don't ask me to have a cup of Murphy's coffee."

The Captain took a cup and held it under the spout. He chuckled to see that someone had tied a pair of scissors by a string to the spout with a note that read, "Good to the Last Piece." And it was signed Murphy. The Captain was pleased to see it was hot. He took a careful sip.

"This coffee is terrible Anderson. How often do you guys clean this pot?"

"Murphy cleans it every time it gets empty Captain."

"When was the last time it was empty?"

"I don't recall it ever being empty Captain."

The Captain smiled and shook his head. He enjoyed the humorous banter of the crew. He pressed a button on the intercom. "This is the Captain. Is my steward in the wardroom?"

"Yes Captain," came the reply.

"Have him bring some fresh coffee to Radio Central from the officer's mess."

"Aye, Aye sir."

He keyed the intercom. "Bridge this is the Captain. I will be in Radio Central."

"Bridge Aye"

RM1 Matthews sat at the C.W. Circuit with headphones copying a Morse coded message. Seaman Franklin was routing teletype traffic. The other members of the radio crew were busy setting up the frequencies that would be used in the new Zulu (Greenwich Mean Time) day which would take place in 6 hours (GMT was 4 hours ahead of EST). They prepared for the twenty three fifty nine to zero-zero change-over of the computers and the new Zulu day paperwork. He brought up WWV Fort Collins Colorado on the computer's receiver and listened to the clock ticking over the circuit. Finally the ticking stopped and a strong male voice said; "This is double-u, double u, Vee, Fort Collins Colorado, when the tone returns the time will be fourteen hundred hours." There was a loud 3 second tone and the radioman punched the two red buttons with the thumbs of his right and left hand and waited. The ticking resumed. After a few seconds the teletype kicked into action and fleet broadcast information was printing out.

Anderson provided the Captain with printouts from Maritime Weather Reports for the Atlantic coast and news printed from Armed Forces and Associated Press. The Captain and Radioman Anderson read the news and shared their comments about the news items while they drank officer's coffee from cups bearing the ship's seal poured from a real coffee pot complimented by Gedunk (pronounced Gee-dunk meaning snacks).

In the meantime, the conning officer was well aware the seas were becoming increasingly turbulent. The helmsman reported difficulty in holding the ships head on a steady course claiming he was constantly spinning the wheel from right standard to left standard rudder in an effort to keep her from yawing. The barometer continued to fall and the Deck Officer observed a noticeable cross-swell.

1430: The Conning Officer called the Captain to the bridge. The Captain put down his paper and stood up. "Well Anderson, enjoy the coffee and Gedunks, It seems I am needed on the bridge. It looks like we are in for some very bad weather. You saw the weather reports they all claim it will not come near our route. But Mister Hooper thinks differently."

"I would go with Mister Hooper," Anderson replied.

The Captain entered the bridge for a first-hand look at the conditions. Mister Winthrop entered a few minutes later. "Mister Hooper seems to think we will be in the storm if we steer our present heading," said Lieutenant Sterling.

"Yes, he told me that this morning and then again in a message before being relieved," The Captain said.

"He has a lot of experience with weather being a northern fisherman. If I had to bet on the weather office or a gut feeling experienced mariner, I would go with gut every time," said Winthrop.

After conferring with ComResDesRon34 on the *Lancing,* the Captain gave the order to continue steaming on the present course since the storm is reportedly 6 miles to the west and was now heading north-north west away from the squadron. The Captain decided to confer one more time with Mister Hooper before altering the course set by ComDesRon.

Off in the distance were fearsome black clouds boiling up with strong winds producing great agitation on the ocean surface. It appeared as though water from the ocean was being pulled into those black clouds and then forced back down into the sea with fierce roaring and slashing about.

The Captain entered the wardroom and found Mister Hooper in a leather side chair reading a novel. Over his head was a painting of the *Card* in a stormy sea. Robert Mills commissioned the painter, a private citizen, as a symbolic representation of the condition of the ship when he took command. On his left was a side table that was bolted to the deck. On the table was a pilot's wheel lamp and a cup holder securely fastened to the table. In the cup holder was a steaming cup of that once contained wardroom coffee. The front of Mister Hooper's shirt was soaked and stained with the coffee. He looked up at the captain with an embarrassed smile. "You would think by now I would know better," he said.

"So, Mister Hooper, your experience tells you we will be in the storm in spite of the naval weather guessers."

"It is my opinion Captain. I may be wrong, but I don't think so. I am not that familiar with the area off the coast of Cape Hatteras, I know it is infamous for being frequently struck by hurricanes and frequent storms and heavy seas that move up the East Coast of the United States. I know about its turbulent water and that many ships have been lost in this area. Mariners call it the Graveyard of the Atlantic. Like I say I am not that personally familiar with this area, but I do know storms, and I believe we are in for some mighty rough seas."

"Dangerous seas?"

"Dangerous seas."

"How much time before the onslaught?"

Mister Hooper consulted his watch. "OK, it is fourteen forty now. The conditions have been steadily deteriorating about every fifteen minutes. I would say if it is going to turn and come after us, ahhh, it will do so in about two hours, maybe less."

"Very well, pass the word I want to see all officers and chiefs in the wardroom at 1500."

1445: The sea state was getting worse. Normal movements on board were becoming increasingly more difficult to continue ship's work on deck. OOD Sterling keyed the intercom to the Wardroom. "Is the Captain there?"

"Yes Lieutenant Sterling, what is it?"

"Captain I recommend we secure from ship's work and rig for heavy seas."

The Captain pressed the intercom. "Thank you Lieutenant, we are working on doing just that. I'll let you know."

"Aye Sir."

1500: The officer's had returned to the wardroom and took up their place for the next meeting that was to take place there in a few minutes. The five chiefs filed into the wardroom and took chairs around the perimeter of the room.

The Captain entered and all stood at attention.

"As you were," he said as he moved to the coffee nook to pour a cup. He smiled at himself. He had just witnessed Hooper's spill and realized, as much as sailors enjoy coffee heavy seas was no time to have a cup. He turned to face his leadership crew and leaned against the counter.

He flipped the switch to the Bridge, Radio and CIC. "Bridge, Radio, CIC this is the Captain. I want you all to hear this, so listen up." He turned back to the wardroom participants. "We are now at sea state 7. We are experiencing High winds with moderate to near gale force. Mister Hooper and Mister Gilliam believe we may get this storm in spite of all we can do. I concur. So just to be on the safe side I want every department to rig for severe weather and heavy seas. Let's be prepared in case the storm over takes us. After evening meal when the word is passed to continue ships work, I want all ammo, water and other commodities available stowed as low in the ship as possible to provide more ballast."

The officers and chief took notes.

"All officers and chiefs will make a thorough inspection of spaces under their supervision to ensure we are rigged for heavy seas."

Heavy seas required that all items not bolted down had to be placed in lockable storage bins, or lashed down with line. This was especially true in the galley with all the free pots and pans and utensils lying around. The sudden movements of the ship in response to the syncopation of the ocean waves will throw any free object against the bulkhead or the floor; this includes the sailors on board.

There was other information passed and suggestions made by the chiefs, all of which the Captain approved. Chief Leon G. Jaquet suggested the galley prepare sandwiches for the crew instead of trying to cook during the storm.

"I agree chief, if Mister Hooper is right we will be riding this one for a while, and I want sandwiches delivered to work stations to keep up the crew's strength and morale. And make sure the galley has plenty of bug juice and fresh water on hand."

"Some of you may think we are a bit pre-mature, but I believe in prudent precautions, especially when you have recommendations from experienced personnel." The Captain spoke into the open intercom to the bridge. "Bridge - Pass the word to batten down the hatches."

1521: "Batten down the hatches Boats."

'Batten down the hatches, Aye sir."

The DBMOW (Duty Boatswain's Mate of the Watch) keyed the 1-MC "Now all hands knock off ship's work and rig assigned spaces for severe weather and heavy seas. Now, batten down the hatches. Close and seal all water tight doors."

Rigging for high seas meant each crewman had a specific task to do in their assigned area in securing anything that was not welded to the ship. Items were stowed in lockers, and the doors shut and locked. Items too large for stowage were lashed down so they would not move during the turbulent movement of the ship. Everything liquid was sealed in containers. Everyone made provision for their own safety, by making sure they had lashing for tying themselves to their work stations. The ship was rocking and pitching so much no one could move around unless they were holding on to some secure structure. Most of the crew remained in their spaces and just hung on. Those at duty stations were strapped in.

No experienced mariner takes the sea lightly. The waters of the globe, while at one moment are peaceful and serene, can in a moment become a terrible, malevolent ferocity, a deathly beauty exuding some profound and fearsome mystery. Few things are as frightening as being tossed about and pummeled, helplessly in the grip of uncontrolled, unbridled power, where there is no stable foundation, no defense against the strength of the wind and great walls of irresistible force.

The weather had begun to turn making it difficult to distinguish the sky from the sea. The Navigator reported 20 foot swells and cross swells. The barometer had dropped to 30.50.

1600: Bridge Log Entry: Lieutenant Grubaugh assumed duties as OOD and the Conn, relieving Lieutenant Sterling.

"We are steaming on course as before; Barometer reading was 30.50 a few minutes ago it is now 30.40 and falling. We have 20 foot swells sometimes going to thirty feet with occasional cross swells. We have slowed to twelve knots in order to maneuver through the seas. Wind variable at 30 miles per hour. The rain began twenty minutes ago and suggests it will gain in velocity as the barometer is slowly but steadily falling. The main battery of the storm is still west although it was now headed south-south east."

"Thank you Lieutenant. Now is there any good news?"

"Yes, you will be pleased to know that the ship is in good hands, the Deck Officer is Lieutenant Grubaugh and your Navigator is Lieutenant Commander McCormick, who is presently in the chart room with Mister Winthrop."

1615: The Captain entered the bridge area. The Boatswain's Mate of the Watch keyed the 1-MC and announced; "The Captain is on the bridge."

"Good afternoon ladies," he said as he gripped the heavy seas handles, welded to the bulkhead at the entrance of the Companionway.

"Captain," they said in unison.

"We are steaming as before Captain, 12 knots due south. We conclude a class 7 sea state with fresh gale. We hoisted the Gale Warning pennant" (Two red pennants).

"Thank you, Lieutenant, you still have the Conn and the deck."

"Aye, Sir."

1635: The bridge intercom clicked. "Bridge, Radio."

"Captain we just got word the storm has suddenly turned and is now headed north-east directly in our path Sir. CIC confirms. We have another message coming to you by Radio Central messenger, one you will need to sign for."

A radio messenger appeared from the gangway.

"He's here now. Stand by."

"Message, from the *Lancing* meteorologist Captain."

"Read it."

"From Reserve Commander Destroyer Squadron Thirty Four aboard *USS Lancing* to *USS Card, USS Roberts* and *USS Granger,* reported storm in your vicinity should be considered as renegade, constantly changing direction and picking up wind velocity. Storm may reach sea state 10 or 11, whole gale to violent storm. If storm overtakes you expect extended hours of very large amounts of airborne spray severely reduced visibility, exceptionally high winds and dangerous seas. Be advised."

Lieutenant Commander McCormick stepped onto the bridge. "Extended hours?"

"That means they have no idea what this storm is doing," said the Captain.

"Is there a reply Captain?" asked the messenger.

"Roger the transmission and tell them we plan to steer clear of the storm."

"Mack I want an After Steering watch in case conditions create a problem at the helm."

"Washington and Inman are there now sir. They should be reporting in any minute now."

"Bridge, After Steering is manned and ready."

"Very well. I hope you secured that set of barbells down there, those things will kill you."

"We secured them sir. If they get loose, they will be the least of our worries."

"Ok I want you to check in with the bridge every fifteen minutes."

"After Steering aye."

1700: The *Card* was now encountering torrential rain and increasingly higher wind velocity but the storm stayed clear enough to maintain the scheduled heading. The torrent made it impossible to see more than a cable's length in any direction. Lieutenant Grubaugh noted the low visibility watch standers, as they strained to see and hear any potential threat to their ship. The pitch of the ship created difficulty in maintaining balance. She rose then plummeted, taking white foam over her bows that washed down the foredeck.

"Captain, I recommend we steer a course east south east to move away from the storm. The barometer was now readying 29.2."

"I agree Lieutenant."

She sent the word to the helmsman with the new course readings."

"The Captain's expression changed to deep concern as he looked across the sea at the ominous colors, swirling clouds and precipitation. The atmospheric pressure created foreboding feeling that went deep into one's chest. He stared forward as he spoke to the duty Quartermaster who was standing on the port lookout balcony. "Quartermaster, pass the word that all hands are to put on life jackets. No one is to go topside without permission from their chief or division officer except for those on the bridge. And call Mister Winthrop to the bridge." The Captain wanted his best navigator available at a time like this.

1800: The first dog watch began. Mister Gilliam took the Conn as scheduled. He was qualified to Conn a ship, but since he had not driven the *Card* Mister Faulk was assigned to assist him. Lieutenant Sterling gave him the status; "We are steaming on course east south east. Barometer reading is twenty eight point four oh and falling. We have 30 foot swells sometimes going to 35 to 40 feet with occasional cross swells. We have slowed to eight knots in order to maneuver through the seas. Wind variable at 48 to 53 knots. I estimate a sea state of 10. We have very high waves - overhanging crests. The signalman has hoisted the Storm Warning pennant (A single square red flag with a black center)"

The bridge crew was strapped in and holding on to anything that was welded to the ship in order to keep their footing. The helmsman was lashed to a stanchion in order to maintain control of the wheel.

Lieutenants Grubaugh and Sterling went below to their stateroom. The Captain joined Mister Gilliam and Mister Faulk on the bridge.

The noise of the raging sea and wind was deafening. "Lieutenant Gilliam, shouted the Captain, "I will take the Conn, you retain the Deck." The Captain said.

"Aye Sir," Said Gilliam as he moved aside and let the Captain move nearer the wind screen.

Mister Gilliam shouted to be heard above the freight-train like sounds of the wind and the waves "We slowed to eight knots, Captain. I don't think we can out run it, sir. I recommend we had into the storm and ride it out."

The captain glanced in the direction of Mister Hooper.

"I concur, Captain."

It was getting very rough now.

I agree Lieutenant," said Mills. "Order a course of zero-two-zero and all hands clear the deck."

"Duty Boatswain's Mate, pass the word. Helmsman come to zero-two-zero. Keep her headed into the wind."

The 1-MC came alive with the husky manly voice, "Now hands clear the decks. Rig the ship ready for high seas.

1900: The wind was 55 knots. LCDR McCormick entered the bridge. The *Card* was rolling, reeling and rocking violently, and footing was difficult. The tell-tale haze of rain advanced across the uneven swells hiding the horizon and surged over the bow and boiled along the decks like a raging river and a deluge of torrential rain. The rain lashed down like needles against the crew standing on the *Card's* flying bridge and splashing up from the steel deck soaking their shoes and pants legs.

Giant plumes of sea water rolled over the sides and onto the weather decks, splashing its bulky, heavy water against the ship's structures, into the gun wells, and gushing out again in white foam and raging currents down the outside passages. There was considerable tumbling of waves with heavy impact.

2000: Bridge Log Entry: *Estimate sea state 11 on Beauford scale. Very high waves - overhanging crests. Large patches of foam from wave crests give the sea a white appearance. Large amounts of airborne spray reduced visibility. Second dog watch commenced. Lieutenant's Gilliam and Faulk were relieved by Captain Mills. Lookouts secured due to WX conditions. The captain declared hurricane conditions. We hoisted the hurricane warning pennants (two square red flags with black centers). On the bridge are Helmsmen Frazier and Gillman, QM striker Smidlap, Lieutenant Winthrop, Lieutenant Commander McCormick and Captain Mills.*

2055: The rain was blowing horizontal and visibility was about 100 yards. The wind gauge showed 63 knots and was howling so loudly it was difficult and sometimes impossible to hear anyone speak. The bridge was 42 feet above the water line, the radar dome and antennae were 110 feet above the water line. Sea water was washing across the bridge, and at times, when the ship was in a trough it appeared as though the water was higher than the antennae. The Captain ordered the bridge watch to go into the pilot house. It was crowded, but it afforded some protection against the rain and the wind.

2115: The Boatswain's Mate keyed the 1-MC and announced "The Officer of the Deck is shifting the watch from the flying bridge to the pilot house. The Captain is in the pilot house."

2130: Bridge Log Entry: *Estimate sea state Beauford 11.*

The Conning crew secured themselves inside the pilot house.

2135: The ship shuddered as the entire forecastle (folk-sul) plunged beneath the surface burying the forward gun mount in the watery grave. Then she pulled herself up out of the raging brine as streaming rivers draining from the decks guns, and aft past the torpedoes and depth charges poured out into the sea astern.

2150: Bridge Log entry: *Sea state 12 – hurricane force. Hurricane warning lights were illuminated (a white light between two red lights).*

The Boatswain's Mate announced the *Card* was taking 40 degree rolls, a fearsome situation. "Say Mack, do you recall the maximum roll the *Card* is designed to take?" asked the Captain.

"The engineering reports say we can recover from a 72 degree roll Captain."

"Was that report adjusted after the radar dome retrofit on the main mast?"

"Yes Captain, even with the top heavy mast the ship is countered to recover from a roll of 72 degrees."

"I hope that report is correct because I got a feeling we are going to find out, if the swells continue to rise."

He turned to the Helmsman. "Keep us into the wind. We will use engines only to maintain steering."

"Aye, Aye Sir."

The turbulent sea was relentless in its punishment of the little 308 foot ship. The DE was a tough, stable little vessel, well designed for heavy seas. Many times the *Card* was standing on end with its bow out of the water and the depth charges submerged. Another swell pulled the fantail out of the water and submerged the bow. It stood on end for what seemed to be five minutes. It was actually more like

10 seconds. She scooped up a mass amount of sea as her bow once again pulled to the surface.

The sound of the wind and rain like an oncoming freight train ran over the ship in a seemingly unending relentless assault rolling side to side and rocking fore and aft. On-coming swells crashed into the forward hull, with a loud bump that felt like it was hitting large rocks. Sometimes the crashing of the sea exploded sprays of powerful gushes flying in all directions.

Each onslaught was followed by climbing a giant wave standing the ship on its stern with the stem out of the water and then falling into the trough the wave created standing on its head with the screws out of the water, the bow plunging into the green and white swirling sea. Without resistance from the sea, the screws would race wildly causing the governors on the propeller shafts to slow the revolutions. If the governor did not slow the shafts, the generators and drive motors would shut down. Then they would have to go through a restart procedure to bring the generators back online, and then start the electric motors that drove the screws all while wallowing in seas without steering or forward control. Situations like that can sink a vessel.

Another mountainous wave lifted the craft higher and higher, then swiftly abandoning its purpose dropping her 20 feet in an abyss with bone shuttering sudden stop landing her back on the beam. There was no respite as once again a watery hand lifted the bow upward and dropping her bow downward once again lifting the drive propellers out of the water. Waves came crashing over the forward gun mount and splattering against the pilot house sending shock waves throughout the ship. Everyone was strapped into a position and had braced themselves between solid bulwarks.

2210: The Captain keyed the intercom. "Radio – Pilot house"
"Radio, Aye."

"Send a message to ComResDesRon on the *Lancing* and tell him we are adjusting course to accommodate the storm."

"Radio, Aye."

2215: The intercom came alive in the pilot house.

"Pilot house, Engine room."

"Go ahead."

"Engine room is experiencing heavy leaking through the air intakes. Water is threatening the electrical switchboard. We are doing what we can to keep it from shorting out." The air intakes supply the engine room with fresh air. Since all hatches to the lower decks are inside and are entered from the topside down they are usually dogged for water tight integrity.

"Very well, keep us advised. Do you need any further assistance?"

"Negative, Sir."

2235: The engine room reported they managed to hook up some hoses from the bilges to pump water out of the engine room. "Don't know how much longer we can keep up with the leaking."

2245: The barometer dropped to 27.20.

2300: The barometer dropped to 26.20.

A giant swell lifted the bow up in the air, rolling along beneath the vessel and then dropped it into its trough.

Everyone was strapped in to their positions. One moment one is walking on the bulkhead, at another they were feet on the deck and other times their feet were dangling in mid-air. It was a frightening experience, but the crew took heart believing the officer on the Conn was an experienced tin can mariner and knew when to turn the ship and how much.

2320: The roar of the powerful wind and the wild sea continued to buffet the ship as all hands held on and adjusted to the surges that manipulated it at will.

2359: Bridge Log Entry: *Captain determined the storm was too powerful to relieve the Conn, helmsman or quartermaster watch.*
In the fury the pilothouse door opened and the startled crew inside jerked their attention to the door, as wind and water rushed in. BM1 Furman entered struggling to keep the door from flying open. He managed to get inside and close the door with the help of Mister Winthrop. Furman leaned hard against the door to keep it from bursting open as a line harness around his torso served to prevent the door from closing completely.

"What are you doing here?" the Captain's tone was unusually harsh. "Orders were that no one was to be on the weather decks during the storm."

"I was just checking the weather decks to make sure all is secure. The life boats are rarely checked and they could come loose during strong wind," said Furman, apparently not disturbed by the heated reprimanding tone of the officers. "I noticed the tarp was coming loose from the motor whaleboat. If it blows off and the ship continues these fifty degree rolls it will fill up with sea water and may make it difficult or impossible to recover from a roll that severe. I tried to secure it myself but I can't. I need help."

"Furman, we are at hurricane force winds and sea! How are you getting about?" asked LCDR McCormick.

"I have a tether to the oh-two railing and the gig hoist and to the pilot house line hook."

"You managed to do all this line connections by yourself in this torrential rain?"

"Hey that is part of my job description. Good sea legs."

"I'll go," said Mister Winthrop.

Furman unwrapped another line he had around his shoulders and chest and made a harness for Mister Winthrop. Together they ventured into the night against driving rain, heavy water surging over the weather decks, the treacherous winds and the abrupt jerking of the ship in the grip of elements that constantly tossed it about. The quick and hard pitching and rolling of the ship against the tempest further complicated their short trek to the endangered life boat. They held onto the tether line and to each other.

Just as they reached the boat a sharp pitch to starboard threw them against the underside of the boat. Mister Winthrop sustained a deep gash on his forehead. The blood rushed in torrents from the cut, but the wind and the rain washed it from his eyes.

"You have a cut on your forehead," Furman shouted to be heard over the raging sound.

"I'm OK, let's get this tied down," Winthrop shouted back. Using the tether on the hoist they managed to pull themselves up to the tie down hooks. The tarp was flapping at such a high rate, getting a hold of the loose ends long enough to thread them through the eyelets was difficult. Several times the tarp escaped their grasp and slapped against their hands, arms and face stinging and bruising. Furman hand signaled for Mister Winthrop to hold the ends while he tied them secure.

That done the two lowered themselves down to the deck and began their trek back to the pilot house. A sudden pitch threw Mister Winthrop against the bulkhead rendering him unconscious. Furman lifted him by the harness and after struggling with the weight of the unconscious officer and the torrents of the weather he managed to get to the pilot house door and up the five step ladder.

Lieutenant Commander McCormick and the Captain aided with holding the door and retrieving the gallant sailors to the relative safety of the inside. Again Furman braced himself against the door, with his feet against the stanchion.

Lieutenant Commander McCormick pressed his handkerchief against the Navigator's wound.

"We better bring the doctor here. We will never get him to sick bay," the Captain said.

"I'll go," Furman volunteered. He exited the pilot house and like a mountain climber he detached his tether and reattached it to other secure places as he made his way down the ladder. At the foot of the ladder he disconnected the tether and attempted to tie it to a "D" handle welded on the bulkhead beside the door. A torrent of sea water hit him dislodging his feet from the deck and lifting him sideways as he gripped the ladder with one hand and the "D" handle with the other. With all his strength he pulled the line through the "D" on the bulkhead and the "D" ring on his life vest. Now stable, he ventured to unlatch the water tight door. He pushed it open, and disconnected the line from his life vest. Gripping the watertight door and the opposite bulkhead he pulled himself into the skin of the ship. Like a roll of lava, water poured through the door way, dislodging the sailor's footing. He pushed his feet against the inside bulkhead and with all the force he could muster pushed the door closed. Furman knew this ship so well, that almost total darkness made little difference. He picked up the interior phone and called the wardroom.

The doctor was there and after much jostling about he managed to meet Furman at the hatch that would give them access to the weather deck and the ladder leading to the pilothouse. Furman connected his tether to the doctor, and with powerful arms, developed over the years working the deck force, he assisted him outside and up the ladder and into the pilot house.

Mister Winthrop was conscious and sitting on the deck with his back against a bulkhead. Mister McCormick had used the navigator's harness to secure him to the bulkhead using the life secure handles welded in place for just such an occasion.

"You're going to need stitches in that gash Mister Winthrop, but not here and not now. These butterfly bands will hold you until after the storm."

"Is it bad doc?" asked Mister Winthrop.

"It's a foot deep – when I open it I can see the back of your skull. There is nothing in there."

"OK, OK. I need a doctor, not a comic."

"You'll be OK."

"How is it you are able to get around outside in weather like this, Furman?" asked the doctor.

"Fourteen years of sea legs outside on Dee–ees," he responded.
Captain Mills clapped him on the shoulder. "Well, you did well by the *Card* tonight Furman." He turned to his XO with a half-smile and in his best cockney accent he said "An extra ration of rum fer the lad number one."

"Eyeee cap'n sur an extra ration it be then."

"I'm just a humble able bodied seaman suh, jes doin' me duty."

Mister Winthrop was pressed against the bulkhead and his legs pushed hard against a stanchion holding the bandage on his head with one hand and holding onto a "steady bar" with the other. (*Steady bar is metal bar welded onto the bulkhead for heavy seas*). He smiled and shook his head. "May I remind you, there's an injured officer over here?" he said fainting jealousy.

The Captain turned his attention to the injured officer, then again to his executive officer "An extra ration of rum for the injured officer number one."

"Jus one sur?"

"Right you are number one, make it two."

"Rah-eete cap'n sur . . . it be two rations fur the officer, str-eye-t a w-eye." *Note: Drinking alcohol is not permitted on US Navy ships except in sick bay, but may not be used without permission of the Captain.*

Doctor Johnson breathed out a big smile and shook his head.
Furman spoke again. "I appreciate your appreciation Captain, but I was just making sure I had a ship under my feet instead of water, a case of self-preservation."

"But few could have done what you did," said the Captain.

2359 The storm was too powerful to relieve the Conn, helmsman or quartermaster watch. The only good news came from the engine room. They had shored up the leak and were managing well.

Note: Drinking alcohol is not permitted on US Navy ships except in sick bay and the wardroom, but may not be used without permission of the captain. In this case the captain was kidding, and those involved knew it.

Executive Assessment
Weathering the Storm and Staying Seaworthy

The organization is the entity that provides the jobs for the crew. It is the entity that offers the prospect for a future for all concerned, both now and in the future. The organization must be preserved and must weather the storms and the turbulent times. When the storms are abated the organizations that made it through will once again provide products for customers and jobs for the community.

The ocean is a fitting metaphor for the human experience. The sea is the strangest and most mysterious of God's creations. Down through the ages the sea has been a mistress and a murderer.

Like life, the sea can be unpredictable. No experienced mariner takes the sea lightly.

The waters of the globe, while at one moment are peaceful and serene, can in a moment become a terrible, malevolent ferocity, a deathly beauty exuding some profound and fearsome mystery. Few things are as frightening as being tossed about and pummeled, helplessly in the grip of uncontrolled, unbridled power, where there is no stable foundation, no defense against the strength of the wind and great walls of irresistible force.

One can navigate over the sea, in the sea and undersea. As in life, and one can protect against the predictable elements that threaten us. We can enjoy the voyage when all is well and learn lessons of life as the inexorable conditions of our lives introduce new and different adversaries, new adventures and new experiences. Like life, sometimes inviting, sometimes forbidding, sometimes encouraging, sometimes foreboding but one thing you can be sure of is that short-lived interludes of pacific are followed by fury sometimes short and sometimes prolonged.

There is a lesson here for us all. Though you may be taking on high seas, though your frail craft seems to be in danger of sinking, don't give up. Head into the winds and the waves and stay the course set for turbulent conditions. Remember you are not alone. You have a crew, and if they are properly trained they will come through for you.

There is a famous proverb that states; a ship, like a business organization, when in turbulent times must not focus on being on course it must focus on being seaworthy.

When a manager is experiencing turbulent times it seems it would be an opportunity to assess the resources available. The mind-set of the manager in high seas is directed toward the protection of the organization and the crew. This would be the time to include others in the analysis and recommendation stage rather than deal with it alone. Of course the decisions must be made by the chief executive as there will be risks involved.

This is a time when a well-developed and practiced *what-if plans* pay off.

We have witnessed here how the preparation for heavy seas indicated an effective *what-if plan* with the exception of missing the tie down on the motor whaleboat.

The Captain chose to prepare the ship for engaging a storm based on Mister Hooper's opinion even though there was no evidence to show the official Navy weather report was wrong. In turbulent times you surround yourself with competent experienced personnel and you listen to them. Of course one would require evidence of past experience when taking someone's word for a recommendation that carries a risk.

BM1 Furman chose to go out on the weather deck to inspect the motor whale boat and the lifeboats during the most ferocious time in the storm in direct violation to the captain's orders. No doubt he thought about the storm preparations by his deck force and doubted the inexperienced sailors would have thought about the consequences of sea water filling the boat. He should have inspected it before securing the deck force. A dedicated employee with a personal investment in the job and the organization would have taken the action Furman took. They should be rewarded for the action they took to correct an error rather than be punished for the error. There are certain conditions when one should take life-threatening risks in order to confirm something is secure or to correct a condition. Those conditions exist where a possible devastating event may or may not be avoided.

No doubt you noticed that the various departments were in constant contact with the bridge reporting on conditions in that department. In some cases their report required some decision or permission from the captain and in other instances it was just to keep the Conn Officer informed. Was this a nuisance or was it a necessary activity? Explain your answer.

Even though there was a qualified Conn officer and navigator on the bridge the captain called Mister Winthrop to assume the navigator duties. This was not an affront to those officers on duty. Other managers should realize that when in turbulent times you want your best people in positions where training, experience and savvy are needed.

"Seaman Thurmond refused to take orders from Petty Officer Phelps because she was a woman. But she is also a non-commissioned officer in the US Navy. No doubt you have encountered people who refuse to perform a task because of some strange personal conviction or because they believe the way they were trained to do it was superior. They must be confronted and informed of the organization's policies for hiring competent people no matter their gender, race, religion or handicap. They will get with the program or get out; there is no room for the dissention that results from negative behavior toward anyone, especially toward the organization's management personnel.

The Navy has a tradition of sending rookies on wild goose chases. They are sent to get some non-existence item. Each person to whom they were sent, sends them to someone else. Eventually the rookie either realizes what is going on or their boss puts an end to their trek. While the veterans get a kick out of jerking the new guy around it has a purpose greater than just fun for the old timers. After a few days of wild goose chases throughout the ship, being sent to every space and to every senior enlisted they learn their way around the ship and they get used to traveling through shin knocker hatches and watertight doors. While this is one way to do it, organizations need to have a thorough orientation of new employees and then they are entered into a three to six month training time where they are brought up to speed and trained to do the job. They are tested during this training time and those who cannot pass those tests should be terminated.

Hillman is a cook (Commisaryman). He is very good at his job, in fact he is the best there is on the job he does. He knows how to do other jobs in his department and does not hesitate to jump in and make things right. He is well liked by all his shipmates. The problem is his outside the job activities often create a problem for his boss and the others in his unit. Action must be taken to bring persons with this problem in line, or they must be terminated. Regardless of how good an employee is at their job these problems will affect others negatively and result in a loss of credibility for management.

Did you notice that when the OOD or Conn Officer was relieved there was a definite procedure for passing information that included some very specific items. You will also notice that there is an underway bridge log where specific information is logged. Such procedures will solve a lot of discovery problems when the oncoming supervisors or managers have a formal information passing procedure. Perhaps an organizational, or department log book would be beneficial for recording events.

The Captain demonstrated his confidence in Mister Hooper, when he chose to prepare the ship for engaging a storm that the experts said would not be a factor. The captain knew Mister Hooper was not given to offering recommendations unless he was absolutely certain that his information was from his own experience.

Command Axiom:

- A ship, like a business organization, when in turbulent times must not focus on being on course it must focus on being seaworthy.

- Do not try to outrun or skirt, head right into the storm and maintain steering.

- When one shows this level of confidence in another's talent and resourcefulness it not only empowers that one, it also encourages others on the team.

Chapter 8
After the Storm - Reinstating Normal Operations

Thursday 16, July 1970
USS Card
At Sea somewhere between Cape Hatteras and Mayport

0030: The engine room reported they had shored up the leak and were managing well.

0400: Bridge Log Entry: *OOD/CONN Captain was relieved by Lieutenant Hooper. The helmsman and duty quartermaster watches were relieved. Sea state 7 – high winds moderate gale. Hurricane lights extinguished gale warning lights illuminated.*

0500: The galley crew reported for work and began preparation for breakfast.

0600: Bridge Log Entry: *The storm abated at approx. 0555. Sea State estimated at 6. Lieutenant Hooper OOD/CONN shifted the duty from the Pilot House to the Flying Bridge. Gale warning lights extinguished.*

The daylight was slow in making an appearance. There was no dawn, just a slow transition from night to a gray cloudy sky. The ship and its crew must still contend with inclement weather and high seas but the ship's rolling and bouncing did not deter the breakfast crowd on the mess decks.

0745: The Boatswain's Mate piped clear the mess decks and began ship's work.

0750: The deck force was busily ensuring all was secure and well on the weather decks. Boats (Furman BM1) stopped by to check on how the work was coming, considering some of the deck force personnel were on their first sea voyage.

"What are we having for lunch Boats?"

Furman looked into the sky and said, "Looks like fried chicken."

"How can you tell we are having chicken by looking into the sky?"

"Anytime you don't see sea gulls flying around you know we are having chicken."

"Why is that?"

"Don't know."

0755: Officer's call. Mister Alexander informed the officers of a radio message received that brought news that the *USS Granger (DD750)* had foundered in the storm and all hands were lost. The *Roberts* sustained damage but was on station. The *Lancing* sustained no reportable damage.

LCDR McCormick spoke up. "Captain, I want to say your prudent precautions as you call it saved our lives. Apparently the *Granger's* Captain believed the fleet weather bureau and didn't prepare for the storm."

"You can thank Mister Hooper, said Mills. "It was his instincts that I relied on. I have learned that prudence takes the side of experience."

Lieutenant Grubaugh was almost in tears. "The *Granger* was the most highly rated ship in ResDesDiv5; it is hard to believe she went down, with that crew.

They are the most efficient crew in the entire East Coast Navy Reserve." She turned to Mister Gilliam with a shocked expression. "That was your ship Foster."

"Yes. I was assigned to that ship and I drilled on her a few times, but I signed up too late to get a billet for the Gitmo cruise."

"What a twist of fate!" cried Lieutenant Sterling.

"Foster recognized the situation the same time I did," Mister Hooper inserted. "He saw it in the Falklands. If he had been on the *Granger* they may not have foundered."

Lieutenant Commander McCormick raised his hand as if he were signaling stop. "I knew Commander Cain, the Captain, and Watson the XO. They both were too arrogant to take advice from anyone but themselves. Foster would have gone down with them!"

Foster Gilliam was visibly upset by the sinking of the *Granger*. All eyes were on him.

Foster Gilliam spoke softly; "Joseph Conrad once said; *Foul weather and a turbulent sea is the irreconcilable enemy of ships and men ever since ships and men had the unheard of audacity to go afloat together in the face of his frown.*"

"Had you planned to take the *Granger* to Gitmo?" asked Winchester.

"Yes I did. But unfortunately, or in some cases fortunately, circumstances always did shape my course different from my plans."

Lieutenant Commander McCormick took the lead. "Captain Mills ordered more drills to ensure readiness for the team activities that included the new reserves that boarded in Norfolk. The first drill will began at 0900 with battle condition X-ray. The crew will stay at battle stations working through simulated combat situations until 1100 when we will break for the noon meal. We will be at drill status during the evening meal. We will secure at twenty-hundred (8PM). The galley will bring sandwiches and coffee to the crew at their battle stations, then come back to collect the waste. Inform your crews of the fate of the *Granger*."

0800: Each department stood for muster and was informed of the battle condition X-ray and the fate of *Granger*. Each member of the crew took heart, their Captain and officers of the *Card* had once again acted with good judgment.

Bridge Log Entry: *Lieutenant Hooper was relieved by Lt(jg) Winchester. Sea state estimated at Beaufort scale 5, fresh breeze.*

0900: Department drills were called for all hands except the galley crew. Meanwhile in the galley the lunch menu plan included Southern Fried Chicken, savory Roast Beef, mashed potatoes, steamed green beans, glazed carrots and cream of broccoli soup. The Commissarymen gathered on the mess-decks for quarters and to discuss the plan of the day and make duty assignments.

CS3 Brown was sent to the Reefer Deck to secure the frozen food for the meal.

The sea state is up but did not appear to be excessive so no changes are planned for the meal time. The Chief reviewed the day's routine and discussed the meal assignments with CS2 Jackson, the watch captain. CS3 Jennings was assigned to make the salad bar items and set up the desert bar. CS3 Brown was assigned to prepare the main entrée; fry the chicken. The routine for this particular item called for preparation three hours before lunch was piped. CS3 Brown gathered ingredients and transported them to the prep table. As he passed the fryer; he lit it up and continued through the galley. In a few minutes the fryer would be ready for the ingredients. He set about preparing the chicken. Instinctively he turned toward the fryer to see how it is coming. A shock wave ran up his spine when he saw the smoke rising from inside the fryer. He made a quick mental run through of procedure and realized he forgot to put oil in the fryer. He immediately turned it off and ran after a container of fryer oil. CS2 Jackson smelled the burning and went to investigate, but by then Brown was pouring liquid shortening into the fryer stopping the smoke. After *"on the spot counseling"* concerning the minor oversight the process of prep continued on.

There is always a considerable amount of moving about in the small galley during meal preparations and today was no different. The sea-state was rising creating some difficulty on the prep tables. CS2 Jackson reminded all his staff to ensure pans are secure for sea when placed on the tables.

0930: CS3 Brown floured the chicken, being careful to put in the special herbs and spices, according to the recipe. He placed the chicken parts it in the fryer basket and dropped the basket into the hot fryer grease and headed off to the sink to wash his hands. The wet chicken hitting hot grease created a series of grease explosions sending grease splashes into the air. The rolling of the ship directed those splashes of grease off the fryer and into the heating coils igniting a grease fire.

The galley quickly filled with smoke, flames begin to rise. The automatic suppression system doesn't go off and the battle is on. CS2 Jackson and the chief call the bridge to report the fire.

The Boatswain's Mate of the Watch engaged the fire alarm setting off a constant barrage of single dings. "Fire, Fire, Fire" he shouts into the 1-MC; "Class Bravo fire in the galley, flying squad away, man repair 5." The bell continued to ring. Once notified the fire team was on station, he disengaged the alarm.

The rolling seas and the rocking of the ship spread the burning grease throughout the galley. Heavy black smoke made breathing difficult. The fire status is reported to the repair 5 locker leader. Repair leader 5 keyed his microphone. "Bridge this is Repair 5 leader. The fire threatens to endanger the mess-decks. I recommend a call to General Quarters- Fire Station."

The OOD approves the recommendation and the Boatswain's mate of the Watch shouts the command into the 1-MC. "Now General Quarters. General Quarters, we have a fire in the galley threatening the Mess Decks. All hands report to your General Quarters fire station." Everyone on the Watch, Station and Quarter Bill had a designated place to report when a fire GQ is called.

The smoke leaked through the galley serving line windows and into the mess-decks. The fire has been raging for three minutes. The Repair 5 hose teams are dressed out and begin moving into the galley area.

Fire hose Team 1 moved up the port side passageway from the mess-decks and enters the galley from the forward galley door. Hose team 2 enters through the aft galley door from the mess-decks.

The hose teams tag-teamed with the flames; hose Team 2 uses the AFFE fire-fighting foam to extinguish the grease fire, while hose Team 1 works to stop additional fires starting outside the main galley. Repair lockers 2 & 3 send out de-smoking teams to work and remove the heavy black smoke from inside the ship by setting up "Red Devil Blowers" with hose to the exterior of the ship forward and aft.

1022: The fire was finally extinguished and the investigation team began its work as the clean-up teams moved in to restore the cleanliness.

The ship's lead investigator, the Damage Control Chief begins with the automatic fire suppression system and discovered that during the last PMS work completed by the damage control division, the automatic melt-able link was inadvertently replaced with a non-melting link. This was problem one which did not prevent the fire from getting out of control. Problem two was that CS3 Brown left the fryer unattended. It was only for a minute but that was enough to allow the situation to explode into a big problem. The problem there was the lack of training for the CS's and Food Service Attendants. Members of the galley team were placed on battle damage control teams, but no training was conducted for galley fire damage control.

In the process MS3 Brown received third degree burns to his face, hands and arms.

1100: The galley fire was out and the ship's crew was secured from General Quarters and returned to normal sea cruising duties. The Galley was behind schedule but managed lunch a few minutes after the posted time.

1300: After the noon meal, battle condition drills were reinstated. The drills called for constant trials designed to go through supper and into the early evening.

1600: Mess cooks delivered sandwiches and bug juice (Kool-Aid) to the sailors at their battle stations.

1850 Everyone thought they would secure from battle stations when the sun went down but instead the Boatswain's mate of the Watch piped Battle condition Yankee and a third of the crew was secured to get rest, and the ship remained at wartime cruising. The Condition Yankee called for one third of the crew to be off for four-hours, then another third, then another third.

GM1 Brenda Phelps and PN3 Robert Benson sat in the forward gun mount going over the battle plans provided by Chief Osborne. Phelps had conducted numerous training exercises with the gun crews in keeping with her assigned training duties. She documented a below standard 2.0 for the mid-ship gun crews and a barely standard 3.0 for the after gun crews.

"I just can't seem to get it into their heads, she would shout. The most basic problem faced by naval guns, is that the guns have to be aimed from moving platforms at other moving platforms, with wave motion adding the third dimension. You ain't firing a shore artillery!"

She was determined that her gun mount would qualify whether any other of the *Card's* guns, torpedoes, hedgehogs and depth charges qualified during the exercises. As they poured over each attack they determined how they would respond. Phelps asked Benson to show her how he would direct the gun using information from CIC to provide a proper shooting solution for specific ranges and elevations. His responses were dead on each time.

Phelps sat on the deck of the gun mount and Benson joined her there. "I think you have a handle on it Benson, I hope you do so well under fire."

"Say Phelps, you are a unique individual. Two perplexing questions come to mind about you."

"Oh?"

"Yeah . . . You are smart, you have a quick wit, and you are independent, confident and competent. You are a cut above the average sailor. . ."

"Hold on there, Benson, where are you going with this?"

"Just this. Why are you a Gunner's Mate and not some high tech rating, or even an officer?"

"I have wanted to be a sailor since I was eleven years old. My Uncle Billy was a sailor . . . well he wasn't really my uncle he was the uncle of one of my foster parents. Anyway he had some great stories about being at sea and visiting faraway places, and strange ports. I decided that was the life for me. I guess I have read every book there is on the sea and seamanship, and the US Navy. When I got out of high school, I joined the Navy. The only billets that guaranteed sea duty were Boatswain Mates and Gunner's Mates."

"Deck Ape didn't appeal to you I take it," asked Benson.

"No! I went to gunnery school. I like this job, I am good at it, and I have been on four steaming ships in five years." I don't care to be an officer and I don't want to sit behind a video screen or any other kind of device that needs a desk. Well that answers that question. You said two questions."

"I think I know the answer to the second question."

"And that is?"

"Why hasn't someone asked a great lady like you to marry them? I figure you have been asked many times but it has always come with a condition that you would not agree to."

"Not many times, but a few, and you're right, getting out of the Navy is not negotiable."

"When you get salt water in your veins, you can't get too far away from the sea," he stated.

"Exactly," she confirmed.

"Now that we are clearing up some ambiguities I have one for you."

"OK."

"What are you doing here? You are bright, a quick learner and bit more mature than most guys that come on board for their first two week cruise."

"When I got out of high school, I went to college for 3 semesters. I took architecture. I thought I would like that. I decided that was not for me so I bummed around the country on my motorcycle for about a year. Then decided I needed a career so I took a job in a temp agency placing people in temporary jobs. The idea occurred to me that if I had a degree in business management I would be in a better position to get a good paying job. So I signed up for night school classes."

Benson shifted his body for a more comfortable position and continued. "I don't know why I joined the Navy Reserves. I was walking by the Navy recruiting station one day and just went in and signed up. I liked boot camp. My first two week active duty assignment was for Commander Richardson, the Liaison Officer at McGuire Air Force Base. He liked the way I did things and talked me into working in his office on weekends. My job was to take care of the office and get transit naval personnel on flights to where ever they were going, so he could party on the weekends. I don't like that guy. When my two weeks came up this time, I called a guy I had met who works in BuPers (Bureau of Personnel), and told him I needed to get away from Richardson. This guy had had some problems with Richardson and was glad to help."

Phelps leaned in closer, showing sincere interest in the story.

"When Richardson found out I was not going to work for him for two weeks, he tried to stop my orders. My buddy from BuPers lied to him, telling him he would try to find the orders and cancel them, but he could not locate them."

Phelps smiled and shook her head. "It's nice to have friends in influential places."

"Very true. He called me one day and asked me if I would go to Gitmo on the *Card*. I told him I would and here I am."

"You are a strange duck, Benson. I have drilled you and grilled you and you learned this job and you have not complained or tried to transfer off this gun. Why is that?"

"Two reasons. I like this job. I like being at sea and I like working with this gun, I like the whole idea about naval firepower. I like it so well in fact I am thinking of changing my rate to Gunners Mate and go active on a steaming ship. You're a good instructor."

"If you are serious about changing your rate, I bet I could teach you enough to test into Third Class. Then you could go to gunnery school and come out an E-5."

"I would like that."

"You said there were two reasons."

"Ah, yeah well . . . I like being with you."

"What!" She was shocked.

"Hey what can I say, I'm a glutton for punishment. I heard bells the first time I saw you."

"You heard eight bells. They ring that at the end of every watch from reveille to taps. A ship's bell could hardly be anything romantic."

"Bells are bells. Nobody said it couldn't be a ship's bell."

She shook her head from side to side and gave him a fake sympathy look.

"I grew up with a girl name Brenda McIntyre. She had three brothers who called her Brennie. If anyone else would call her that she would punch them in the chops. One day our neighborhood gang was at a high school football game, when a guy from the opposing school came over and introduced himself. We took a liking to the guy and we all went out for a burger after the game. He called her Brennie and she just smiled. They were married right after graduation."

Executive Assessment
Managing in Turbulent Times -Reinstating Normal Operations

We stated earlier the organization is the entity that provides the jobs for the crew. It is important to re-iterate that now and recall how the organization is the entity that offers the prospect for a future for all concerned, both now and in the future.

The organization must be preserved and must weather the storms and the turbulent times. When the storms are abated the organizations that made it through will once again provide products for customers and jobs for the community.

The loss of the *USS Granger* is an example of an organization that counted on outside experts to tell them when and how to prepare for future events. Senior executives would do well to develop their own systems, their own barometers and their own internal experts who are constantly taking the readings and recommending a proper course. Each department head; sales & marketing, purchasing, production, accounts receivable, accounts payable, to name a few must have systems for reading the operational climate and make weekly or monthly reports to the senior executive or to an executive committee, with predictions and recommendations based on evidence they can point to, and supported by historical records.

When a ship is fighting a storm, they do not run headlong full speed ahead. They head into the storm and reduce the speed to just enough to maintain steering. Organizations facing uncertain times, with no visible end in sight slow the pace of daily operations in order to conserve resources and to keep a grip on the current events and make preparations for the future.

Financial integrity becomes one of the critical elements that are slowed. In many cases, I have witnessed the freezing of certain expenditures. Hiring may be curtailed. The introduction of new products are delayed, expansion and other future plans are delayed. In some cases lay-offs are necessary in order to protect the cash flow. I have worked with organizations that were caught up in an industry, or national credit crunch, who themselves had cash, but delayed spending until a clearer economic forecast could be made.

Many executives have a problem informing upper management on the status of their department, especially if the news is bad. Get there right away. It is better to hear it from you than from someone else or from the boss' own discovery. No alibis. Just the straight facts, no matter how damaging. The discovery of a cover-up would be devastating to your career. Be Sure of Your Facts before approaching your boss. Be sure you're armed with pertinent information.

Anytime you approach a senior executive particularly when that senior manager is your boss, provide deference but not obsequiousness. Properness does not mean submissiveness. Submission is not a characteristic of courtesy, respect, politeness, or manners. Courtesy requires a prompt reply and a polite response. Obsequiousness will cause the boss to see you as one with no backbone. Deport yourself in a respectful manner when interacting with your boss. Anything submissive reduces proper courtesies to duteous and servile practices. Don't talk apologetically. The boss must see you as a mature adult who has their self-respect intact.

Inattention and careless mistakes resulted in a fire in the Galley. There plans in effect that were employed. Even though some things went wrong, because of improper maintenance the fire was extinguished. What followed the fire was an important item in organizational management. They conducted an after action investigation to determine the cause, the methods for dealing with it and what to do in the future. All that was followed by fire brigade drills.

Command Axiom

- When encountering hard times face it head on - reduce where necessary, keep your bread and butter items and stay on course.

- One cannot be victim unless they want to be.

- Keep Going "Diligence is the mother of good luck." Successful people deal with failure. They tackle their demons head on. They pick themselves up and keep going.

- Do not try to protect your boss from bad news.

- Your relationship with any executive who is senior to you should be Professional. You are both professionals with a mission.

Chapter 9 (SNAFU) Situation Normal All Fouled Up

Thursday 16, July 1970
Destroyer – Submarine Piers
Mayport Naval Base

The ship pulled into the D&S piers in Mayport at ten hundred hours. They were berthed on the outer portion of the nest, meaning one had to cross over five other ships in order to reach the pier. They were to tie up against the *USS Roberts (DE 749)*.

Mister Goldsmith had the Conn; Mister Gilliam stood next to him. Lieutenant Commander McCormick and Lieutenant Winthrop were in the chart house busying themselves with charts for Gitmo. The Captain was visiting CIC. Both Mister Gilliam and Mister Goldsmith had experience placing a DE on the end of a nest. Everyone on the bridge and anyone on the *Roberts* who were paying attention knew they were coming in too fast.

The *Roberts* OOD ran to the railing and shouted; "You're coming in too fast, reverse engines."

Too late, the *Card's* port anchor connected with the side of the *Roberts* and the ship's forward movement peeled the paint off the *Robert's* numbers and left a nice score mark on the *Robert's* starboard hull. The ship stopped directly alongside the *Roberts*. The duty Quartermasters on both ships hit the collision alarm, bringing everyone to attention.

The Captain, McCormick, and Winthrop ran to the bridge. "Belay that alarm," shouted the Captain. "Belay the alarm," shouted the *Robert's* OOD.

The officers of both ships examined the damage. The *Robert's* Captain came to the Quarterdeck to inspect the situation. "Bob," he said to the *Card's* Captain, "We wondered if your ship could ever put to sea, now it seems you guys have trouble coming into port, first Norfolk and now here."

"I will send a crew over to repair the damage," said Captain Mills.

The line handlers from the *Roberts* and the *Card* threw lines and threaded them through the line chocks tying the proper marlinspike seaman knots, securing the two vessels close enough to lay a brow but with enough distance to allow for drafting and sea movement.

1020: The first mooring line was made fast. The Boatswain Mate of the Watch passed the word to shift colors. The ship's call sign and steaming Ensign were hauled down, and the jack and Ensign were raised.

1030: The deck force connected the ship to shore power lines. Mister Goldsmith shifted the Officer of the Deck from the flying bridge to the Quarterdeck. GM2 Hargrove assumed the Petty Officer of the Watch.

1035: The five minute countdown began and the ship shifted from ship power to shore power without a glitch.

The reports of the damage to the *Roberts* showed the damage was slight and posed no concern for the integrity of the hull. But the numbers would need to be repainted. By eleven hundred Furman had a crew hanging over the *Robert's* starboard side repainting the numbers. "Remember lads, its 749 not 383."

1100: Harold Hillman arrived on the Quarterdeck shackled between two burly base police petty officers from the Norfolk Navy Base. They were accompanied by a Lieutenant from the Norfolk Judge Advocate General's office. The Petty Officer of the Watch was dispatched to notify the Captain of Hillman's arrival.

Mister Hooper arrived on the Quarterdeck wearing a Master at Arms arm band. He wore a webbed gun belt with a holster that held a .45 automatic pistol. He was accompanied by BM1 Furman who also wore a black arm band with yellow MAA (Master at Arms) letters. He was armed as well.

Hargrove returned with orders from the Captain for Mister Hooper to take custody of the prisoner and send Hillman's handlers back to Norfolk. He ordered the Petty Officer of the Watch to call all parties having business with the Captain's mast to report to the Quarterdeck. The prisoner exchange was made and the Norfolk Navy Base law enforcement officers left the ship.

Hargrove keyed the 1-MC and announced; "Now all parties having business to bring before the Captain's mast will lay to the Quarterdeck immediately."

Mister Gilliam, Lieutenants Grubaugh and Winthrop arrived on the Quarterdeck. Mister Winchester, Chief Jaquet and two other petty officers from the Galley followed them. Yeoman Williams had the case files in a file folder with the ship's seal imprinted on the cover.

The Captain arrived on the Quarterdeck.

"Attention on Deck," cried Yeoman Williams.

Everyone snapped to.

Williams surrendered the file folder to the Captain.

"At ease."

Harold Hillman stood at attention; his white hat was in his right hand down by his side. His head was bowed in submission.

The Captain ordered Hillman's release from the shackles. Petty Officer Furman unlocked the shackles and removed them. He opened the case-file. He peered down at the charges and without looking up he began. "This Captain's mast is now in order under the authority of Article 15 of the Uniform Code of Military Justice."

He turned his attention to Hillman. His face was stern, his voice low and deliberate. "CS3 Hillman, you have a history of drunk and disorderly. In every previous duty station you have been delivered to your ship by shore patrol, civilian police and base police on numerous occasions throughout your career in the Navy. You have been incarcerated for several days making you absent over liberty 12 times. Because of that you have been reduced in rank 4 times and transferred off four ships in the past eight years. Now, you have committed this same offense on my ship. As a consequence of this act you missed movement. There was a fire in your galley causing injury to one of your shipmates. It may very well be that if you had been on your station that fire would not have gotten out of hand and no one would be suffering burns at this time."

The Captain paused to let the charges sink in. He closed the file folder.

"Tell me why I should not throw you in the brig and order a general discharge for the benefit of the service?"

"Captain, I am guilty of immaturity and poor judgment. When I am on the beach, I just go stupid. I had a lot of time to think on my way here. This is the worst thing I have ever done . . . Missing movement, because I was in jail due to my stupidity. Captain. . . I don't want to be kicked out of the Navy. This is all I have, this is all I want. I have no family. I have no other place to go. When others leave this ship they go home, then after a while they come back to the ship. Going home for me is returning to the ship. This is my home. I have learned my lesson. I will not jeopardize my home again, I assure you."

The Captain stood for a minute observing the accused. He was acutely aware of the cook's shipmates standing in somber repose. Every one there knew Hillman was guilty of an offense that came with harsh consequences. Justice was demanded by the offense for his behavior ashore. Hillman was a good sailor, a good shipmate and a dependable component of the ship's mission. This was not going to be an easy decision for the Captain, but whatever he chose to do the crew would be hard pressed not to agree.

Finally, the Captain opened the case files in a folder, wrote a few lines on the top paper then closed the file. His attention went once more to the accused and without taking his eyes off Hillman he stretched out the hand holding the file to Yeoman Williams. Williams took the file.

"Harold Hillman, I am ordering Yeoman Williams to write up a general discharge for the benefit of the service for you."

Hillman's countenance fell, he slumped his head lower.

"I will not reduce you in rating but you will forfeit one-third of your pay for 60 days. You will be confined to this ship for sixty days. For the next sixty days you will work for BM1 Furman on the deck force. If you can clean up your act and not, as you say, *Get stupid* for the next six months I will shred the discharge papers."

In spite of the crowd on the Quarterdeck, the only sound was the low continuous gentle swooshing of the in-port waters splashing against the hull of the ship.

"Do you have anything to say?"

Hillman looked up at the Captain then lowered his eyes to the deck. He was standing with his feet together, turning his white hat in his hands like a driver turning a steering wheel. He quietly said; "No Captain. I appreciate your leniency."

"It's probation . . . with dire consequences for violation."

"I am yours to command Sir."

"Does anyone else have anything to add?"

No one made a move. Everyone was staring off into space. No one was looking at anyone else. In spite of a sense of relief that Hillman would remain on board, the atmosphere was tense.

"Very well, these proceedings are completed. Mast adjourned." The Captain turned to Ezra Furman. "Boats take charge of the prisoner. And see he is properly dealt with."

"I will see he gets what's coming to him Sir."

1200: The Captain turned about face and walked down the 01- weather deck and into the skin of the ship, up the ladder and to his quarters. The Duty Boatswain's mate of the Watch keyed the 1-MC "The captain is off the quarterdeck."

The officers' club on base was the *Fiddler's Green*. The Captain joined his subordinate officers there for lunch and drinks. It is a Navy tradition that ship's Captains do not usually go ashore with junior officers but Captain Mills felt that since the officers had gone through some difficult times in the past six months and a terrible storm and humiliating bad luck in Norfolk, they deserved some social time with the Captain.

BM1 Furman provided Hillman with a paint brush and a metal water bucket. In the bucket was a quart of water with gray food coloring, giving it a look of weak gray paint.

"Hillman, the Captain put me in charge of your punitive duties so you will do exactly as I say. You will carry this brush and pail with you at all times. You will paint every square inch of this ship." Hillman took the bucket and the brush gave his undivided attention to his new supervisor.

"You will begin after breakfast," Furman continued, "and you will paint all day, stopping only for meals. You will begin again after the evening meal and you will secure after the eight O'clock reports at which time you will muster with me and the duty MAA (Master at Arms) and duty officer."

At any time during working hours that you are not painting you will be with me in my office, which is the First Lieutenant's locker" (storage space for deck materials).

Hillman nodded in compliance.

"Any Questions?"

"No. I think I understand completely."

"Good, I will report your activities to the OOD every hour." He handed Hillman a yellow memo card. "This is a pass allowing you to take head calls and meal privileges. If anyone should see you doing something other than painting, show them this pass."

"Aye, Aye Boats."

There is an unwritten rule on board navy ships. Two people you do not want to hassle are cooks and Boatswain Mates.

1630: The officers gathered in the wardroom in preparation for the evening meal. The table was set but no one dared sit down since the official partaking was set for 1700, and not even then if the Captain had not arrived. Mister Goldsmith was sitting in one of leather side chairs. A worried look prompted Lieutenant Sterling to ask: "What's with the worried look, Marshall?"

"It was me who rammed the *Roberts* when we came in. It was me who was on the Conn when we lost our anchor coming into Norfolk. I think I may be in deep porky pine poop with the Captain."

"Has he given you any indication you were in trouble?" asked Lieutenant Grubaugh.

"The Navy has a reputation of eating its own," said Mister Winthrop. "Any time there is a mishap some officer gets the shaft and it is usually the one who was present at the time."

"Has he said anything to you Commander?"

"Well he said he would handle it, so I am letting him handle it, whatever *it* may be," the XO answered.

The wardroom steward entered the area. "Will the Captain be joining us for the evening meal?" asked Mister Winthrop.

"Oh no sir, the Captain will be going ashore in about an hour. He has a evening meal appointment with the DesRon senior officers."

'Well, then," said the XO, "I think we can all be seated and begin our meal."

The metallic sound of the intercom system clicking on drew all officers' eyes toward the speaker box.

"Wardroom, this is the Captain. Is Mister Goldsmith there?"

"I am right here Captain."

"May I see you in my cabin, please?"

"Certainly Sir I am on my way."

The speaker clicked off.

All the officers' eyes then turned toward Ensign Marshall Goldsmith. A rush of anxiety overtook him. He found it hard to catch his breath or control his worried expression. "Well I guess I will be learning my fate for embarrassing the Captain and continuing the *Card's* poor reputation with the fleet."

He took his hat from the rack, placed it under his left arm and exited the wardroom door. Standing just outside the door he placed his hat on his head, squared it, took a deep breath and ran up the two flights of ladders and paused outside the Captain's stateroom. He tried to get his breath and calm his nerves. He knocked on the door, uncovered and poised his hand on the door handle.

From inside the stateroom he heard the Captain's voice. "Enter."

He tried to surmise if the tone of that one word was friend or foe. He turned the handle, pushed the door open and stepped inside. He stood with his back to the door with his hat under his left arm. He pushed the door closed with an outstretched finger of his right hand.

The Captain did not look up, but continued his study of the day's reports.

The Ensign snapped to attention. "You wanted to see me Captain?" he asked breathlessly, still trying to calm his labored breathing. He tried not to show his fear, but was pretty sure he was not doing a very good job of it.

The Captain looked up and smiled. "Yes Mister Goldsmith, sit down." He waved his hand in the direction of a leather side chair flanked by small table on which was a plate of coffee cakes, a silver coffee pot similar to the one used in the wardroom. There were two cups next to the pot. Mister Goldsmith sat in the designated chair and placed his hat under it.

"Have a cup of coffee and some of this coffee cake. Hillman sent it up. Apparently Furman gives him a break from time to time to help in the galley. He assures me Hillman is keeping up with his punitive assignments. Anyway that guy makes a great coffee cake."

Shock and amazement seized the j.g. when the Captain stood up and poured coffee into each cup and then sat down on the leather chair on the other side of the table. The Captain leaned back and crossed his legs as he took a sip of coffee from his cup. Mister Goldsmith lifted his cup and took a sip. Still under stress by the summons of the Captain and the scolding he was sure was coming, and still winded from climbing the ladders, he tried to calm himself, steady the hand that held the coffee and control his breathing.

The Captain lifted the plate of cakes and extended it toward the young officer. "Here have a coffee cake."

Goldsmith considered it more of an order than an offer so he complied.

"I hear you have a 1929 Navy Blue Chevrolet. Is that right?" he asked with look of pure fascination.

"Yes Sir."

"Tell me about it."

Startled by this unusual beginning of a certain reprimand and perhaps some bad performance notes in his official record, he shuddered a bit as he tried to think about what the Captain wanted to know.

"Well . . . Sir . . . My Grandfather bought it in 1929 when he graduated from college and received a commission through NROTC. I think he paid $600 for it."

"How did you come about it?"

"He gave it to me when I received my commission. He drove it to my commissioning ceremony, and then handed over the key and the title. He said it was a Navy car and it had to stay in a Navy family."

"Is it just a pastime or is that the car you drive?"

"Oh it is the car I drive. My grandfather said he saluted it every time he got out of it. I keep up the tradition."

"Sounds like he loved that car?"

"Yes Sir. He named her Lizzie."

"Lizzie. Hmm. Like Tin Lizzie."

"I suppose so, I don't know. It makes sense now that you mention it. Grandfather was a tin can sailor. I have heard him speaking of her as his tin can."

"Is it original or have you had to do a lot of plastic surgery on it?"

The Captain was showing a lot of interest now. He was smiling and leaning forward with great enthusiasm. Mister Goldsmith began to relax a bit. He liked talking about his car. He took a small bite of the coffee cake and washed it down with a large sip of coffee.

"All the sheet metal and wood are in very good condition. It has new rubber all around. A very solid ride. It will cruise at 55 mph without a rattle or a shake. It has an overhead valve six cylinder engine. I have been told that this is very rare. Chevy only produced the overhead valve engine in '29 and '30 I think."

The Captain finished one coffee cake, followed by a healthy sip of coffee, and reached for another.

Mister Goldsmith finished his cake, and the Captain pointed to the dish as he said: "tell me about the styling and how it feels to drive it."

"It has bumpers," he said as he secured another cake. "Bumpers were an option in 1929. It had other options as well, such as, wire wheels, running-boards, step plates, a radiator-cap hood mascot and a spotlight." He realized the Captain showed pleasure that he had taken another cake so he decided he should take a bite. He hastily chewed the morsel and washed it down with a hefty sip of coffee. "I really enjoy driving it, especially in warm weather with the top down."

"I would like to take a ride in it sometime."

"Any time you say Captain."

Their conversation went on for another ten minutes, then the Captain patted his junior officer on the knee and said. "This has been delightful Mister Goldsmith. I wish we had more time to talk. Unfortunately I have a evening meal meeting with the mucky mucks from ResDesDiv5 to go over the Gitmo Bay Plans."

The Captain stood up. Mister Goldsmith quickly sat his cup in the saucer, snatched his hat from under the chair and raised himself to his feet.

"Thanks for having tea and crumpets with me," the Captain said as he extended his hand to his subordinate.

Mister Goldsmith extended his hand and the Captain took it, squeezed it slightly then let it go.

"I enjoyed the time also Captain." He walked to the door and turned the handle. As he pulled it toward him he turned to the Captain and said; "My offer stands, you name the time and I will arrange it."

"I will, Mister Goldsmith, I certainly will, as soon after we get back as possible. Good evening now."

Mister Goldsmith exited the state room and bounded down the ladders and into the Wardroom.

Lieutenant Grubaugh was the first to ask. "How are you doing Marshall?'

"OK, I think."

"Did he come down on you or just ask you a lot of questions until you had to come up with a plan to correct the problem?" asked Lieutenant Sterling.

Mister Goldsmith sat at his usual place at the table. The steward brought his plate and a cup of coffee.

"Well he did ask a lot of questions. But they were all about my car."

"He just wanted to know about Lizzie?" asked Mister Alexander.

"We drank coffee and ate coffee cake and talked about Lizzie. After a while he looked at his watch and said he had a meeting with ResDesDiv5. He told me he enjoyed the conversation and the tea and crumpets and I was on my way out."

Lieutenant Commander McCormick peered down the table at Mister Goldsmith and said. "It was not just tea and crumpets, Marshall. It was an instruction period. Think about it. You are a smart man Mister Goldsmith. What was that all about? What was he showing you? What did you learn from that?"

"Well," his face took on an internal investigative look. "I think he was showing me I was still OK with him in spite of the glitches in coming into port. But I think I better get my act together if I expect to stay in his good graces."

"I think you are correct, Marshall." He turned toward the others. "I think it is an instruction for us all. We have come a long way, since he came on board, but we have to really have our act together when we get to Gitmo."

"I plan to tighten up. I gotta make a good showing from now on," said Goldsmith.

"You'll get a chance to correct that, Mister Goldsmith. You will have the Conn coming into Gitmo. I suggest you begin your Gitmo port entry preparation now. Consider the tide, the weather, the location of the berth and our spot in that berth. Decide the appropriate approach speed, what you will need from the sea and anchor detail or the line handlers and any shore assistance you may need. All this is standard stuff, but have it all in your mind. I will be standing with you, but you are on your own."

"Oh that's good news," he said unconvincingly.

Executive Assessment
Dealing with minor crises during the Crises

Other situations will come up in times of turbulence. Some are just minor annoyances, like attendance or discipline problems. Others are major situations such as the loss of essential personnel or materiel. Frustration is usually the emotion of the day and these other unforeseen or blindsided events only add to those frustrations. They must be dealt with dispatch and clear heads.

Command Axiom

- It is imperative that top management insist on staying with the strategic plan and the subordinate objectives that guide and measure the process.

- Plans in the form of company policies and procedures guide the action that will need to be taken. In most cases these items can be handled at the lowest competent level, and that usually means first line supervision and Human Resources.

- In those cases that have a crucial relevance to the plans for turbulent times, a member of the executive team will need to take charge. The *What IF* plans will then be called into play.

Chapter 10 Anticipating the Onslaught

Friday, 17 July 1970
War Game Preparation
The Caribbean Sea, near Guantanamo Bay, Cuba

0500 The maneuvering watch was posted at zero five hundred at which time the ship shifted from shore power to ship power and the officer of the deck, Lieutenant Winchester, shifted the watch from the quarterdeck to the flying bridge.

The last mooring line was dropped and the Boatswain Mate of the Watch blew a long whistle blast and passed the word to shift colors. The Jack and the Ensign were hauled down smartly and the steaming ensign was hoisted on the gaff and the ships call sign was hoisted from the signal bridge.

On the bridge was the Captain, Mister Winchester, who had the Conn, Mister Winthrop the Navigator, Commander McCormick. The *Card* pulled out of Mayport bay and turned east to the shipping lane that would eventually lead them south toward Guantanamo Bay and their next big adventure.

"We are in the shipping lane." Said Mister Winthrop.

"Very well." Acknowledged Mister Winchester.

The Captain slid off his chair and headed for the gangway to the lower decks. He stopped just before he entered and turned to Mister Winchester. "Mister Winchester."

"Sir."

"Point her south and let her eat."

"Aye, Aye Sir."

The morning meal was piped at 0630. Secure the mess decks was piped at 0700.

1000: The ship cleared the channel and entered the open sea.

1030: The clanging of the ship's bell and the echoic blast of the quartermaster's voice came over the one-MC. "Now General Quarters, General Quarters, all hands man your battle stations, this is a drill, this is a drill, all hands man your battle stations."

The crew hopped up from where they were and ran to their battle stations. Those stationed on the weather decks donned their battle helmets and life jackets. They waited for further instructions.

The one-MC came alive and the Boatswain Mate of the Watch shouted; "Now stand by and give ear to the Captain."

"This is your captain speaking. Between here and Gitmo we will remain in battle condition x-ray. We will have constant drills to prepare us for what we will in the drill exercise zone. We must learn to work together under battle conditions. We must know that each sailor on the ship is committed to the task at hand, and committed to each other. And furthermore we must know that each sailor is competent to do the job that is needed done when it is needed done. We must develop faith in ourselves as individuals and faith in ourselves as a team; we must learn this ship and learn to have faith in our ship and in our equipment."

The Captain stepped away from in 1-MC and the Boatswain Mate keyed the toggle and announced; "That is all – Carry on."

The drills began again. Drill after drill. There were man-over-board drills, abandon ship drills, damage control drills, and casualty drills. The bridge and CIC also conducted evasive action drills. With the defensive drills were the offensive drills, torpedo and gunnery drills, depth charge setting and firing drills as fast as they could be initiated. The officers and chiefs served as umpires, taking time readings and accuracy checks, correcting mistakes and repeating the event until time objectives were met. All this lasted through lunch. GM1 Phelps made rounds to each gun position offering corrective measures. Everyone noticed a distinct change in her tone of voice. She was almost friendly.

1400: The order to set condition Yankee was piped. One third of the crew was secured to get rest and chow and report again in four hours while another third took their turn followed by the next third.

Donaldson had spent the last seventy-two hours in radio central in enemy contact drills. He entered the gangway through the after hatch and descended the ladder. He did not remove his clothing but fell into his rack and slept for the four hours he was allowed before relieving the next watch. He was so exhausted he slept through gunnery exercises. For four hours there was a constant barrage of torpedoes, hedge hogs and depth charges as well as anti-aircraft and surface to surface cannon fire just above where he was sleeping. When he awoke, he took quite a ribbing from the ship mates in the same berthing area who remained awake because of the ear piercing noise and the bone jarring vibrations that the little ship endured.

The entire ship's company drilled on G.Q. as well as their daily jobs under the worst conditions possible. These drills helped them to get very good at calculation the needed response to each event and making the correct responses within a few seconds.

GM1 Phelps and PN3 Benson met again in the forward gun mount. Sundown was coming on and Phelps wanted to go over some last minute preparations and practice before the big day that would consume their attention and tax their skills to the max. Phelps tested Benson from the Second Class Gunner's mate manual. When Lieutenant Grubaugh came by to check on them, Benson was reciting as Phelps followed along in the manual. "The projectile consists of fine distinct parts the ogive (o-jive) is the nose, the streamlined forward part. The Bourrelet is the forward-bearing surface of the body, which steadies the projectile in the gun barrel . . the body. . "

1500: "Excuse me gunner," Ms. Grubaugh interrupted, "we need you in the wardroom. We are going over some Gitmo attack problems and we need the benefit of your thinking. "I'm on my way Lieutenant."

Lieutenant Grubaugh did not wait for her, she proceeded to the wardroom.

"Ok Benson, keep at it and I'll be back as quick as I can. There will be a test!' Not to worry may-tee (matey), " said Benson in his worst Long John Silver accent. I'll be right here and I give yee me aff-a-davie I will not slip me cables."

"Then see ye don't ye ole sea dog or I'll have ye clapped in irons." She responded in the same tone.

"RRRR," Benson replied. They both laughed.

1400: GM1 Phelps and PN3 Benson met again in the forward gun mount. Phelps wanted to go over some last minute preparations and practice before the big day that would consume their attention and tax their skills to the max. After rehearsing the sequence of action for the ump-teenth time correctly Phelps turned to face Benson. She leaned against the gun mount, and placing her hand on Benson's right shoulder, she looked into his eyes and said: "You know, when we are in the heat of battle at Gitmo, I may shout at you in a way that will not be lady like. . . I . ."

The apprentice held up his left hand to stop her in mid-sentence. "Not to worry," he interrupted. "You know what you are doing and what needs to be done, and it needs to be done quickly. I will try to stay up with you, but if you need to get tough, have at it."

"I like you Robbie, you're a good man. I think we will do alright out there."

"Robbie?" He thought to himself. Not Benson?" He smiled at his boss. "I like you Brennie, and I think you're right."
She smiled.

"Well she didn't punch me in the chops for calling her Brennie," he thought to himself.

Lieutenant (Junior Grade) Gilliam loved the feel of the ship under him as it sped along toward its next port of call. He hadn't had much opportunity to experience a ship at sea in a long time and he missed it. He bathed in the pounding, and bounding over the main as his ship moved steadily southward, her screws churning up a white and cream colored wake astern. No sailor ever grows tired of the experience of a sturdy ship beneath them and the vast latent power of the sea around them, and a crew of competent professional seafarers on duty. Ahead of them the open sea and the horizon which never seemed to get nearer.

As he stood on the 0-2 weather deck, near the number two aft gun, he peered out across the open waters. "Not a speck of land, just sky and ocean. "You can see the edge of the earth," he thought. He always marveled at the slight curvature coming out of the sea on the port side, arching over and descending back into the sea on the starboard side and how it rose and fell with slow, timeless regularity. He directed his focus to the hum of the engines and the vibration on the deck and everything attached to the ship. After a few hours on board a ship at sea the brain's natural sensory reduction mechanism kicks in and you don't hear it or feel it. But there are times when you want to hear it and feel it, like a new born baby listening to its mother's heartbeat.

Saturday, 18 July 1970
Entrance to the Gitmo Training Area

1500: Those of the crew who had access to a porthole, an open hatch or a weather deck watched the Guantanamo section of the Cuban island come into view and watched as it drew nearer. They were entering the "War Zone" where a new adventure awaited those who were here for the first time. Those who were here before actually looked forward to another exciting and challenging experience. The drills were tough, now they were over. The next drills would be under the scrutiny of umpires in hostile action conditions.

The *Card* was the last ship in the squadron to enter the Gitmo training area. Sundown was two hours away and the Caribbean skies were beginning to streak with pink and peach colors. Mister Goldsmith had the Conn. Lieutenant Sterling was lounging in CIC sipping a cup of tea and reading armed forces news delivered from radio central.

The Radarman turned to the CIC Lieutenant. "Lieutenant, this is a peculiar bogie. It is streaming commercial fisherman radar, but there is a lot of other interference like a thermal barrier. The bogie, whatever it is, is not shaped like a fishing vessel."

The CIC boss shifted her chair over to take a look. "Let me hear it," she said. The Sonarman handed over the headset.

"Hmmm. That is peculiar. Get Jawarski up here."

"Bridge, CIC."

"Bridge, Aye."

"Sir we have a bogie on the scope. It looks very suspicious. We will give you a better idea of what it is in a few minutes."

"Very well."

The messenger found Jawarski in the galley, with Hillman and Furman sipping a cup of coffee and snacking on a 'Bundt' cake. Jawarski hurried up to CIC with anxious enthusiasm. He loved the peculiar and the strange. He had the opportunity to experience many such phenomenon both unexplained and cleverly devised.

He took the Conn on the scope and the headphones as the other CIC crew looked on.

"Have you ever seen anything like this?" Sterling asked.

"Not exactly like this, mixed signals, like a fishing vessel with a thermal over modulation. I can tell you what I think it is, and I'll bet you a cup of Radio Central coffee I'm right. The *Amberjack* has been known to come out to get a signature on the ships it will be battling. They get the scent of each ship and that gives them an advantage in the big show. They come out disguised as a fishing vessel or some other benign vessel or as an ocean phenomenon. The ships pay no attention to it."

"The Captain would enjoy this," said Lieutenant Sterling. "The last word was that he was in his cabin. Messenger go fetch the Captain."

"On my way."

The CIC messenger knocked on the Captain's door.

"Enter."

The Messenger opened the door and stepped inside. *(Messengers with duty belts or those under arms do not remove their hats when addressing others, including officers.)*

"Captain, CIC has a bogie on the screen. Lieutenant Sterling thinks you may be interested in it."

"Has Jawarski seen it?"

'Yes Sir. He has a good idea what it's all about."

The Captain grabbed his hat and stood up. "Let's go see it."

The messenger was pleased with the Captain's enthusiasm.

The code entry system buzzed and released the door. As it popped open the Captain stepped into a dark room illuminated with light green and yellow glow from the computer monitors. Additional lighting came from small incandescent lights around the perimeter. There were overhead lights of course but they were not used when CIC was in full operation.

"Got something interesting I hear," said the Captain as he navigated the narrow pathway between operator positions with their computers and monitors and other interesting looking equipment. He stood behind Jawarski.

Jawarski remained seated but turned toward the Captain. "I am willing to bet this is the *Amberjack*, playing possum and getting the signatures of his adversaries. But we can get his signature so we will know who it is next time we see him."

"So what I think you are saying is that the *Amberjack* is going to sneak up on us before the actual drill begins. He will come into range under this cloak, then turning on his systems at the last minute and catching us before we have time to go to G.Q."

"Isn't that against the rules?" asked Lieutenant Sterling.

"Well it is a gray area in the rule books but as long as they are active before the drill they are legit," Jawarski replied.

The Captain touched his finger to the monitor. "Show this signature to all the CIC crew, Jawarski. I want you here before the drill begins. When this fox shows up looking innocent we know it's him and we will be ready."

"Bridge, CIC," the Captain called.

"Bridge Aye."

"Send your messenger to assemble all the Officers, Chiefs and First Class Petty Officers. I will meet them on the mess deck in fifteen minutes."

"Aye, Sir."

The Officers, Chiefs and First Class Petty Officers were assembled on the mess deck as ordered. The Captain entered through the forward door. "Attention on Deck" one of the Chiefs shouted. Everyone sprang to attention.

"At ease ladies and gentlemen."

Every one sat down, and turned their attention to the Captain. These types of meetings in the mess deck were not unusual but when they included officers, chiefs and certain enlisted it was usually something that pertained to each department, something the enlisted would need to know since it would probably be them who will take the first action. It was also something the Captain wanted to keep under wraps.

"Jawarski believes the *Amberjack* will sneak up on us in some disguise just before the drill begins. When he does I will call to prepare for General Quarters. When that word is passed, I want everyone to go to their battle stations quickly and quietly. When the battle drill begins we will sound GQ. At that time we put on the gear and we are set. I have a suspicion we will get one shot at the *Amberjack,* and if we don't get him he will get us or we will lose him, then we are in for a major run. Any questions?"

There were none.

1600: "Very well then. This may be a good time to take another look at the strategic plan we made in Baltimore. Let's run another situation analysis of the events we will likely face at the Combat Readiness Exercises. I don't believe there is a sailor aboard that doubts we can actually score enough to qualify, and frankly I think most of us believe we can actually win most of the contests in spite of or because of our dubious reputation. We have been through some learning experiences, our drills have been so successful we can perform at combat level in our sleep. We been in some harrowing experiences these last few months, especially the past few days. We have proven to ourselves that we are professional sailors and our ship has with-stood the challenges. I think we need to have some arrogance as we take on the adversarial forces."

He smiled as he placed his right foot on a nearby bench and leaned in, placing his right elbow on his right knee. "We have talked about this back in Baltimore and I think we know what we are supposed to do and, if our drill results are any indication, I would say we know how to do it. We all realize we will encounter some unexpected surprises but I am confident we can overcome any tactic they try. I don't want to be overly optimistic but I think we can win."
He paused for a moment to get a reading from his crew.

"All in favor of winning say Aye.

The all shouted "AYE."

All oppose Nay.

Everyone Laughed

"Get a good night's sleep. We have a big day tomorrow." Said the captain. With that he saluted his crew, retrieved his hat from the table in front of him and walked out the door.

Attention on Deck," Mister McCormick shouted.

"The all stood up. If the captain was attempting to motivate his crew to make a good showing at the 'games' as Mister Falk called them, He did indeed succeed.

It would be near sunset when the warship would be berthed at the Destroyer-Submarine piers at the south end of the Navy Base. Ships are usually tied up to each other side by side creating a nest of ships. The first ship in got to be tied up to the pier, the second in was tied to that ship, and so on and so on. This time the first ship would be the one carrying the Admiral's flag. the *USS Lancing (DD770)*. Two ships from ResDesRon35 were next the *Longmire (DE 219), Bruzzard (DD 734), and finally* the *Roberts (DE 749),* from ResDesRon34.

The *Card* pulled into the Combat Drill piers at twenty hundred hours. They were again berthed on the outer portion of the nest, meaning the crew had to cross over the other ships in the squadron to get to dry land. Couldn't be helped, but to be tied up to anything that connected them to land would be welcome after all they had been through. As in Norfolk and Mayport, they were up against the *Roberts (*DE 749).

It seemed like every sailor from both ships lined the railings to see if the *Card* would scratch up those new numbers. If they could not do this in the day light, they were sure to goof it up in the haze of dusk. As the XO had promised Mister Goldsmith had the Conn. Mister Winthrop stood next to him, expecting to make docking suggestions, if needed. Mister Goldsmith had done his homework and they pulled in correctly the first time. A cheer went up from both ships. Mister Goldsmith breathed and Mister Winthrop gripped the OOD's shoulder and said; "Well done Marshall, all is forgiven, you may come home." The Captain of the *Roberts,* chuckled, shook his head and waved at the Captain of the *Card,* who returned the wave and head shaking from side to side. The two Captains then retired to their respective cabins.

Line handlers from the *Roberts* and the *Card* threw the thick mooring lines and threaded them through the line chocks tying the proper marlinspike seaman knots securing the two vessels close enough to lay a brow but with enough distance to allow for drafting and sea movement.

As soon as the first mooring line was made fast on the pier, the Boatswain Mate of the Watch passed the word to shift colors. The ship's call sign and steaming Ensign were hauled down, and the Jack and Ensign were raised.

The ship shifted from ship power to shore power and the OOD shifted the watch from flying bridge to the Quarterdeck.

2030: The Captain went below to the mess deck to see for himself if what he suspected was true. No one was in the mess deck area so he stepped back in the galley. Sure enough there was the OOD, the duty MAA, the doctor and Furman eating steak and eggs, homemade biscuits and gravy while Hillman looked on with pride and pleasure.

Hillman noticed the Captain enter the galley and shouted; "Attention on deck."

The OOD, the doctor, Furman and the MAA jumped to attention, all of them looking like one who was caught with their hand in the cookie jar. The Captain surveyed the situation and then said; "I see we have added a new item to the plan of the day; Eight O'clock report rats (*rations*). I trust you will care for the Midnight OOD at mid-rats as well."

"Sir," Hillman tried to explain in embarrassment.

The Captain held up his hand to stifle any attempt at explanation from either of them. "Carry on." He walked out of the galley smiling and shaking his head from side to side.

The Captain expected as much. Hillman did not report to the OOD at twenty hundred to muster as a restricted person, the OOD reported to him and ate elegant food. Hillman was reputed as doing this every night since he has been on board the ship. He maintained his political standing by feeding the Officers and Petty Officers who manned the quarterdeck and security watches at twenty hundred. He was also available to assist the mess cooks during midrats (midnight rations), even when he was not on duty.

Executive Assessment
Employing the Team when The Plan is threatened

We explored the S.W.O.T. analysis earlier. It is difficult to identify all the threats before your engagement. You can expect unidentified or newly introduced threats during the engagement. When your executive team discovers a possible threat, pull the team together to determine how each department head should pro-act toward it. The final decision is the chief manager's, of course, but a focused team effort is always the most effective. Jawarski and the CIC team discovered the *Amberjack* and decided it was using clandestine methods for sizing up their adversary, a tack not against the rules but definitely the gray area of fair play. The captain made a plan to deal with them before they could get a jump on them.

He knew the *Amberjack* would sneak up on them before the actual exercise began and catch the *Card* off guard, He decided to call prepare for General Quarters a code that meant for all hands to quietly and quickly repot to their GQ stations. When the word was passed to commence the operation, the official pipe to general quarters would be piped, and at that time they would don helmets and life vests. The *Jack's* radar would go on and CIC would identify their position and the *Card* would commence attack operations. This method was also in the gray area. Using that same *gray area* analogy one must ask; Is it appropriate to use the same tactics on an adversary they are using against you? Is it ever appropriate to use a **dark gray** area as a defense or an offence to counter their plans?

Mister Goldsmith was the Conning Officer when the other entry mishaps occurred yet the captain and the XO insisted on him being the Conning Officer when entering the nest at Gitmo in the dark. I am sure Mister Goldsmith was wondering why they would put him in that precarious situation again. A third time may very well cripple his self-esteem not to mention his influence on the other officers and crew.

But we have come to know Mister Goldsmith, and we have witnessed his attention to detail and ability to learn from mistakes, his and others. When you have an executive with these character traits the risk of another mistake similar to the one(s) he/she made in the past is greatly reduced. We can expect this executive to make good on the next attempt. They need encouragement, and recollection of their skills and mental abilities, from their boss and the admonition to be better prepared next time. Usually the next time will be a success because the executive will ensure it. It is amazing what that does for their self-esteem as well as their influence on others in the organization.

Executives make mistakes of course, and sometimes they make several in succession. While those mistakes can cost the company money, lost market share or some other missed opportunity and of course embarrassment to the one who made the error this is not usually the most memorable, or hurtful outcomes of a mistake. Consider those time when you or colleague made a public mistake or failed, either for wrong action or inaction in some way that affected the organization. What was that most difficult issue to bear? Their failure to live up to the obligation to others, and filed to meet the expectations of subordinates and peer executives. We should also mention the despair of not performing for their boss. This is a great mechanism for learning more about themselves. When the executive has acted with unearned pride and self-assurance a failure will usually bring them back to reality. Pride goes before the fall.

For those executives who exercise appropriate leader behavior a failure or big mistake will call attention to their limitations. A person needs to know their limitations. No one is perfect and the executive needs to be cognizant of that, not only in their own experience, but in the behavior of others.

I read once where an R&D executive took on a project that appeared to have a great potential. The decision cost the company one hundred thousand dollars. She went directly to the boss and informed him. He told her to be more careful next time. "You mean I'm not fired?" I can't fire you now I have too much invested in you," he said.

Hillman was on restriction. The captain noted that the restricted man did not report to the duty officer, but instead made a meal and invited the duty officer and the watches to enjoy the meal. Was this good leadership to have this breach of policy? Sometimes there are circumstances where it is permissible to allow a breach in policy or protocol. One just documents the event and makes it apparent this is not establishing precedence but is dealt with on a case-by-case event.

Command Axiom:

- "The enlightened commander who will use the highest intelligence of his command for the purposes of spying, and thereby achieve great results." (*Sun Tsu Art of War*)

- "The end and aim of spying in all its variety is knowledge of he enemy, and this knowledge can only be derived, in the first instance, from the converted spy. Hence it is essential that the converted spy be treated with the utmost liberality." (*Sun Tsu Art of War*)

Chapter 11 – The Fun (If you can call it that) Begins
Sunday, 19 July 1970
War Games Day One
Guantanamo Bay Combat Drill Zone

0400: "Now Reveille, reveille all hands heave out and trice up. The smoking lamp is lighted in all authorized spaces." The crew came to life. Breakfast was completed by zero five hundred. The umpires reported aboard at zero six hundred.

0700: Each ship in the nest broke off and set sail for the combat drill zone taking their place in their squadron formation. The ResDesDiv5 battle group scenario was a typical war time cruising formation screening an imaginary carrier group. The squadron would come under attack by the Gitmo adversary force. From zero eight hundred to twelve hundred hours the squadron would be involved in an ASW exercise with the *Amberjack*. That means that every ship in the squadron was responsible for finding the foxy sub and coordinating a pattern of sub detection and destruction.

The Command Flag was on the *USS Lancing* (DD770). In the squadron were the *Card* (DE 383), *Longmire* (DE 219), *Bruzzard* (DD 734), and *Roberts* (DE 749). Each ship had a job to do for the squadron in this screen scenario. Along with performing the normal operations of screen escort service, the umpires and those in drill assignments on the Guantanamo Bay Navy Base, were required to present problems to each department that could happen during normal operations. The problems each had a time limit in which they were to be identified and solved while all time being graded by umpires.

The Bridge umpire was Commander Jack Garrett an officer with three years' experience in these games. He had met Robert Mills several years ago when he was XO of the *Rogers*. Commander Mills was assigned to the *Rogers* to assist in some organizational development work. Other umpires managed grading operations in Radio Central, CIC, the Engine Room, and one at each torpedo, hedgehog, gun mount and depth charge rack. There were umpires in the galley and the pilot house.

It was at exactly zero seven thirty, the umpires were in place on the *Card* when the intercom came alive on the bridge.

"Bridge – Combat." It was Jawarski.

The Captain keyed the intercom; "Bridge."

"We are all set down here Captain." That was the code they had set last night to inform the Captain the bogie seen last night had showed up.

"Very Well," He turned to the Boatswain's Mate of the Watch. "Prepare for General Quarters Boats if you please."

The Boatswain's Mate of the Watch keyed the IMC and announced; "Now Prepare for General Quarters."

Every member of the crew preceded quickly and quietly to their battle stations. The umpires noted the movement and suspected the sub had been recognized without its standard signals present. They noted the account. Nothing was said. Maybe the plan was not only working but approved by the umpires. The umpires would call foul if the crew did anything that was not in line with rules of the game. The *Card*'s officer corps and most of the higher enlisted personnel suspected not all the rules were published and most favored the adversary force. In the meantime the *Card* moved through the waters in line with the other ships in the squadron.

At that moment a messenger from CIC entered the bridge and handed the Captain a note. It read; "zero-zero-five 1500 yards 75 feet." The Captain read the note. He tapped his XO on his upper arm with the back of his hand. "Mack." The XO looked over at him. He handed him the note. Commander Garrett noticed the transaction. He was curious as to the contents of the note, but said nothing.

The XO passed the note to the Deck Officer. The Deck Officer handed the note to Mister Winthrop. He folded it and handed it off to the messenger who took it Lieutenant Grubaugh. She read it and put it in her shirt pocket.

At precisely zero eight hundred Commander Garrett, keyed the IMC and announced; "Begin the Drill."

At that moment the *Amberjack's* electronics came on, and was spotted by all the ships in the squadron.

"Bridge - CIC, sub sighted bearing zero-zero-five."

"Sound General Quarters," the Captain ordered.

There was clanging heard from the GQ bells on all the ships in the squadron, but while the other crews were scrambling to their battle stations the *Card*'s crew simply donned their battle gear. Each person's battle gear had a built in communication system allowing all connected to hear and respond to every word spoken, by all battle stations during the encounter. Strict radio protocol required no one to speak unless it was their turn.

Each department began reporting in;

"Radio manned and ready."

CIC interrupted the report; "Bridge – CIC - Bogie zero-zero-five – range 1500 - depth seventy-five feet."

"After steering manned and ready."

"Forward watch manned and ready."

And it went on until they had all checked in. As all this was happening, the *Card's* battle crews were preparing for the attack on the sub. While the *Amberjack* set torpedoes to fire at the *Lancing*, the *Card* had the sub's bearing.

The Captain stood on the starboard porch, off the bridge area gazing over the forecastle. He could see the gunners dressed in their life jackets and steel helmets were crouching behind the breech. They looked every bit the gallant combat sailors he had been preparing for just such a moment as this.

"Come right to zero - zero - five and hold steady. All ahead one third."

"Zero - zero - five Aye."

"All ahead one third. Aye."

The ship came around and increased in speed.

"Range 1500 and closing."

"Set depth charges to 75."

"Depth charges to seventy five, Aye." The Ordinancemen had prepared the depth based on information from the note before the official GQ was piped. Depth charges were also armed and set at the proper depth.

The *Amberjack* recognized the *Card's* attack and broke off and began the dive.

"*Jack* made us. He's increasing speed and diving."

"Make ready the hedge hogs."

"Hedgehogs ready Captain."

"Sub is going deeper."

"Fire hedge hogs."

"Fire!"

The hedge hogs were shot in front of the ship and sank to the correct depth. An electronic beam signaled ignition.

"Bridge, CIC. We lost him."

"Rats!" The Captain spat.

"You can bet we will be their number one target from here on out." said McCormick."

"You are correct Mack. We have wakened the dragon."

"*Jack* has reversed direction and is now heading for us range two thousand yards seven zero feet."

"Come, right zero-niner-zero and heavy on the gas. Ready on the depth charges."

The little ship turned to reverse direction.

"Set depth charges to 70 feet. Reduce speed to 8 knots."

"Eight knots Aye."

"He'll catch us."

"He'll catch up. Right now he thinks we're running. By the time he realizes we have slowed he will be on us and we can drop the cans on him."

"*Jack* at 50 yards and slowing."

"Fire starboard depth charges."

"Fire starboard charges." repeated Grubaugh.

The firing process shot the depth charge into the air enough to clear the ship, and then it dropped into the water and sank. At seventy feet the ordnance sent a signal that served as the detonation.

"Fire port charges, and continue at will."

The *Card* made a pattern run dropping ash cans into the ocean and recording the detonations. The umpires noted the depth charges were set at the correct depth, but they missed the sub. There would have been some minor damage, but no sink.

The *Amberjack* reversed engines, backed off, made a right turn then dove with increased speed.

The umpire entered information into his umpire log. Without taking his eyes off his book he said; "You made the sub break off, otherwise your flag ship would be in an abandon ship drill right now. You picked up some good points on this one."

An hour went by with no sightings. Finally the silence was broken.

"This is CIC, sub sitting at one hundred feet. Not moving . . . two thousand yards dead ahead."

The destroyer *Lancing* and the DE *Longmire* both sighted the *Jack*.

"The *Lancing* is circling. It looks like he is doing a three sixty to trick the sub into thinking he's breaking off. I think he's hoping to catch them from behind," said McCormick.

"Shall we run a pattern Captain?"

"A DE can do a three-sixty in 400 yards the Captain thought out loud, it takes a DD almost nine hundred yards. We could do the same and the *Jack* will think we have both broken off, but we can catch him before he knows what we are doing."

The Captain ordered the helmsman to do a three hundred and sixty degree turn, while the engines revved up to 12 knots. The little ship tilted hard to port as it cut a circular slice into the sea.

The *Amberjack* was not fooled. It disappeared and settled on the bottom.

"Good idea people," the umpire said, "but he got away. No points for you or the sub."

An hour dragged by, then another, finally the Bridge intercom crackled.

"Bridge. CIC, I think he is directly below us at 150 feet."
"All stop."

"All stop."

"Where is he now Sonar?"

"Hanging with us Captain. He ain't none to happy with us I think. He is ignoring the bigger ships and is focusing on us. "I recommend, all ahead one third and run pattern seventeen," came the voice of the ASW officer.

"Set depth charges to one-five-zero. We will go pattern seventeen," the Captain ordered.

"Come left 90 degrees."

"90 degrees - Aye."

"Engine Room, give me eight knots."

"On station Captain."

"Eight knots Captain."

"Fire depth charges in pattern seventeen salvo."

"Firing depth charges."

"If we can get him to surface we can fight him topside."

The ship ran 1500 yards dropping depth charges then reversed direction continuing the same pattern.

"The sub is gone Captain."

"What?!! How did he get away?"

"Two Torpedoes in the water and closing off the port beam, Bridge!"

"Submarine sighted off port beam seven hundred fifty yards heading away."

"He fired stern torpedoes and is high tailing it out of town," said CIC.

"All ahead flank come left to two five two and get us out of here!" came the order from the Captain.

The ship bore heavy into the waves. The torpedoes missed by less than two yards off stern.

"Shall we try another pattern Captain?" Mr. Winthrop asked.

"Negative. Continue the search."

The bridge umpire spoke up. "You can secure from GQ Captain. You missed him."

"He's a fox, I'll give him that."

"That he is. But you gave him a run for his money, and he will not soon forget that. Usually the first day he hits the first two ships and plays with the others. It has been a while since he has been chased away. You'll get another shot at him tomorrow."

"And he will get another shot at us."

"You can count on it. The other ships in your squadron may get a day off, at least until they get you."

"The next time I need a builddown, Commander Garrett I will remember to call you," the Captain said as he slapped the umpire on the shoulder.

"That's what I'm here for Bob, any time."

1700: The *Card* pulled into the assigned slip at the piers. All hands were elated at their success today. Everyone did their job and did it well. There would be celebrating at the EM Club and the Acey-Ducey Club tonight. For Chief Petty Officers *The Goat Locker* club was their destination located on Guantanamo Bay's historic Marine Hill.

1800: The Boatswain's Mate sounded the word for liberty call.
"Now liberty call, Liberty call, Liberty for all hands in sections Alpha, Charlie and Delta except those on the depth charge reclamation crew. Liberty expires on board at twenty three fifty nine tonight. Now liberty call."

Lieutenant Grubaugh removed her hat, opened the wardroom door and entered. She placed her hat in its designated spot and went directly to the refreshment counter and poured a cup of tea. Lieutenant Sterling entered the wardroom from the back where she and Miss Grubaugh shared a stateroom.

"How is Benson doing with your top gun?"

"Actually, they are getting along quite well. When they think no one can hear them, she calls him Robby and he calls her Brennie."

Sterling raised her eyebrows at the sound of that.

"That is not for re-broadcast you understand."

"Roger that."

The sailors with liberty passes took turns crossing the *Card's* Quarterdeck, saluting the Ensign, and then saluting the OOD. "Permission to go ashore."

"Permission Granted."

Each member of the liberty party then stepped across the brow onto the adjoining ship, turned toward the fantail in the direction of the Ensign, saluted the Ensign then saluted the Quarterdeck OOD. "Permission to cross to the pier."

"Permission Granted."

This continued until they had crossed the ship that was tied to the pier. From there they stepped on to the pier where they awaited the bus ride to the enlisted clubs. The officers either walked to the "O" club or took a car.

1830: A small mine sweeper pulled up next to the nest with the spent depth charges from the channel. The reclamation crews from the ships in the nest secured those with their ship's name on them and stowed them in the area for reclamation.

Those who were in Gitmo for the first time were surprised when the bus that pulled up was a tow motor tractor pulling three cattle cars connected by a trailer hitch. There were no seats in the cars, everyone was required to stand. They were all crowded into the cars and held on as the tractor towed them out of the dock area and down the road to the clubs on base.

Recognizing the cattle car type transportation a loud Maa-ooooo chorus began and soon every sailor onboard added their own Moos to the chant. It lasted all the way to the clubs. The Moo chorus was louder and in a happier vein coming back to the dock area from hundreds of sailors very well under the influence of adult spirits.

1930: Captain Mills decided to visit the officer's club. Perhaps he may get a chance to see the Captain of the *Amberjack*. Captain Sorenson had told him the *Amberjack* skipper enjoys hanging out at the bar collecting accolades for his boat's successes. It was a good night for a walk so he chose that mode of transportation instead of ordering a car. He enjoyed the warm fresh Cuban air as he strolled along collecting salutes from sailors and junior officers who were returning to the *nest* after exploring the base.

As he passed The Windjammer Club he recalled the brochure the Navy Base distributed telling of its fine cuisine. "Maybe I'll stop in there on the way back," he thought. "A steak would be nice. A pleasing end to a successful day."

Rick's lounge, located inside the Bay View Complex is the only officer's club on Guantanamo Bay. It serves as a safe haven for all military officers assigned to the base and those from ships visiting the Bay. The door opened with a pull on the long highly polished brass door handle. He stepped inside.

The voice of *Brook Benton* greeted the Captain's ears singing *A Rainy Night in Georgia* playing over the sound system compliments of Radio Gitmo, the base Armed Forces Radio Station. He found the bar and settled in. The bartender had just brought him a stein of beer when a voice three stools down captured his attention.

"So you are the Captain of the *Card,* is that right?"

"That would be me. Robert Mills." He turned to face the Commander who asked the question.

The voice came from a young handsome man in khakis wearing a floppy officer's hat with a salty looking officer's crest. He had an athletic build and a day-old beard. He was chewing an unlit cigar. His attempt at a nonchalant look was compromised by a bright shiny belt buckle and spit shined Cordovan shoes.

"I am Jack Westaway the skipper of the *Amberjack*. You can call me Jack."

"We have been calling you Jack all day."
"We have been calling you some names as well, none of them as clean as the word Jack."

"The word *Jack* was not used cleanly I can assure you."

"I was told your crew was a bunch of shanghaied ner'-do-wells that could not make it on a real navy ship. That reputation was not apparent today."

"We came to Gitmo to change that reputation."

"Well, your crew made a good showing today, and I'm not used to being chased around by any ship and especially a reserve ship. I gotta tell ya, I didn't like it. I got a reputation too you know and its one I intend to keep."

"Foxiest sub in the U.S. Navy, I heard."

"Foxiest sub in any navy. You were lucky out there today. But luck does not last against skill and experience. I am giving you fair warning Captain Mills, you have won the dubious honor of being number one on the hit parade."

"I would expect nothing less. Let me buy you a drink Captain Jack. What are you drinking? Oh no, let me guess, Jack and water."

"You figures me right mate. But save it. In a few days you can buy my entire attack crew a Jack and water."

"Or you will buy my entire ASW crew a round of beer. Deal?"

"The most sinks win?" asked Captain Jack holding up his glass of Jack and water.

"Most sinks, or disables."

"Deal."

"If we get you to surface that will count as well."

"Deal."

"I'll see you on the surface."

"I'll be there taking on survivors."

"We'll see who takes on survivors," Mills responded. With that he took a last swallow from his stein, swiveled around, slid off the stool and exited the building.

"I think I made him sufficiently mad, he thought, and mad men fight like fools. He is an arrogant sort. In spite of our performance today he still thinks it was luck. Let's hope he is so obsessed with sinking me that he will get too haughty and take risks that will favor us.

2100: The captain called a meeting of the officers, chiefs and senior enlisted to review the day's activities and analyze the tactics used by the Amberjack as well as their own offensive actions. They gave particular attention to the times they had to improvise and react to the opponent's methods. The captain took an axiom from the Art of War; do not repeat the tactics which have gained you one victory but let your methods be regulated by the infinite variety of circumstances.

Executive Assessment
Functioning As a Team in the midst of the Crises

The normal daily operations of any organization consists of groups of people working together to accomplish worthwhile objectives for the benefit of that organization. Whether unusual major operations or daily routine operations those groups of people must function as a team. An ops team is made up of individuals each with a special set of skills honed to excellence.

The effectiveness of those teams depends on how well each individual applies those skills in a team setting.

You have heard the cliché that there is no "I" in team. That being said there is an "I" in victory. For a team to be victorious every individual ("I") must apply their individual ("I") skills for the benefit of the team. It is the committed contribution of the expert individual in concert with other expert individuals that win the day.

Each member of a successful team prides him or herself on being the best at what they do, and consider it their ethical and moral responsibility to ensure the other team members can rely on them to apply those individual skills and personal integrity to the mission at hand. Effective operational teams begin with the individual performer. Management assists in building top rate performance teams by hiring individuals with the operational skills needed to ensure organizational success, or hiring individuals who are trainable to high levels of performance. Those individuals should receive on-going training and educational opportunities to ensure their continued competence, and by rewarding them for their individual efforts.

One does not surrender personhood or individual pride in their skills when they become part of a team. On the contrary their personality, their personhood and their skills are employed in concert with others on the team as each individual person and skill is focused on the accomplishment of the objective. Like an orchestra it is the uniqueness of the flute and the technique of the flutist playing a part separate and distinctly different from the part played by the skilled trombonist that creates the beauty or the grandeur of the piece. They may each have a turn at a solo in the piece that brings out the talent of the player and the grace of the instrument that when the piece is over the listener is blessed.

Like each member of an organization team they must play the part they were prepared to play, and do it so the others' contributions will not go to waste.

After every victory on the battlefield, individuals are rewarded for their part in the success of the operation. After the individuals have been decorated (honored with medals or commendations) they then receive team commendations. If individuals are recognized for their individual contributions there is an incentive to exceed for the team at another opportunity.

You will notice the executive team considered the suggestions of the senior enlisted, and made decisions based on their recommendations. It is axiomatic that before an executive would authorize an action that affected the integrity of the organization's operation, they would need evidence the senior hourly employee was competent and probably correct. This confidence comes from giving those who *flip the switches* and apply the *tread to the road*, a chance to become that dependable, and then allowing them to prove their worth in everyday events.

Captain Mills made it his business to meet with the captain of the *Amberjack*. Maintaining professional relationships with executives from other organizations, both in the same field and in different fields, is recommended as a method of accumulating a *rolodex* of contacts. Professional associations put the executive in touch with other executives where information can be shared as a way of keeping abreast of the business climate. Attendance at association meetings, industry conventions, conferences and expos keeps the executive in the know. One never knows when those associates can help you out of a jam. Networking and politicking is how business gets done and problems are worked out. The most effective executives are those who know who to call and how to get in touch with other executives when needed.

The captains agree on a friendly wager on the outcome of the events. Friendly wagers add to the excitement of competition. One must never wager company resources on such adventures.

Command Axioms:

- "Those skilled at making the enemy move do so by creating a situation to which he must conform. They entice him with something he is certain to take a lure of ostensible profit they await him in strength" (Sun Tsu – Art of War).

- The strength of individual experts banned together make a formidable defense.
- "There are no more than five primary colors, yet in combination they produce more hues than can ever be seen" (Sun Tsu – Art of War).

- Causing the opponent to lose perspective by being so intent on winning at all costs thereby making mistakes give you the upper hand. One wins battles by making no mistakes. Making no mistakes is what establishes the certainty of victory, for it means conquering an enemy that is already defeated.

- "Do not repeat the tactics which have gained you one victory but let your methods be regulated by the infinite variety of circumstances" (Sun Tsu – Art of War).

Chapter 12 Fear and Faith During times of Crises

Monday, 20 July 1970
War Games Day Two

The *Card* pulled away from its berth alongside the *Roberts* and headed toward the war zone. They cleared the sea channel and crossed into the war zone just leeward of the outlaid island. Suddenly and without warning the *Card* came under attack.

"Bridge, Sonar, bogie spotted." The coordinates were given. "Bogie confirmed enemy submarine and the bearing zero, zero, zero. It's the *Amberjack.*"

"Where is the J*ack* CIC?"

"We lost him."

"We gotta find that fox or we're going to be sunk."

"I got him Captain," came the word from CIC. "I think he is directly below us."

"He likes to get under us like he's hiding then bust out and either take off and shoot at us with after torpedoes or back out and hit us with forward torpedoes," Said Jawarski.

"He tried both of those tactics yesterday to no avail," Said Sterling.

"It would not surprise me if *Jack* came at us head on," said Mills. "Where is he now combat?"

"Still beneath us."

"He knows we know he's there. He's vamping," said Sterling.
"He's diving," shouted the Radarman. "75 feet and heading straight ahead at full speed."

"Reduce speed to two-thirds," shouted the Captain. "His blank-stare revealed he was picturing the sub's actions.

"Shall we try a pattern Captain?" asked Sterling in CIC.

"Negative. He's going to make a head to head run on us . . . The arrogant sea dog. He's playing gun slinger."

The gun-slinger slowed to a stop just out of range. The *Card*'s crew watched as the *Jack* made a turn and came to periscope depth.

"Here he comes Captain," said the forward watch. "Here he comes," CIC repeated.

"Set torpedoes for periscope depth and prepare to fire," said the Captain to the Gunnery Officer.

Grubaugh repeated the order.

"Ready on the Hedgehogs."

"Ready on the Hedgehogs."

"Fire when he comes into range. Helm and Engine Room, the *Jack* is making a run on us. He may draw first but we will fire when in range. Engine Room be prepared to get us out of here quickly. Helm when I give the word give me right full rudder and quickly if you please. Engine Room - don't spare the beast."

"Range three thousand . . . twenty five hundred . . . two thousand."

"Fire tubes one and three."

"Torpedoes away running straight. We got him unless he does something quickly."

"Torpedoes in the water! Dead ahead!"

"Helm right full rudder. Engine full throttle."

The sturdy little DE cut a sharp edge in the sea, as it surged ahead pinning everyone against the port bulkhead. The *Jack's* torpedoes sailed past with no hit. The *Jack* hit the dive plane at full speed and the *Card's* torpedoes zoomed over the sub's head.

1700: The sub was gone and the *Card* tracked back to the area and commenced a search. The day passed slowly, the crew remained at G.Q. Sandwiches, coffee and bug juice was delivered to the crew at their battle stations.

1830: Word was passed that the *Card* and the *Roberts* were to engage in nighttime submarine hunting. The *Amberjack*, the *Hammerhead* and the *Red Fin* would be running sorties on them. All night G.Q. instead of a cold beer at the EM club ashore was not what the crew had in mind.

2100: After what seemed to be an eternity the night began to overtake the day. Patches of light blue sky peeled from behind dark gray clouds with yellow and pink striations. The light blue grew darker and the yellow and pink transcended into dark red and the dark gray clouds shifted to black. A few stars peeked out from behind the clouds as the sun faded away, replaced by the glow of the moon that sent a shimmering aqua-pearl carpet runner from the horizon to the forward beam of the tiny warship.

2130: All was quiet. The sea was still and the moon was full and bright and cast a romantic image across the sea in front of them. The *Card* was now running abreast of the *Roberts* about 500 yards between them.

2145: The forward look out called out "bogie off the forward beam." All binoculars turned to the forward beam. There, sitting on the sea was the black silhouette of the adversary submarine that moved across the moon's bright image on the water giving the eerie appearance of a ghost ship adrift. The crew, weary at their stations, ready and willing to continue until the need to continue had passed. They were ready to take orders and carry them out with do or die determination.

"Bogie off the port beam," came the word from CIC. All binoculars turned to port. It surfaced just out of range. It was the *Amberjack*. The Fox's sailors scrambled onto the conning tower and focused binoculars toward the *Card*.

There was another sub surfaced off the starboard beam, out of range.

"Can you tell if it is the *Red Fin* or the *Hammerhead*," asked the Captain.

"Bogie off starboard beam is *Hammerhead*," came the answer from CIC.

2146: CIC reported a submarine off the after beam. There was a loud bump against the starboard side of the fantail. The umpire informed the Conn officer the *Card* had taken a torpedo and to sound the alarm. The night was blasted by the clanging of the alarm and the announcement: "Torpedo hit the fantail. Damage control to quarters."

The Deck Officer called for damage control. The umpire on the fantail informed the Weapons Officer the starboard depth charge rack had been destroyed and there were three casualties. The casualty crew removed three of the ordinance men from the rack and sent them to the triage area on the quarterdeck, Damage control came over with hoses and foam and explained what to do to extinguish the fire. They were required to explain what the scene would look like had it been an actual explosion.

"Those rascals set us up. The *Hammerhead* and the *Jack* were just out of range on the surface distracting us from the *Red Fin* who was sneaking up from the rear."

"CIC," the Captain called, "how did you miss that sub on our tail?"

"I can't explain how we did not see him, Captain," Lt Sterling replied, "no excuses sir."

"Keep on your toes and your eyes glued to that scope."

"Aye, Aye Sir."

"At least it was not the *Jack* that hit us," said Mister Winthrop.

"No but he was in on it and he'll claim it," said Lieutenant Commander McCormick.

Lieutenant Grubaugh requested a three man crew from Mister Hooper's deck force, who had training with depth charge racks.

2155: Another bump against the side of the fantail. The bridge umpire notified the Captain that the sub had taken out the propellers.

The Captain keyed the intercom: "Engine Room cut your engines. We have lost our propellers."

"This is CIC. The sub is beneath us and moving forward."
"Prepare to fire hedgehogs."

"CIC, tell me when the sub's bow clears ours. He'll fire a stern torpedo at us."

"That would be now Captain," he shouted.

"Fire hedgehogs."

"Fire hedgehogs," Grubaugh repeated.

Twelve hedgehogs fired three in succession.

The *Red Fin* surfaced.

"Cease hedgehog fire. Forward guns prepare to fire on the sub if they man their deck guns."

"Aye Aye," Phelps replied. Benson loaded the gun.

2205: "Stand down the umpire shouted." Signals were sent to Gitmo control to order the subs to stand down.

The umpires informed the *Card* to start engines and cruise at four knots in the vicinity. The other umpires came to the bridge to report.

"OK, you were not sunk but you sustained heavy damage. The fire was extinguished in good time. Serious casualties were moved to the quarterdeck. That was a good move. Most move their wounded to sick bay. Your quick action moving them to the correct area where the doctor would triage and deal with the worst was worth one hundred points, and you would have saved some lives. It is too difficult to move injured and dead to sick bay. In the case of heavy wounded the wardroom would be the hospital."

The entire bridge crew had directed their attention to the bridge umpire, while everyone connected to the combat communication system stared into space, listening carefully to catch every word the chief umpire had to say.

"You did not sink the sub but you caused him to surface and would have sunk him had he attempted to engage. That was a capture which is worth considerably more than a sink. You continued the battle even though you were badly damaged. Well done. You may be interested to know the *Roberts* was sunk by a torpedo from the *Amberjack* while surfaced."

"They tagged teamed us," thought the CIC boss.

"You may secure from General Quarters," said Commander Garrett. "Go back to your birth at pier 4."

"Do you suppose the *Roberts* kill satisfied the beasts craving?" asked Lieutenant Grubaugh into the communication set.

"I wouldn't count on it, said Garrett. He usually has several kills by now."

"And you can bet he is not going to be satisfied until he takes out this ne'r-do-well weekend warrior training ship that has been such a pain in the fantail for him," added Mister Winthrop.

"He will want to reclaim his Fox reputation, and we are in his way. He will certainly be gunning for us tomorrow," added Mister Hooper.

2245: The 1-MC blared the good news. "Now Secure from General Quarters. On deck section Bravo."

The crew of the *Card* kept the faith for the ship and for their shipmates. It was the experience of those difficult times on the *Card,* all the drilling that prepared them for the big show. It was working together for a purpose that they came to trust each other.

When the real test came there were no doubts that each crew member would keep that faith and perform remarkably. That faith formed a bond between them all that they intended to protect at all costs.

Executive Assessment
Fear and Faith During Times of Crises

Faith is trust, and that trust must be earned by consistent performance to that standard, whatever that standard may be.

In the narrative we could hear fear in the voices of those responsible for calling the plays, and we could sense it in those who aimed the weapons and pulled the triggers. Fear is an inevitable consequence of any battle, including those organizational and commercial battles that take place in turbulent times when so much is at stake, not only for the organization but for all those who claim a paycheck from the organization.

Just as a military unit in a combat situation, an organization facing turbulent times faces an enemy. That enemy or enemies are a reality and an intangible, difficult to identify sometimes, unpredictable and potentially hazardous to the organization's existence and the continued employment of those in the organization. The enemy is any force that opposes the efforts of the organization to reach its long and short term objectives. The organization exists for specific purpose and an enemy is any deliberate and consistent force that threatens the effective continuation of that purpose.

Some institutional enemies may come in the form of national economic downturn, pivotal changes in the marketplace, government or union restrictions, scandal, embezzlement, destructive natural disasters, unwise investments, the loss of certain suppliers or customers. Sometimes the crises are created by the loss of key personnel or misdiagnosis of future industry trends leading to misdirection in corporate strategy.

Fear is not the enemy. It is uncontrolled fear or undisciplined fear that becomes detrimental to the behavior of the employee and the mission. I cannot emphasis enough the need for training and education for the management team and the employees who do the aiming and pulling the triggers. It is through education and training that allows the crew members to focus on some directed activity designed to handle the situation.

With training and application, one is so familiar with the equipment, and the methods that have proven effective in simulations and in actuality that they are able to think and perform within the focus of the event. Being good at one's job, and being recognized for the high standards one holds for themselves fosters confidence, not only confidence in one's ability to perform, but knowing they have the confidence of others who are willing to rely on them to do the right job on a level that will produce success for them all. Confidence is the greatest source of emotional strength. Confidence reduces fear and panic and aids in handling deprivations, minor setbacks and extreme stress that comes from an onslaught of circumstances that require optimum performance. Confidence in one's own abilities and the abilities of the others on the team makes it much easier to advance into the unknown and handle situations that may not have come up in planning sessions or that are totally unique in the current crises.

Another factor that is so vital to effective operation under adverse conditions and is too often overlooked, is discipline. In book one of this Stewardship of Management Series, I provided a great deal of ink to the concept of discipline. Discipline is the maintenance of standards. There are behavior standards, quality standards, dress standards, performance standards and equipment maintenance standards. When organizations maintain every aspect of discipline each individual practices a disciplined approach to each circumstance and performs in a disciplined way. Discipline should also include a personal code of honor

While the officers and crew of the *USS Card* had a battle plan, and a set of contingencies that included offensive and defensive actions, they had to improvise many times as the wily *Amberjack* continued a creative set of attacks and retreats that were designed to confuse their opponent. Often the onslaught of circumstances or demands does not allow much time to develop detailed and elaborate planning. If the organization's management team has its *What If* plans or *Back Up* plans or *crises management plans* the management team can turn to those plans and tweak them. It may be that the executive or the front line employee, in the thick of it has to make quick estimates of the situation and develop a plan covering only what is absolutely necessary to address a particular set of circumstances. Again training to the familiar is a key factor in the ability to think on one's feet and take the action necessary.

Command Axioms:

- As in combat fear and panic is the crew's greatest internal threat against waging a successful campaign against the enemy.
- Too often hasty decisions made in panic thwart progress toward a successful outcome. Actions taken by the leadership must address both survival of the organization and the defeat of the enemy.

Chapter 13 When Bad Things Happen in Clusters During the Crises
Tuesday, 21 July 1970
Guantanamo War Games Day Three

The *Card* was moored to the *Roberts* through the night, in relative peace. Each four hour watch coming on and going off as scheduled. Certain hands getting out of the rack to take care of the ship's business and others climbing into their rack after taking care of their watch obligations.

0500: "Now Reveille, reveille all hands heave out and trice up. The smoking lamp is lighted in all authorized spaces, now reveille." All hands except those coming off the 0400 watch hopped out of their racks and began taking care of the early morning personal preparations.

0600: Breakfast was piped.

0615: The shipboard intercom came to life; "Now turn to, scrub down weather decks, sweep down all compartments, empty all trashcans, now sweepers."

0700: "Now clear the mess decks. Turn to and commence ships work."

The *Card* pulled away from the nest at zero seven thirty. The Conn Officer was Lieutenant Grubaugh.

0800: Lieutenant Commander McCormick assumed the duties of Officer of the Deck and the Conn as the ship arrived in the war zone. The drill was to officially begin at zero eight thirty. The *Card* would be the only ship in the morning's agenda. He keyed the intercom; "Ready underwater search gear. Maintain present course and steady as she goes."

He turned to the bridge umpire. "Are we considered on station at GQ or is this war time cruising? The drill P.O.D. (Plan of the day) was not clear on that."

"You go to GQ when the sub is sighted." He placed his hand on the XO's shoulder and leaned in close to his ear and said in a low voice; "And Mack . . . this time make no preparation for General Quarters to give your crew a head start."

"Oh you noticed that did you?"

"I cut you some slack because the *Jack*, as you call him, was playing in the gray area of the rule book, and because your CIC had located him when he was sending a false signal. Today we are all playing it straight."

"But *Jack* is patrolling at GQ right?"

"Not until he spots you. You may spot him first. In any case you both go to GQ when you realize you are in an attack situation. They have an umpire on board also."

At ten hundred the *Card* had been in the war zone for almost two hours with no contact or sighting of enemy vessels.

"This is too eerie Captain," said Mister McCormick. "I get a feeling we are about to get hammered from out of nowhere."

"Our only adversary for the morning run is the *Jack*, or so that is what the agenda reads," the Captain said.

The intercom came on. "This is CIC," said Lieutenant Sterling, "I got a feeling the *Jack* is planning some get even program just for us."

"I am sure you are correct Lieutenant. You and your crew keep a sharp eye on the ASW gear."

"Roger that," she answered.

1035: The bridge intercom lit up. "Radar contact off the starboard bow course . . . one-four-zero speed . . . ten knots bearing 124 true. She's on the surface."

"There!" The forward lookouts shouted as each one pointed at the fearsome figure of a genius submarine bent on winning this round of war games.

"Bring us around to one two four and all ahead flank. Sound General Quarters."

The 1-MC blared its metallic sound. "Now General Quarters, General Quarters, all hands man your battle stations. All hands man your battle stations, this is a drill, this is a drill, sub sighted off the starboard bow."

The crew had been waiting for the GQ announcement and they scrambled from their waiting areas to their positions. The crew on the weather decks donned their battle gear and life vests.

The air shuddered as the Boatswain's pipe and the sound of the X.O's voice over the 1MC that sounded like a great trumpet. "Attention Crew. We have found the *Amberjack* and we are going to make a run on him. Step lively people."

"Target bearing 6000 yards."

"Ready tubes one and three."

"Tubes one and three ready."

"Ready on the forward gun." Benson slammed a shell into the gun.

"Ready," he said to Phelps.

"Forward gun ready."

"Torpedoes in the water off the starboard beam."

"Fire torpedo tubes one and three. Come around to one-four-zero."

"Torpedoes away."

"Engine Room, give me full power and don't spare the beast."
The mighty tin can turned sharply and moved away from the deadly fish that was meant for them.

"Come back around to one-two-four and steady up."
"Where's *Jack* CIC?"

"700 yards and closing. *Jack* is diving now Sir."

"How did she get turned around so quickly?"

"Torpedoes in the water, they're going to be too deep to hit us."
"Are you sure Jawarski?" shouted the Captain. "If you let them sink my boat I will have a word with you."

"They were distracters Captain. He's working on something we are not going to like. I think *Jack* is still mad about yesterday."
"Ready the forward gun. We'll hit him before he gets underwater. Fire when ready."

"Range 700 yards elevation 25 degrees," came the word from Fire Control.

Phelps repeated it as Benson made the adjustments.

"Ready."

"Fire."

The pyrotechnics blasted from the blank shell and the gun ejected the spent shell.

"Missed . . . too short," shouted the umpire.

"Rats!" shouted Phelps. She turned to Benson and gave him a "I don't agree," look but she said nothing.
"We have lost him Commander."

"How can we lose him?" asked the XO. "He can't be that far away or deep."

Lieutenant Sterling keyed the intercom to the bridge; "Captain I think *Jack* was moving toward us in reverse. That's how he got turned around so quickly. The fox just backed up. The next set of torpedoes will be to the stern and not too deep. You can count on that."

"*Jack* is now 500 and closing about fifty feet deep."

"Is he still diving?"

"Negative, steady at fifty feet."

"Set hedgehogs and ash cans for fifty feet."

"Hedgehogs at fifty Sir, we changed them when we heard CIC give us the depth."

"Fire hedgehogs."

Hedgehogs away. The dummy hedgehogs were fired into the air and they quickly dived into the sea set to explode in clusters at fifty feet.

Had the hedgehogs been real the explosions would have erupted the water pushing the *Card*'s bow upward and sending shock waves throughout the ship.

"*Jack* went under us and is now behind us and still moving in reverse."
"The hedgehogs were effective," shouted the umpire. "The *Amberjack* has been notified of damage sufficient to force it to surface."

"Oh *Jack* is not going to like that," said McCormick "Good shooting Lieutenant Grubaugh. If that had not worked he would have fired from forward torpedo tubes and made another run on us. Might have been too fast for an effective ash can response."

The *Amberjack* surfaced just off the after starboard beam. Captain Jack appeared on the sub's conning tower. He pointed toward the *Card's* bridge and threw up a right hand salute. "You earned the beer Captain."

Captain Mills stepped toward the bridge railing and returned the salute. "That was my Exec and the ASW this time Jack," he shouted.

The umpires' decision was to give the *Card* a capture. The *Card* now had two captures but no sinks.

"This is better than we ever did before," said McCormick. "Every time I have been here we were sunk in every scenario."
This entire encounter lasted only one hour. It was now eleven forty.

The bridge umpire keyed the combat communication talk switch. "The *Card* will remain on station but stand down until thirteen hundred. What happens at thirteen hundred depends on your Radio Central cryptographer. If the cryptographer can decipher the coded operational order, the *Card* will rendezvous at a specified place and begin another exercise. If the encrypted message is not decoded, the *Card* will return to the base and today's exercises will be concluded. Radio will receive the message in approximately twenty minutes. The supervisor of the watch must receive the message, send it to crypto, it will be deciphered and Radio Central will deliver the message to the bridge for action."

"So we are in a time window, is that correct?" asked the Captain.

"Your cryptographer has fifty five minutes to decode the message and take action on it. You may secure from General Quarters and commence condition III normal wartime cruising."

When cruising under Condition III, the ship's company stands watch on a basis of 4 hours on, 8 hours off; about one-third of the ship's armament is manned in the event of a surprise attack.

Those hands on the outer decks not on watch, at this time, removed their helmets and combat gear. Those who were scheduled for a watch reported to their normal work station, those not scheduled either went to their racks in the berthing quarters or just sat around on deck.

As the crew was securing from GQ the bridge intercom again lit up; "Captain this is Perez in the galley. We have sandwiches and chicken soup ready. Shall we prepare to serve?"

"Affirmative. We have about an hour before the fun starts again."

The 1-MC echoed again as the Boatswain Mate of the Watch announced; "Chow is ready on the Mess Deck." followed by the warning: "We have one hour ladies and gentlemen." Supervisors of the watch sent personnel to the Mess Deck in shifts. The officers had sandwiches and soup in the wardroom.

1205: "Twelve fifty-five. The magic number," said Mister Winthrop.

"Mister Alexander is skilled at Crypto, we will be OK," said the Captain.

1240: Still no word from Radio Central. The Captain made his way to Radio Central to see how things were going. The radio crew, was sitting at their positions waiting, all was quiet. The umpire was sitting at the supervisor's desk reading a *Stars and Stripes Newspaper.*

"How's Mister Alexander doing?"

"He's in irons at the moment Captain," said Donaldson jerking his eyes and head in the direction of the crypto door. The Captain's eyes followed Donaldson's direction and nodded. He sat on the edge of the desk.

"He's never taken this long before Captain," said Electronics Technician Second Class Harbaugh. "This must be a tough one."

"Are you sure you copied that right Donaldson?" asked Anderson.

"It looked OK to me, everything was in the proper sequence, but how do you know? It's all encrypted code."

The clock ticked on past 1246. They waited. The clock ticked past 1250. There were just a few minutes remaining. If the message was not decoded in the next few minutes the *Card* would be sent back to the pier, and out of the day's exercise.

1254: The crypto door opened. Mister Alexander stepped out. His shirt was drenched in sweat, his black hair plastered to his head, beads of perspiration rolled down his temples and onto his cheeks. He looked like a doctor coming out of surgery. Looking around he could see the concern and anticipation on the faces of everyone in the room, including the umpire. He smiled, stretched out his right hand catching the Captain's right hand and pumped it. "Congratulations Captain it's a boy." he said handing him the message. Everyone laughed in relief. The Captain read the message, keyed the bridge intercom and relayed the coordinates for the next exercise to the OOD.

"Had you worried, huh Captain?"

"Not in the least Mister Alexander. The Navy has paid too much for your education to let a little thing like this get the better of you."

He was trying hard to not let it show that he indeed was concerned. It was not just Mister Alexander who had to get the message correctly. There were other hands involved that had to be correct as well. And if radio had gotten it wrong, we would have been sent back to the pier with a much lower score in both our combat exercise and our reputation. The Captain turned again to the radio crew.

"Well done."
The Captain exited the room, out the door and up the ladder to the bridge. The Radio Central umpire stepped out to get some fresh air.

"Donaldson, you were one letter off on the entire code. You typed S for A and L for K and so on through the entire message. It took me a while to figure out what was going on but as soon I got it, I retyped it to make it fit. Still it was complicated; there were three ciphers for each letter."

"Gee I'm sorry Mister Alexander. I was nervous and that code was coming over faster than I am used to receiving."

"How did you figure out the problem, Mister Alexander?" asked Anderson.

"I remembered I did the same thing myself in Gitmo about four years ago. My name was mud for the rest of the cruise."

1300: The umpires announced a new drill had now commenced. The *Card* reached the rendezvous point. Ten minutes later CIC announced they had picked up a submarine on the sound gear. A target moving at zero five oh about five thousand yards approximately eight knots. It is very deep, maybe 100 feet. The 1-MC blasted again; "Now General Quarters, General Quarters, sub sighted, all hands man your battle stations.

"Engine Room, all ahead. Make twelve knots."

"Engine Aye."

"Helmsman come right zero-five-zero and steady."

"Helm Aye."

"Set depth charges for 100 feet. Ready on the forward gun. Ready on the hedgehogs."

Just then a plane flew overhead pulling a target. "Aircraft spotted . . . enemy . . . range two thousand. . ."

"Lieutenant Grubaugh you have the plane."

Fire control orders for range and trajectory. The mid ships gun and the after gun called out the range and trajectory.

"Fire when ready," came the word from Lieutenant Grubaugh.
"Fire." shouted the mid ships gunner. "Fire," shouted the aft gunner.

Dummy shells flew toward the target passing behind it too far to call it a hit.

"The submarine is gaining speed and going deeper bridge."

"Engine Room increase speed to fifteen knots. Depth Sonar?"

"One twenty feet Sir."

"Set depth charges for one two zero."

The guns continued with three more shots each further off than the first.

"Cease fire," said the umpire. "Return to base." He turned toward the captain. "Your crew did very well Captain Mills. Your ship has qualified. Congratulations."

Wednesday, 22 July 1970
US Naval Station Guantanamo Bay, Cuba
Combat Exercise Command Center
War games Conference Room

1000: The officers met with the war games umpires at the combat exercise command center to receive combat readiness exercise reports and scores. They scored high enough to qualify and were released to proceed to their designated liberty port of call. Following the liberty port they were to proceed to the deep water firing rage 100 miles off the coast of Dominica.

Wednesday, 22 July 1970
US Naval Station Guantanamo Bay, Cuba
Weapons and Ammunition Depot

1300: The *Card* took on ammunition they would need for the deep water firing range exercises.

Executive Assessment

A team in combat must be goal oriented. All efforts, performances and resources are centrally focused on a single objective. Usually more than one person will be responsible for some specific element in the accomplishment of critical application, so we stress again the importance of including everyone who will be involved in the training and the planning.

Sometimes bad things happen in clusters. At such times you must have your own experts on board who have been trained, and tested to know how to handle those contingencies, and you must be able to rely on them to do it. Each department head and resident employee experts will mean the difference between defeating the adversaries (Whatever that may be) and being sunk or so critically injured reparations drain time and assists needed to hold your position in the marketplace. When there are too many crucial enemies attacking, you may need more expertise than is available on staff. That means the team needs to be supplemented by contract personnel. Executive management would be well advised to contract with professional consultants, financial experts and the like.

Multiple crises may mean reducing products and services and focusing just on those bread and butter items with the best opportunities for meeting crucial obligations. These are times where employee investment pays off. Your investment in their training, especially dealing with critical matters and taking action they are trained to take without waiting for approval, and investment in a better than competitive paycheck and benefits. This is the time when an investment in their future with a good retirement program that is based on time in grade. An investment in employee morale and loyalty by providing an environment that rewards initiative and offers comfortable physical amenities. The investment you make in employees will pay off in times like these.

In cases where the organization is a public entity, such as a utility or a company with restrictive unions or several competing unions, where wages, promotions and lack of funds limit employee investment top management, with the help of subordinate managers and hourly employees, need to be creative in discovering ways to involve employees in the operation. For those who are members of an industry association that offers training to its members, those in charge must take advantage of those services at every opportunity.

All departments must be in a communication loop. Every member of the executive team and those experts in the lower ranks need to know how the battle is going and how it affects them.

For those cluster headaches experienced only by you, it would do well to have an administrative staff delegated to research projects and their status and report to back to you. Many senior executives are involved in industry and community projects and actions directed toward the continued growth and health of the organization.

Command Axioms

- Invest in your employees now and they will invest in you when their involvement is critical.

- Sometimes a creative program of employee involvement will produce a better training and employee development than hiring an outside expert with *canned* material.

- In times of crises, frequent face-to face staff updates are imperative for keeping all parties informed and forewarned and forearmed.

- There is no substitute for well trained, motivated employees who have dedicated their competence to the company's well-being because their competence is the result of the company's investment in them.

Chapter 14 Finally a Break!

Friday, 24 July 1970
USS Card
Cruising to Ocho Rios, Jamaica

0900: The *Card* pulled out of Gitmo and headed South West to Jamaica.

1030: The word was piped that a Sea Bat had been captured on the fantail. All sailors who would like to see this rare bird should lay aft. The deck force crew had set an orange crate in the middle of the after deck between the depth charges. While others gathered, four of the Petty Officers from the Deck Force were standing around with brooms in their hands. Those who came to see the Sea Bat were instructed to stand in a circle around the crate. Boatswain Mate Second Class Watson proceeded to tell them the Sea Bat was a very aggressive animal and if someone got too close to the crate the sea bat would reach out through the slat with its very sharp claw and could seriously rip their skin, resulting in a trip to sick bay.

Two Petty Officers hit the crate with their brooms to provoke the sea bat while two other Petty Officers stood outside the circle. Since the Sea Bat did not make any noise, some questioned if there was, in fact, anything in the crate. Those who had captured the Sea Bat challenged them to bend down close enough to look into the crate to see for themselves. One brave reserve took the challenge bent over and approached the crate.

As the sailor slowly inched closer to look through the slats of the crate, those Petty Officers with brooms instructed everyone in the circle to watch and pay close attention to the openings in the side of the crate. It is a small, but dangerous claw.

Those, whose job was to provoke the bat, began beating on the crate and the onlookers crowded closer for a better look. The Petty Officers, who stood outside the circle, swatted the curious sailor in the butt with their brooms. The startled shout from the one bent over intensified the interest of the others, and they crowded closer. Since all the others were so intent on seeing a claw comes out of the slat, no one saw the petty officers swatting them with their brooms. After each one experienced a few swats, they realized what was going on. It is just a matter of time, before the Sea Bat initiation is experienced by all.

1400: Tranquility prevailed on the bridge as the stout vessel moved along with a fair wind. Off in the distance white sprays take turns appearing over the top of the sea in rhythmic motion then settles back into its ever moving bed. The seemingly endless sea meeting the vast expanse of the sky joined together a way out on the curvature of the horizon. The entire world seemed at peace. The only interference in the clean un-marred seascape was a lone freighter off the starboard beam heading east.

The alert Quartermaster noticed the Captain coming up the ladder to the bridge and keyed the 1-MC. "The Captain is on the Bridge."

"Good afternoon Mister Goldsmith."

"Good afternoon Captain.

"So how do you like driving the ship?"

"It can be nerve racking but I think I can get to enjoy it."

"Well you have the intelligence and the temperament for it. How fast are we going?"

"18 knots sir."

"Excellent."

The Captain peered over the portside bulwark to the very large ship moving due east.

"That's some large ship. You don't see many freighters that large."

"I would say it was one of those new Norwegian freighters. I hear they are doing a booming business in the large ship business. I read that you can book passage on some of them. They have private cabins. They also have dormitory areas with bunk beds."

"Have you ever thought what it would be like being billeted on one of those steaming freighters sailing all over the world?"

"I have Captain. I looked into it. They pay good money for my skills. I don't think I would like it."

"What do you suppose is the displacement and speed of those new freighters?"

"I would say they displace six thousand tons, and can probably do 20 knots."

"That much?"

"It's only a guess you understand. From what I have read 13 to 14 knots is standard on most freighters but these new ones have a unique gear drive."

"Oh . . . I think you are right. It looks like she's doing about 20 knots now." He paused a moment still looking toward the ship still moving fast off the port beam. "No telling where she's heading."

"Due East, maybe Cuba," was Mister Goldsmith's reply.

Captain Mills moved over to the Captain's chair and sat down.
The Quartermaster Striker timidly approached the captain.
"Would you like a cup of coffee Captain?"

The Captain turned toward the voice. "Yes, yes I would thank you. Say I am curious about something. It seems that I see you on the bridge quite a bit. Don't you ever get a break?"

"I am a Quartermaster striker Captain. I want to be good at it. The pubs (publications) give me knowledge, but I need experience and I can only get that from being here where the action is."

"Well good for you. What's your name sailor?"

"Smidlap sir, but everyone calls me Smiddy."

"Smitty?"

"Smiddy sir, with two "Ds".

"Smiddy it is then. Thank you Smiddy, I will have some coffee."

"It's just a couple of hours old. The off-going watch brought it up from the galley just before we took over."

"Ought to be mellow by now."

"Ought to be sir."

The Captain opened a metal box on the bulkhead in front of his chair and retrieved a coffee cup with the word *Captain* imprinted on it. He handed it to Smiddy. "Cut off about three inches there Smiddy."

The Quartermaster Striker smiled as he poured the coffee from the thermos. "This is not Radio Central or Engine-Room coffee Captain, this is some good stuff! I get this directly from the galley while it is still fresh." He carried the full cup to the Captain who remained seated in his big chair.

"Is this your first voyage?"

"Yes Sir. I could never of realized how grand and majestic the ocean is. How it can be so restless, and yet so calm and forgiving, then in an instant can be fierce and dangerous. You just can't take it for granted. You know, it's a siren, a mysterious nymph that calls you and you just can't resist."

"Wow, Smiddy. You have become a sailor overnight."

"It was the storm, Captain. I have never felt so scared or so alive in my life. It was like she was challenging us, and then the next morning all was forgiven."

Mister Goldsmith felt a sudden curiosity about the Captain's presence and his questions. While it was not unusual for the Captain to visit the bridge during normal underway cruising, it seems like he has something on his mind. He seemed particularly interested in that freighter off the Starboard beam. If anyone had knowledge of displacement and speed of ships, large and small, it would be him. He glanced at the speed and direction indicators on the dash in front of him. He looked again at the freighter. "A warship has the right of way," he thought "but large freighters cannot change direction easily. That was it! He must have seen the freighter from his balcony and was curious as to whether I noticed the predicament. Collision course!" he thought.

He turned toward the Captain who was staring at him over the brim of his coffee cup. He keyed the intercom and very calmly spoke into it. "Helmsman left two degrees if you please."

"Helmsman two degrees left, aye."

"He stealthily looked around to see if any others on the bridge caught on. Apparently no one noticed.

He glanced at the Captain, again who gave him no indication that he noticed anything out of order. The Captain then slid off the big chair and handed the cup to the Quartermaster. "Thank you for the coffee Smiddy. You were right, it was excellent."

As the Captain entered the companion way where the ladder would take him from the bridge. Smiddy keyed the 1-MC "The Captain is off the bridge."

Saturday, 25 July 1970
USS Card anchored out in the Ocho Rios Bay.

1200: The still clear water of the Ocho Rios Bay was momentarily disturbed when the *Card* pulled in and dropped anchor.

The order was given to swag out the gig. The ship's whale boat was swaged out and lowered with the Coxswain standing at the wheel. Once the boat was settled in the water, it was tied to the ship.

Almost immediately the bay was filled with small boats laden with trinkets, local island food and fruits. Some were being paddled by local boys others were driven by outboard motors. They circled the ship calling to the sailors who were hanging over the side to buy their merchandise. They were holding up advertisements and souvenirs shouting like barkers at a carnival.

The XO came onto the quarterdeck and called out to the merchants. "You are free to set up tables on the pier and our crew will purchase them from you there. We can have no one approaching the ship."

He turned to Mister Winchester, the Quarterdeck Officer of the Watch. "We made arrangements with the mayor and the local police that we would not have brokers coming out to us. Contact Radio Central and have them put a phone patch, we will call to the mayor." Before Mister Winchester could react, the bay police had arrived and disbursed the tradesmen.

1300: "Now all personnel assigned to shore patrol duty will lay to the quarterdeck for transportation ashore." The shore patrol personnel were assigned to patrol the city ensuring sailors from the *Card* would not give any trouble to the local police or citizens.

1315: Seven sailors, assigned to shore patrol appeared on the Quarterdeck dressed in shinning white, pressed uniforms, spit shined shoes and brightly polished brass belt buckles. The letters, "SP" was prominently displayed in the front center with a black strip that circled their highly polished white helmets. They wore a white web belt that holstered a black night stick. On their upper right arm was a black arm band with the letters "SP" in gold. They loaded into the liberty launch and were transported to their designated stations on the beach.

1350: As the liberty launch returned to the ship the 1MC came alive with the announcement the crew was waiting to hear; "Now Liberty Call, liberty for sections Alpha and Charlie. Liberty to expire on board 2300 hours tonight. Now liberty call."

The sailors from ship's port watches, Alpha and Charlie, stood on the quarterdeck in their starched white uniforms and freshly spit-shined shoes waiting their turn to take the liberty launch (Ship's motor whale boat) to the pier.

Robert Benson waited until Lieutenants Grubaugh, Sterling, Lieutenant (jg) Gilliam and Ensign Alexander climbed down the ladder to the liberty launch. He then climbed down and took a seat near the stern where the Coxswain was stationed. It was a smooth and speedy ride from the ship to the pier.

Benson felt a thrill of pride fill his chest and spill into his smile as he turned around to take a good look at that magnificent vessel, the USS. Card, as she rode her anchor in the bay. He took in the fresh battleship gray color of the hull the large white numbers shadowed in black. He savored the numbers Three – Eight - Three (383). He admired her tall mast with the radar dome at the top, the superstructure and the dark gray non-skid coated weather decks.

He stared at the forward gun mount, like a new father looking at his first born child. He thought about being in that gun mount with his boss, his favorite person in the world, GM1 Brenda Phelps. He was a real sailor. This was the Navy. Not an office in some Air Force base, this was a Navy warship anchored out in the bay while its seafarer crew went ashore.

The liberty launch pulled up next to the pier. The Coxswain threw a line to a civilian line handler who held the boat in place as the riders climbed out and onto the pier. Lieutenants Grubaugh, Alexander and Sterling exited first, followed by Lieutenant (jg) Gilliam and Ensign Alexander. Then Benson and his enlisted shipmates climbed out of the boat and onto the pier. Once the excited crew was safely on the pier, the Coxswain took in the line and sped away toward to the ship for another load of the liberty party.

Robert Benson asked one of the souvenir vendors where he could rent a motor scooter for the day. He pointed to an intersection. "Left at the intersection about two blocks down on the right." Benson made haste to get there. He had to have one rented before Brennie came ashore in the next launch.

He paid for two bikes for the day and waited for his boss to show up.

GM1 Brenda Phelps asked the same vendor for directions and was given the same information. She was careful not to make eye contact or conversation with any of the ship's crew. She did not know how she could talk herself out of spending the day with her old shipmates instead of her new friend. She arrived at the rental place and joined her protégé at a table where he was sipping a soft drink. She sat down and pulled her waiting drink toward her.

"Hi boss," he said.

"Hi Gunner," she answered back in a tone rarely heard by anyone else.

"This is Ocho Rios," Benson explained, as if he were an experienced island guide. "Eight Rivers, which is a misnomer since, I understand, there aren't eight rivers in this lovely village, or in the Parish of Saint Ann. Today I will show you this island paradise. We will start out at the Reynolds' mine, a Bauxite mining operation.

They are the fine people that built the nice pier we just came from. Then into the countryside. I got us two really sweet bikes."

"Robbie, we only need one bike. You drive and I'll sit behind you."

"You'll have to hold on to me."

"Oh, I intend to, believe me."

The two mounted their gas powered steed and headed out of the bay area and into the country side through the Fern Gully, a rocky gorge of tremendous depth which zig-zags four miles from the Ocho Rios coast up to the central mountain area of the island and into Dunn's River Falls.

Lieutenants Sterling, Grubaugh, Junior Grade Gilliam and Ensign Alexander found Rex Sterling at the pool bar of the Ocho Rios Hilton. Rex stood up when he saw the *Card's* officers approaching. His attention went immediately to his wife, with a big smile and outstretched arms he said, "Hey sailor, come here often?" She moved inside his arms and they encircled her. She embraced him.

"Hi there big guy."

The word *guy* barely escaped her lips when his lips came down on them. It was not a prolonged kiss, just enough to announce to all who looked on that they were in love.

"Oh give it a rest you two. Married five years you still act like newlyweds," said Grubaugh.

Lieutenant Sterling introduced her officer friends to her soul mate. "Rex, this is Foster Gilliam, Lance Alexander, and of course you know Phyllis."

The civilian husband shook hands with the two men, and kissed his wife's roommate on the cheek. "How ya doing Phil?"

"Rex has been in Mexico City all week, making arrangements with one of the local manufacturing companies to use the manufacturing control systems his company makes," said Sterling.

They had a few drinks and appetizers at the poolside bar then they all boarded a tour bus and took a tour of Ocho Rios. Benson and Phelps passed the bus riding together on the same motorbike. The officers smiled at each other knowingly, but no words were spoken of it. Their suspicions had been confirmed.

1700: After a pleasant ride through the countryside, Benson and Phelps stopped at *Cap'n Ron's Sea Side Bistro* in the city. They enjoyed an American style Hoagie sandwich and a local beer. They rode back to the rental office and returned their bike.

"Now what?" asked Benson.

"Back to the ship?" she asked.

"Let's walk around town for a while we still have a few hours."
They were nearing an outside snack shop when the sky opened up pouring rain down on the laughing couple. Ducking and running they rushed toward a

concrete table protected by a large umbrella. They stepped up on the concrete seat and sat on the table top. They both basked in their cozy little dry world as the rain cascaded down all around them.

The full length of Benson's left leg from his hip to his ankle was pressed up against Phelps' right leg. It pleased her. Surely he was also aware of it as well but took no effort to move. Her left hand was holding onto the edge of the table while her right hand rested on her knee.

She felt the loader's hand cover hers. Instinctively she let her hand roll over and his fingers meshed with hers. He squeezed slightly and suddenly her life took on a clarity she had never known. The vacant space in her life was thought to be the lack of parents to love her and allow her to love in return. Her career in the Navy was very satisfying but it did not fill the space. Now that space was filled. She realized she had been living only a half a life. "Now here was the other half of my life, this guy, this fool that I was going to harass because he was not the experienced gunner I had requested, this guy, who calls me, Brennie." She let out a ragged breath. She felt an excitement in her chest and stomach that she had only felt once before. Yes only once before. When was that? The first time she saw Benson.

Neither of them spoke. Neither of them had ever been here before. Neither of them really knew what to do or say. This was a new experience. They sat there staring out into space, in a trance of sorts. Both appreciating the other's body touching and their fingers entwined. This was new to both of them. Neither wanted to move, neither knew what to do next.

She thought to herself, "One doesn't know what they can have, so one does the best with what they have. One doesn't know what they have been missing, until they find it!"

Their revelry was interrupted by a scowling voice saying; "I said can I get you something?"

There in front of them standing on dry pavement was a waiter with a pad in his hand. They looked at each other in amazement. They had been in another world, for who knows how long.

"Yes two cokes please," said Robbie. "No wait, one coke and two straws."

Phelps leaned in toward Benson fully intending to whisper something to him, but whatever it was, was forgotten when Benson leaned toward her and kissed her lips. It was a stolen kiss, a quick kiss but it was a kiss. She returned the Kiss.

They spent the next hour sitting side by side on the cement table sipping out of a straw from one large cup of coke, staring at each other.

1800: Grubaugh, Alexander, Gilliam, Sterling and her husband had an American style evening meal at *Cap'n Ron's Sea Side Bistro*. At the conclusion of the dinner, Grubaugh, Alexander and Gilliam caught a cab and went back to the ship. Sterling having been granted overnight liberty retired with her husband to a rented condo on a private beach on the south-side of the Ocho Rios Hilton Complex.

1800: Harold Hillman sat on the fantail in a chair he had brought up from the galley. He was enjoying the view looking off into the distance. He enjoyed this part of every cruise, staring out to sea while the ship was lying at anchor. In about four hours the ship pivots on its anchor providing anyone who is on the fantail a three hundred and sixty degree panoramic view.

It was times alone when the letters came to mind. He had read them over and over. They were the reason he was here. The letter from his mother was dated 15 March 1964 telling him his brother had died of an overdose of heroin. They had no idea he was even using heroin. His father and mother had not been getting along for several years, and the death of Richard gave them the perfect reason for ending that relationship. She was moving back to Boston where she would be teaching at Boston State. He would be moving to Phoenix taking over a new division with his company. He will be taking his secretary with him. Apparently their relationship was more than professional. The last lines put some finality in the family relationship. She wrote: "You have found a home in the Navy. From your letters I read that you are happy there, your shipmates are your family. Good for you Harold. There is no more *home*, as we used to know it, we must each establish a new home. You are the lucky one. You established the Navy as your home years ago."

He had been in the Navy only eleven months when Richard died. He was in the Sea of Japan and did not hear about it until he got the letter from his mom. They didn't even tell the Red Cross so I could come home for the funeral. There was no funeral.

I will send you my address as soon as I am settled," she wrote. She would have been settled years ago, and still no address, not even a letter. He felt abandoned. "If I ever get to *Bean-Town* again I will look her up," he thought. "Maybe not."

The other letter was from Kate. "Kati-did," as he used to call her. This one was dated 17 March 1964. He received at least one letter a month from her since he left home. He wrote her twice a week.

"Dear Howie." She called him Howie, not Harry as everyone else did. It was her pet name for him. "It was good to hear from you again." The letter continued. "I really enjoy all the exciting descriptions of all the exotic places you have been and all the fun things you have done. I saw your mother yesterday. She told me about Richard. She told me about your father running off with that woman. I am so sorry. She had a good point, though, Howie, she said you have a home in the Navy."

It was hard to really know when he met her or what the circumstances were. He had known her all his life. They grew up next door to each other on Honeysuckle Lane in Fayetteville Arkansas. The neighbors would say where you find Kati you find Howie. He felt it was his obligation to be her protector, since she had no brothers or sisters of her own. They played together. He enjoyed watching her play and laugh. They were in the same classroom at school. He thought of the many times they camped out in his backyard. He made it his business to keep the wolves away. "There is no telling how many times I had to bust someone's head when they upset her," he thought. He did what he could to make her happy.

He was there when she fell off the teeter totter and knocked the breath out of her. He held her until she was able to breathe again. He helped her pull her first baby teeth. He encouraged her when she had to wear braces. Oh yes, he remembered the times when he counseled her when she had "boy trouble" but he always knew she was his girl and she always came back to him when the other relationships didn't work out. He had a *few side trips* with other girls himself, but it was never serious. He always went back to her. Even when they were going with someone else, they still hung out together. That was usually the reason the other relationships didn't work out. Everyone knew Howie and Kati were a couple.

It was her who helped him to the principal when he fell off the monkey bars and broke his wrist. She insisted on going to the hospital with him and was there, with mom as his wrist was straightened and set. He recalled how they were walking home from a pre-teen dance one Saturday evening just about dark. It was raining and they shared an umbrella. "I must have been about 13," he thought. "That's when I realized I was in love with her." He told her so, and she confirmed her love for him. They had kissed a few times, but she was reticent to get too physical and he respected that. He let his mind run the memories of the night he took her to the junior high prom. How beautiful and grown up she was in her prom dress. He felt like a little boy escorting a young lady to a grand affair. He never really noticed before how she had matured, until he saw her in a strapless prom dress instead of jeans and a pull over shirt.

His mind ran a fast forward to the high school senior prom. Again her female charm and beauty captivated him. He was proud to be the man, yes man, who was with this lovely thing. Every male in the class was jealous. He had gone to the punch bowl to get them a drink and was delayed by one of his classmates who just had to tell him about being accepted at Ole Miss. He was trying to break away and find his date when Kati came to him. She had a big smile on her face and was pulling some guy behind her by the arm. "Hey Howie this is George Breckenridge. He just moved here from Tulsa. His father bought that furniture store over at Pierson's.' He recalled how she pulled the young man up beside her. "George, this is my big brother Howie." He stretched out his hand. "Well he isn't really my brother," she confessed with a big excited smile, "but we grew up together. I love him like a brother."

"I was stunned!" he remembered. "Brother! She was smiling big, and seemed happy to have me as her big brother. I was thinking of her as my future bride and she was thinking of me as her brother!"

The letter ended with, what almost appeared as an afterthought.

"Oh do you remember George Brackenridge? I have been seeing a lot of him lately. Well he asked me to marry him. How about that? Who'd a thunk, me and Brackenridge? I know you are happy for me big brother. It will be an informal affair just his Mom and Dad and My Mom and Dad. Next time you get leave, and you are not in some south sea island surrounded by beautiful women, come and visit us."

"She laughed, she played, she lived, she cried," he thought to himself. "I thought it was all for me. But it was all with me. I have since realized it is a rare thing when one marries someone they grew up with."

He came out of his self-imposed altered state of consciousness realizing his memories took one complete rotation on the anchor.

Someone he didn't know moved in beside him and placed a foot on the railing. The uninvited guy spoke; "Too bad we aren't on the beach huh? I go tomorrow. I'm going to rent a motor scooter and travel all around Ocho Rios. I'll get some souvenirs and photographs." He turned toward the direction of the pier. "Then I'll go to the hotel they reserved for us, shift into a swim suit and find out for myself if what they say is true about the water being so salty one can't sink."

He continued to stare out towards the pier. "Then I'm going to find an outdoor bar and drink every kind of native drink I can, then back to the ship in a slightly stupor condition." He waited for a reply. When none came, he turned toward the salty cook and asked; "You going ashore tomorrow?"

"No. The Captain has restricted me to the ship."

"Oh man that's too bad."

"No, no it isn't. I want to be right where I am."

"Don't you want to see the island?"

"I have been there. I have been in a lot of ports over the past seven years." His stare suddenly turned from focusing on the beach to some memory of a south Caribbean port in his not-too-distant past.

"Let me tell you what I see when I go ashore. I see the first outside bar I come to. I see bamboo chairs around a bamboo table, with a bamboo and thatch roof. I see a constant stream of pretty girls bringing me an endless supply of booze, I see some guy that looks a lot like me buying rounds for everyone and starting a fight to prove how clever I am. I wake up to a rusty set of bars in a small concrete arena where a bunch of ragged, smelly ugly men who don't speak English are counting money that used to belong to me."

Hillman continued to stare past his intruding shipmate. "Or if I'm lucky I wake up surrounded by a set of gray bars the shape and size of a bird cage in the bottom of a Navy ship where I am waiting for Captain's mast. A few times I have awakened in the back of a shore patrol van where some guys I used to know hauled me around until I was able to walk up the gangplank from a pier or up the ladder from a liberty launch. No thanks, those days are gone. I will stay on board ship until I can grow up."

"Say, are you that guy Hillman?"

"That would be me."

"You got a lot of friends on this ship Hillman, even the officers like you. But I just can't understand why someone would want to be stuck on board, like a prison, instead being of out having fun."

Hillman finally turned his face toward the shipmate that had interrupted his reverie. "This kid has not had the experiences that bring an appreciation for life on board a US Navy ship. It was time for some reality indoctrination," he thought to himself.

"Well," he said, "I like the familiar surroundings. I get to do a job that I enjoy. A job I am good at and it is appreciated. There is always something to do and someone to talk to. No matter what time, day or night there is always someone awake, always someone looking out for you." He could see he had the young man's attention so he poured it on.

"There is always something to eat. And when you get tired of a place, either the ship moves or you move to another ship. And friends? The best friends you will ever have, because you share an experience known only to a select few. Some people say you should not have friends in the service, only buddies. Not so in the Navy. I have friends, lots of friends. And that is not the half of it. Once you experience the open sea, where all you can see is the ocean and the sky, and feel the breeze in your face, or lying on your back on a warm deck, feeling the vibration of the engines and the smell of steel, diesel fuel and salt water, man there is no greater feeling in this world. No, give me a steaming ship and a good crew and I am in my element."

1900: Hillman found Chief Jaquet sitting in the chief's lounge. "Chief, I would like to recommend a celebration for the crew tomorrow afternoon on the pier. I was thinking since we scored so well in Gitmo, after coming through some frightening and some embarrassing moments that we have a party."

"A party huh?"

"Me and the mess crew could light off some barbeque grills and cook up some hamburgers, hotdogs and the like. Maybe the captain could authorize Mister Goldsmith to secure some beer for us. We could do it on the pier over there."

"That is an excellent idea Hillman. I will speak to the Captain about it."

"And the beer too?"

"Beer also, Hillman, but none for you."

"Oh, no Chief, none for me."

2000: After eight O'clock reports Chief Jaquet found Hillman in the galley serving up his usual twenty hundred fair to the OOD. "The Captain liked your idea, Hillman. It's all set. Gather a crew and have at it."

2100: "Now rig for Movies," came the voice over the 1-MC.

2130: "Now Movie call, Movie Call on the fan tail. Tonight's thriller is *The House* starring James De'Angelo and Jennifer McCoy."

**Executive Assessment
Awareness Learning Under Pressure**

Even during peacetime underway cruising there is a potential for bad things to hit you from the blind side. One must always be vigilant, and keep a *weather eye* out for situations that may appear to be mundane at first but if not watched can go dreadfully wrong. On the bridge an underway log (journal) is maintained, where events are recorded that not only tell what has happened, but what could happen, and what is scheduled to happen. Each on-coming watch reads the log anticipates and prepares for future events. Every manager should have such a log, with barometer readings (items that may affect morale, or position in the market place), and remarks about unusual activities by competitors or suppliers.

Included in the log are items discovered in trade journals regarding news of activities and trends in the industry, and advertisements that display products that may affect the industry in the future. Daily status reports from subordinates should include current trends in their particular field and predictions of future events that may call for pre-emptive action or pro-action now. Entries should be made while they are fresh in the mind. The log should be consulted at designated intervals. Constant vigilance to one's field and its affect on the organization is the key to knowing when to take prudent investments or precautions.

One could achieve expert status within the organization after such research information is collected. One could be a valuable asset when armed with predictive information useful in future planning.

The Right Person in the Right Job

Hillman made a good case for being in the right job. We spend more than a third of our lives in the workplace. It should be enjoyable most of the time, if not we are in the wrong job. When a person is in a job for which they are well suited, they can be trained to reach levels of performance that will bring great satisfaction. There are elements of every job that is not enjoyable, but the one who is enjoying a feeling of contribution will step up and do what needs to be done. What is even more remarkable is their ability to see what needs to be done, why, when and how to do it.

We have discovered why Hillman was a loner and why he was so reckless when on liberty. Management does not usually know what is behind a person's behavior but we know something is eating at them. While it is not the business of senior management to know what is going on in the life of subordinates, it is necessary to get to the bottom of the reason for unexpected and unprecedented behavior.

Command Axioms

- Daily status reports from subordinates should include current trends in their particular field and predictions of future events that may call for pre-emptive action or pro-action now.

- We spend more than a third of our lives in the workplace. It should be enjoyable most of the time.

- The one who is enjoying a feeling of contribution will step up and do what needs to be done

- While it is not the business of senior management to know what is going on in the life of subordinates, it is necessary to get to the bottom of the reason for unexpected and unprecedented behavior.

Chapter 15 The Hits Just Keep on Coming

Monday, 27 July 1970
USS Card
Western Caribbean - Steaming to Deep Water Firing Range

0300: The *Card* was a day's run from Gitmo and two days from any other civilized land mass when the engine room supervisor of the watch woke up Chief Gruber with some bad news.

One of the deuce firemen (Fireman Apprentice E-2), a reserve from one of the centers out west, was on EVAP watch and inadvertently pumped all our freshwater over the side. The Duty Officer and XO were notified immediately. Mister McCormick notified the Captain at zero three thirty. (*Evaporators take in salt water from the ocean separates the salt from the water and pumps the fresh water into a holding tank and dumps the brine back into the sea*).

The Captain did not lose his composure but it was clear he was very dissatisfied that an E-2 inexperienced Fireman Apprentice was alone on the Midnight Evaporator watch.

"O . . . Kaaaay," he said with a long sigh. "Did we lose all of it?"
"All of it Sir."

"How long before the evaps can give us enough water for normal operations?"

"About 48 hours Sir. But I checked with the galley and they have plenty of bug juice for drinking if it is rationed and enough water for two meals."

"Draft a message to Gitmo and to the . . . what is the destroyer that is operating in these parts?"

"*Williams,* Sir."

"See if the *Williams* can come along side and give us about ten-thousand gallons."

0400: The oncoming Boatswain Mate of the Watch was notified of the water situation and to announce it at the revile call.

0530: The mechanical sound of the 1-MC being keyed was usually enough to wake most of the crew. They knew what was coming next, the sound of the Boatswain's pipe and reveille. The familiar sound of the harsh authoritative voice shouted "Now reveille, reveille, all hands heave out and trice up. Now hear this . . . Due to a malfunction in the evaporator system the ship has no fresh water. There will be no showers or other water use until further notice." There was another boatswain's whistle "Now light ship."

There was no water but there was the familiar smell of bacon and diesel fuel wafting through one's nostrils like a sweet savor to the wakening mariner, a welcome aroma that will be remembered long after their time at sea has ended *(Diesel fumes is part of every smell on board a DE).*

0600: The shrill whistle of the Boatswain's pipe followed by his booming voice barked, "Now breakfast is served on the mess decks."

0730: Again the 1MC blasted, "Now secure mess line. Clear the mess decks."

0745: The Boatswains Mate of the Watch once again barked into the 1MC, "Now muster all stations." Each petty officer in charge met with their crew and passed the information from the ship's plan of the day and the department's scheduled activities for the day. Included in the meeting was a muster to ensure everyone was on board and where they were expected to be. It was rare that anyone fell overboard on a DE but every person needed to be accounted for.

0800: Eight bells sounded and the word was passed over the 1MC "Now turn to, commence ship's work. Officers call, officers call."

The Stewards had cleared away the breakfast dishes, and the officers sat down for the daily briefing. After all pertinent information was passed the officers went about their business *(Stewards are now called Mess Management Specialist, Cooks are Culinary Specialists).*

The plan of the day (POD) was posted and the morning ship board routine began. Every sailor had a job to do, even those who were not scheduled at a working station. The lookouts were vigilant on all the weather decks scanning the open sea for changes in the weather, the sea, any sign of movement, whether friendly, hostile or otherwise.

The POD called for a meeting of all officers and chiefs at zero nine hundred in the wardroom to discuss the events that were to unfold over the next two days. Mister Hooper had the Conn.
As the officers were being seated around the wardroom table, Lieutenant Sterling spoke; "Mister Faulk, was that Evap problem that lost our water in your contingency plan?"

The officers laughed as Mister Faulk replied; "No it was not. But it is now thank you. And it goes without saying that an inexperienced Fireman Apprentice should not have been alone on the Evaporator watch. Fortunately for us all it was part of Marshall's (Mister Goldsmith) Plan. His galley crew thought to stock up on water so they could cook."

They were all seated and Commander McCormick began the meeting.

"Good morning all, let's get started. Okay, we are headed to a firing range in the Dominica area fifteen degrees latitude and minus seventy five degrees longitude. There we will fire live ammo at the targets we brought from Gitmo."

There was a knock on the wardroom door, it opened and in stepped a messenger from Radio Central. "Pardon me Sirs. I have an urgent message for Mister Alexander. Anderson, the Petty Officer of the Radio Watch said this may be something you will need to see right away."

"I'll take it Baker, thanks, and thank Anderson for his attention." The messenger passed a yellow folder to the Communications Officer. It had an imprint of the ship's seal in the middle.

Across the top was written **NOTICE TO MARINERS URGENT**. The messenger did an about face, and exited the room.

"Let's hear it Mister Alexander," the Captain said.

The Communications Officer opened the file folder and lifted a yellow sheet of paper. "We just received this Notice to Mariners only ten minutes ago that the Russian made Cuban destroyer *Restolf* was hijacked off the coast of one of the Islands in the area. It was taken while the crew was on liberty and only a skeleton crew was on board at the time. The ship was believed to be taken by pirates who kept the remaining crew alive and serving as support personnel. There is speculation that some of the ship's crew may have been in on the hijacking. There is also a report that the pirates may not be familiar with a war ship of this caliber but intend to use the warship as their own weapon. So far no demands have been made, but there have been reports of a Cuban warship shooting into one of the uninhabited islands in the area."

"Well," the Captain began, "something to keep in mind anyway. We will need to be particularly careful during our deep water ordinance and firing practice session, both going and coming. Unlike a war ship from a sovereign nation, these pirates, if that is what they are, answer to no authority but their own Captain. That makes them unpredictable and extremely dangerous."

"So . . . do we try to avoid the ship if we encounter it?" asked Mister Alexander.

"As far as possible. We will report it, just as we would any other enemy contact."

"And if we are ordered to engage, how is that done?"

Mister McCormick decided to handle this question. "First we fire a shot across its bow as a warning for them to stop."

"And if they don't stop?"

"Then we fire a shot at their screws to disable it. We tell them to heave to, stand down and prepare to be boarded."

"What if they resist?"

"We overcome the resistance," Lieutenant Grubaugh interjected.

"Exactly," the Captain confirmed. "But I doubt very seriously the Navy will let us anywhere near that ship. Pass the word to all lookouts to be alert to this vessel, Mack. Do we have a photo to pass around?"

"I am sure we have a photo of a Cuban Corvette we can copy and pass around."

"In less than twenty minutes scuttlebutt will have the entire ship on alert for the pirate ship," said Mister Gilliam.

0900: Ezra Furman BM1 was making rounds on the weather decks to inspect the work his crew was doing on the daily maintenance schedule. Hillman exited a door with a very large cup of coffee in one hand and his paint bucket in the other. "Coffee Furman?" he asked.

"Got some," he said holding up his cup. "When have you ever seen a Boatswain Mate without a cup of coffee in his hand? How else can we keep this permanent crook in our forefinger?"

"Thought you may be ready for a refill," he said as he sat his cup on the deck and pulled a thermos from the bucket. "Still hot." He filled the Boats' cup. "This is fresh, just made it. And if you may be still a bit hungry," he said as he put his hand back into the bucket, "how about a pastry? Still hot right out of the oven."

"You know a thing or two about taking care of the boss I see. I hope you are learning your lesson."

"Oh I am Boats, believe me I am."

"I'm on my rounds, why don't you join me?"

The two walked along together around the Forecastle (foks-el) inspecting each item to see if they were in need of attention. As they rounded the corner on the oh-one level on the forward starboard side near the water hydrants they noticed some sailors, in swim suits, showering under fresh water deck hoses they had rigged for the occasion. Boats quickly shut the valve.

"Hey what's the big idea Boats? This is water used to clean the deck. We weren't drinking it. We were just using it to shower and shave out here. There is plenty of this water."

"It has high strength detergent in it that will burn your skin. Lay to sick bay now." He keyed the intercom on the bulkhead near the forward hatch. "Bridge this is Boats. Call for the doctor to lay to sick bay on the double. We got sailors covered with deck detergent."

The sailors begin to feel the heat and itching as the redness showed up on their skin and they scampered below decks to sickbay.

The call of the 1MC once again disturbed the tranquility of the cruise and the almost unnoticeable sound of the engines, and the beat of the ocean against the ship with the loud metallic sound of the duty Boatswain's Mate's voice; "Now the doctor's presence is requested in sick bay on the double."

Those sailors spent the next hour under a salt water shower hose. Not the most pleasant of experiences and they would be sticky and salty until they could get under a real fresh water shower and that did not look like it would be anytime soon.

1100: Mister Gilliam was asked to join Mister Hooper on the bridge. "You wanted to see me Frank?"

"Yes, Foster. I was just thinking. You say you were a substitute teacher just filling in until a real teacher could take over."

"That was the plan, but I ended up staying the rest of the school year."

"But you were at one time an executive with a large manufacturing company is that right?"

"A junior executive, but yes."

"When we get back to Baltimore, I will be leaving the *Card* to take over a fleet of deep water fishing boats for my father's fishing business. The company I now work for will need a replacement, someone with your background, and the *Card* will need a deck officer, someone with your experience. Would you be willing to relocate to Baltimore and fill those two slots?"

"Are you serious? Are you authorized to offer those two jobs to me?"

"I am responsible for my replacement at Babcock and Huntington, so yes I can. We can discuss salary, but I think you will find it satisfactory and there will be good benefits and bonuses. Can I offer you the Deck job on the *Card?* I asked the XO and the Captain, but more importantly I asked Williams and they all said to offer it to you. Williams can have orders before we get to port."

"Well that sounds like an offer I should not refuse. I am inclined to accept both offers contingent on an approval to relocate by my skipper at home."

"Good. I will have Williams draft the orders for the *Card* and I will consider you my replacement at Babcock and Huntington unless I hear otherwise."

"I will take the job on the *Card*, Frank, but I need to think about the position with Babcock and Huntington."
"What!"

"I was offered a teaching position at Ocean High, to take 11-F. My charges from 10-F will be in 11-F in the Fall. I just don't know now, what I want to do. I may have done all I can for those kids, or maybe they need one more year of guidance. I don't know. I don't know if I can be any more affective even with another school year."

"You really enjoyed teaching that much?"

"No. No, I didn't enjoy the grind, the constant sparring and trying to stay one thought ahead of them. What I enjoyed was seeing the outcome. I saw them grow, and mature, and move from irresponsible aggression, to responsible assertion. That made the battle worthwhile. Do I want to do that again? I don't know. Do I want a great job like the one at Babcock and Huntington? You bet. Where am I needed most? That is the question."

"That is the question only you can answer, ship mate. But you have until the first of September to make up your mind. The school year begins after Labor Day and the position at Babcock must be filled at that same time."

Tuesday, 28 July
USS Card
At Sea heading toward the deep sea firing range.

1300: The Destroyer *Williams* came along side prepared to pump ten-thousand gallons of fresh water into the *Card's* fresh water system. Mister Winthrop, the Conn officer, ordered all available hands on deck to ensure the lines would get over quickly and safely.

The Boatswains Mate of the Watch piped "Attention" and passed the word; "Now station the Underway Replenishment detail. The ship will come alongside the USS *Williams*, Port side Mid-ships station. All stations report manning to the bridge."

Line handlers assigned to the UnRep Detail donned their life jackets and hardhats. Final checks are conducted by BM1 Furman and LT(jg) Hooper to ensure all personnel are ready and where they need to be. The station phone talker notified the bridge that all hands are on station and ready to begin. Word is passed to Lt Winthrop who notified the Captain.

"Let's get the show started Lieutenant, have the Signalman raise the Romeo Flag to the ready to approach position."

The *Williams* repeated and dropped the flag to approach position. Lt Winthrop shouted "Bos'n tell the Signal Bridge to drop flag to approach position. Increase speed to 12 knots and move us alongside."

Furman, the Boatswain Mate of the Watch, passed the word; "All hands stand by for shot lines forward and mid-ships. Step lively lads, we have done this before we can do it again."

As the *Card* approached, the *Williams* signaled the *Card* to maintain 12 knots and move alongside at a distance of 125 yards. The Conning Officer, with the help of Lieutenant Hooper ensured the distance between the ships is maintained at 125 yards.

Once alongside, the *Williams* signaled to reduce speed to 10 knots and maintain course of 095 until finished. Once the *Card* was about three-quarters of the way alongside the *Williams*, the Boatswain Mate of the Watch on the *Williams* shot lines across to the *Card*. The replenishment rig was set mid-ships with the distance line on the bow. Boatswain Mate Furman assigned two squared away seaman to the distance line forward, one on sound powered phones with the *Williams*, and one on the line. Each step of the exercise is reviewed in detail to ensure everyone involved knows what needs to be done and how. Lieutenants Hooper and Gilliam were being as complete as possible to keep the *Card* from looking like they have never done this before. The *Williams* set tension to the cable and sent over the riding block rig to commence the transfer of the needed water.

It was a real feat in seamanship to watch as they rigged lines connecting the two ships. They ran a large hose from the water lines of the *Williams* to the water lines on the *Card*. It took about two hours to rig as both ships were being tossed about by the restless swells of the southern Caribbean. It took all of 40 minutes to pump ten-thousand gallons of water into the *Card's* water system.

The little DE was dwarfed alongside the bigger DD. A message from the *Williams'* signalman asked if the *Card* would be interested in exchanging movies with them. "We have seen the ones we have four times and we are getting sick of them." Mister Goldsmith authorized Yeoman Williams to exchange movies which they did using another rigged line between the ships.

Once the water and the movies had been transferred, the *Williams* signaled ready to "break-away." The crew on the *Williams* set a de-tension cable and the pelican hook was released and the cable was let over the side carefully, so as not to cause any damage. Once the cable was clear and the leader line was off the ship, Lieutenant Winthrop increased speed to 15 knots and changed course to 125 to move away from the big double "D".

Mister Hooper keyed the sound powered phone. "Boats select a good break-away song and play it loud and proud over the topside 1MC speakers as we pull away." Furman was not new at this game. He had "Stars and Stripes Forever" keyed up on ready.

Furman called to all hands on deck to line up and at attention. "OK lads," he said. (several of the line handlers were women) "Look squared away for the move. We want to impress the regular Navy folks that we aren't as bad as our rep has us."

The music played loudly, and the *Card*'s crew stood proudly.
The crew of the *Williams* waved, and the Captain shouted, "Well Done *Card*, well done."

Wednesday, 29 July 1970
USS Card
At Sea heading toward the deep sea firing range.

2330: It was nearing time for Lieutenant Faulk to assume the OOD and Conn duties. Following the normal underway OOD watch relief schedule, he checked into the Combat Information Center (CIC) to determine any necessary actions that will be expected to occur during the watch. Then to the bridge. The bridge at night is a fascinating place. The total darkness requires a few minutes to make adjustment. All was still. One could scarcely hear the ripple of the ship's motion. There is almost an atmosphere of sacredness about it, almost like there is a requirement of silence. While loud discussion was discouraged conversation was of course necessary for the work of the bridge. Bright illumination is not permitted. The instruments were illuminated by dimly lit red lights.

He checked the navigational track, read orders pertaining to the ship and the current situation and to determine the position of all nearby ships. He then withdrew his ball point pen to make an entry in the log. Reading and writing at this time on the bridge of a warship at sea would be impossible if it were not for the dim red light provided by a flashlight held over the book by the duty quartermaster. One learns quickly not to write anything in red ink, as it would be impossible to read under red lights.

After this is complete, Lieutenant Faulk faced Mister Winchester and said, "I am ready to relieve you, sir." Mister Winchester replied, "I am ready to be relieved." He then briefed Mister Faulk on any additional information that the replacement should be made aware of, reconfirming the information that Lieutenant Faulk has previously gained on his own. Lieutenant Faulk, satisfied he had all the information he needed, he then stated, "I relieve you." Mister Winchester said, "I stand relieved. Attention in the Pilot house and on the bridge, Lieutenant Faulk has the Deck and the Conn." Mister Faulk replied "This is Lieutenant Faulk, I have the Deck."

0300: Steaming through the night toward the practice firing range making about 18 knots the solitude was broken by a loud scraping and crunching noise and a violent shaking of the entire ship, the fantail scooted sharply to starboard and decreased speed abruptly. Every sleeping sailor sat upright in their racks bumping their heads on the rack above them or on the overhead for those on the top rack. This was a situation no one on this ship had experienced before bringing about curiosity and shock.

The Helmsman pulled hard on the wheel to keep the ship on course. "Bare a hand Frazier," he shouted to the QM standing beside him. Together they managed to steer the course, suddenly the screeching stopped and the ship righted itself and stabilized at 8 knots. The Engineman on watch flipped the intercom key for the pilot house and the bridge.

"Bridge this is the Engine Room. Is Mister Faulk on duty?"

"This is Mister Faulk," said the officer on the Conn.

"This is O'Connor Sir. We have had a bearing burnout on the turbine shaft of the starboard engine. I shut it down. We are on the port engine only, and limited to eight knots at the moment. We called for Chief Gruber."

"I dare say Chief Gruber was on his way thirty seconds ago. You did well to identify the problem so quickly and shut her down before any more damage. Keep me informed. Have Chief Gruber call me after he evaluates the situation."

"Aye Sir."

Sleepy eyed and groggy the Captain sat up and keyed the intercom. Knowing Mister Faulk, the Engineering Officer, was on the bridge. He addressed him directly. "Mister Faulk, what is going on with your Engine Room?"

The Lieutenant explained the situation to the Captain and of the quick action by O'Conner, the supervisor of the watch, and that Chief Gruber was responding.

"Very well, keep me updated. What is our speed?"

"Eight knots Sir."

Chief Gruber and Engineman Brewer both responded before anyone had time to call them. They quickly assessed the situation and agreed O'Connor had acted appropriately. They began immediate work on the starboard engine.

Executive Assessment
Staying Abreast of Trends that Affect Organizational Health

Mariners have organizations that constantly survey conditions that will affect maritime travel and send Notice to Mariners regularly. Air travel has their own organization that sends constant Notice to Airmen reports. There are many organizations that monitor the conditions of each commercial industry. Executives would do well to subscribe to these reporting agencies and include their information in their strategic and tactical planning.

These notices and the subsequent plans may prevent turbulent times, or at least reduce the adverse effects. If the organization or the industry is already in turbulent times, these notices can help with *TT* exit strategies.

No matter how many safety programs you conduct, somebody is going to do something stupid. Sometimes damage to equipment or an injury occurs even when good people are doing the right thing. There needs to be a well-designed and well-rehearsed action plan for handling those incidents. Specific people should be assigned to specific tasks, for which they have technical ability, and have no operational tethers to prevent them from responding at a minute's notice. Whether a personal injury or unfortunate incident, horrendous or routine, there must be a plan and that plan must be executed without delay. An after action report should be made and based on that report, future action is to be determined.

Command Axioms

- Executives would do well to subscribe to these reporting agencies and include their information in their strategic and tactical planning.

- No matter how many safety programs you conduct, somebody is going to do something stupid.

- An after action report should be made and based on that report future action should be determined and preparations made.

Chapter 16 - Facing the Unexpected Threat

Friday, 31 July 1970
USS Card
100 Miles off the Western Coast of Dominica, West Indies in the designated firing range

0500: Reveille was piped. All hands, except those coming off the 0400 watch hopped out of their racks and turned-to taking care of the early morning personal preparations. They were glad to have the water restored, and were anxious to take a shower and brush their teeth.

0530: Chief Gruber reported they had made headway. The shaft was out and in the machine shop. The machine shop is small but Brewer would be able to fabricate a part that sheared off during the malfunction. Chief Gruber informed Mister Faulk they should have it back in and operating in about eight hours.

0615: The shipboard intercom came to life; "Now turn to, scrub down weather decks, sweep down all compartments, empty all trashcans, now sweepers."

0700: The shrill whistle of the Boatswain's pipe again broke the general ambiance of a moving ship at sea; "Now breakfast is being served on the Mess Deck. Uniform of the day is working uniform."

The officers submitted their breakfast requests to the Stewards. Some had waffles, others, had pancakes, still others went with the traditional eggs, toast and their choice of meat. They ate in silence for several minutes until the Captain spoke. "Mister Faulk, your team responded very quickly to the loss of the starboard engine. I don't recall seeing that particular situation in your crises management plan."

"No, Captain, that particular situation was not part of the plan but there were situations similar to that in the plan and as you know when you have a well-trained team like those guys, they have a knack for improvising. Each person in the Engine Room is assigned a particular job, but when something goes wrong, they feel their job includes everything in the engine room. I gotta say, I am very impressed with the way they all take a personal interest in what goes on down there and they don't mind being cross trained to handle some other rating's assignments."

"Well I am also pleased with the performance in the Engine Room Mister Faulk, you are to be congratulated."

"Chief Gruber deserves the credit for that Sir, as I am sure you know."

"Yes, I know that very well. Pass my compliments to Chief Gruber."

0720: "Now on deck section Bravo, lifeboat crew of the watch to muster."

0750: "Now officer's call."

0800: "Now all hands turn to and commence ship's work. The Officer of the Deck is Lieutenant (jg) Hooper."

0815: "Now sick call. All hands having need report to sick bay."

1100: "Now clear the Mess Decks."

1115: "Now knock off ship's work and prepare for the noon meal. Sweepers man your brooms. Make a clean sweep down fore and aft. Clean all lower decks ladders and passageways, empty all trash cans. Now - sweepers."

1120: "Now mess call for on-coming watch."

1130: "Now the noon meal is served on the Mess Deck."

1300: All was under normal peacetime cruising conditions, with the exception of the starboard engine. Mister Gilliam had the Deck and the Conn. The Captain was enjoying the cruise lounging in his chair on the portside of the bridge. Mister Winthrop and Lieutenant Commander McCormick were leaning against the railing gazing out across the sea. The weather was pleasant. The sea breeze generated by the slow forward movement of the ship was refreshing. There was a quiet ambiance on board, with the gentle vibration of the engines, the up and down motion of the ship in the low level swells, and the gentle sideways sway.

Lieutenant Commander McCormick was in one of his *Long John Silver* moods as he turned toward the OOD. "The old girl seems to have taken to ya sur . . . If you'll pardon tha liber-dee."

"Eye-eve taken to tha ole girl me self may-tee," Mister Gilliam responded. "She's a fine vessel to be sure . . . that she be."

Everyone on the bridge smiled big and shook their heads from side to side.

For those at their working positions there was nothing particularly exciting going on, affording everyday conversation between shipmates. Many not actually on watch chose to sun bathe on the fantail and some on the 02 level near the stack and the BRT. Others chose to play cards in the various berthing areas. Still others were just lounging around enjoying the ride. Robbie and Brennie were in the number one gun mount, apparently making preparations for the firing range activities. The scuttlebutt says they were romantically involved, though neither would admit it. But then how would you explain Phelps' change in attitude?

1330: The peaceful atmosphere of the Bridge was disturbed by the metallic click of the bridge intercom interrupting each sailor's wandering thoughts.

"Bridge, Combat," came the female voice over the intercom.

"Bridge Aye."

"We have spotted a bogie just over the horizon. It is in our target practice area. It has fire control radar and is believed to be Cuban."

"The Cubans have been notified of our practice session and the location. Not even the Cubans would interfere with that," said Lieutenant Winthrop.

The Captain keyed the intercom. "Combat what is the bogie's heading?"

"It seems to be milling around in the target area, no particular heading at this point."

The Captain pressed the ship wide intercom so that all stations and general crew area could hear. "This is the Captain. CIC has spotted a warship just over the horizon in our target practice area. We will proceed to that area as planned. At this point we are not considering it hostile."

"I see it," said Smiddy the forward lookout.

They all saw it, a small speck on the horizon dead ahead and growing larger by the second.

1340: "Bridge, Combat."

"Bridge Aye."

"The bogie is headed this way at flank speed. It has full electronics alive and fire control in the active mode. We are now considering it hostile. We think it is the hijacked Cuban.

"It is Cuban by the cut of 'er," came a response from a salty old Quartermaster.

"Bridge CIC."

"Bridge."

"Sir Based on our intelligence, we can't place any warship in the area except the pirate ship."

The captain pressed the intercom keys to CIC, engine room, the pilot house and radio central. "Any thoughts?" asked the Captain.

Mister Winthrop spoke up. "We could try to outrun them, they are far enough away. We might get clear. If they follow we could lead them right into the path of the *Williams* and let the Regular Navy handle them."

"Is that your recommendation Mister Winthrop?" the Captain asked.

"Negative, Captain, I say we engage. We may be a reserve ship but we are a U.S. Naval fighting vessel."

"Mister McCormick."

"Sir a Cuban Corvette has a flank speed of 26 knots, we can only produce 8 knots at best."

"CIC?"

"Sir," Lieutenant Sterling began, "The Williams is approximately 71 minutes due north at flank speed of 26 knots if they head this way now. We could turn north and try to stay ahead of them until we meet the Williams."

"Miss Grubaugh."

"Sir we have a 1500 yard range advantage on the Cuban with guns and torpedoes. If we are heading north in an attempt to stay out of their range our fantail is vulnerable if they get in range of their forward gun or torpedoes."

1343: 'And our forward gun is far more dependable than our after gun?" the captain asked.

"Yes," Miss Grubaugh confirmed, "And with only two live rounds, one in the forward gun and one in the after gun mount and four live torpedoes two aft and two amidships we need to be sure we are on target the first time, as I am sure you are aware, captain."

"Mister Winthrop what is your best possible guess as to the chance the Cuban will catch us before we meet the Williams?"

"It will be very close sir."

"Captain, any activity with the Cuban will create an international incident," said Mister Hooper.

"Yes, Mister Hooper," said the captain without looking in Hooper's direction. "We are all aware of that fact." He turned and looked directly into Mister Hooper's eyes and said; "But it needed to be said and we needed to hear it said, Mister Hooper thank you. We may all be explaining whatever happens here today to a Naval inquiry or a senate sub-committee."

"Or a Court Marshall," Mister McCormick said with a sigh.

"Or a Court Marshall, yes. Whatever happens here today I will have to answer for." The captain said.

"If we survive it," said Mister Hooper.

"Once again Mister Hooper you have been an anchor in reality."

"Sir, I apologize, I didn't mean for that comment to be audible."

"We were all thinking it Mister Hooper," the captain said with a sigh.

Executive Assessment

Taking risks – making what could be irrevocable choices under conditions of uncertainty

In any organization there is never a question as to whether we should take risks. In order to grow and develop or in order to maintain our present position we must make decisions and take action to make some change that makes something happen. We cannot avoid risks. Avoiding risks is like not making a decision to handle some situation, the lack of a decision is a decision we have no control over. The same is true with risk taking. There are small risks, there are great risks and there are life or death risks.

As managers of managers who have responsibility for the health and stability of an organization and the people employed in it we have to know how to take reasonable risks. How the executive handles the risk affects one's career professional and personal growth.

Earlier in this series we explored the art and science of risk management. When a critical situation occurs, in spite of your risk management initiatives one is faced with the need to take some action that is riddled with risk with no clear assurance that any decision will be the right one.

The confrontation with the Cuban is not the only major risk the captain had to address in the course of his command of the *Card*. He took risks getting the organization to cooperate with getting the ship seaworthy and then combat ready. He took a risk taking the ship out to sea knowing it would lose all power without foundering. He took a risk taking on the storm when top management and other commanders thought it was not necessary. He took a risk agreeing to take on the adversarial force in Guantanamo. And now he is faced with the greatest risk yet, the prospect of taking on a hostile warship from another sovereign nation bent on the destruction of his command and its crew.

Risk taking requires some responsible thinking. Depending on how much time one has in making the decision to go ahead with a risky action that thought process will take as long as your time allows. Sometimes it is months, weeks, days or hours. Sometimes, like this one, we have only a few seconds to consider:

Your assignment is to make a risky decision as to whether to take on the Cuban. You will make this decision using the following risk assessment model.

1. **Assess the risk:**
    - Can you, as an executive in charge afford the consequences of failure?
    - How severe is the risk? What is the worst that can happen?
    - Can your organization sustain the loss and recover from the loss if the decision goes badly?
    - Is there the possibility that your actions could cost lives or put somebody in jail?
    - Are the expected positive outcomes worth the risk?

2. **Assess the pressures that are influencing the risk.**

In risk situations there are two massive pressures: External and internal.

External pressures:
- Top management's expectations of the outcome and the probably it will be positive. In times past ComResDesRon and ComResDesDiv gave Captain Mills plenty of freedom to, almost carte blanch, to do what he thought was correct. They even interceded with the higher ups to excuse the anchor and the ramming incident. They made arrangements to put the *Card* ahead of all other regular navy ship repairs in order for it to make the trip with the rest of the division. But now they were restricting the use of fire power.
- Taking on the Cuban would create an international incident that would involve not only the captain of the *Card* but all its officers and crew, but also ComResDesRon and ComResDesDiv, the US Navy and the executive branch of the US government.
- There is the possibility of loss of the ship and the lives of its crew.
- What were some other pressures the captain and his executive had to cope with?

Internal Pressures:

There are inevitable internal pressures that instantly muster in one's mind at the first realization of the situation that requires some risky action.
- There are those self-generated pressures; one's own feelings of inadequacy to deal with this particular crises, doubt, fear, anxiety, lack of trust in the capability of subordinates to lend credible assistance, "wait and see" or take time fact gathering as a general management style.
- The captain had never had command of a ship at sea and while he did offer opinion as to how other commanders should approach a circumstance there was never a life or death consequence. And while he was responsible for the outcome of the projects he was engaged in, he was never responsible for the outcome for some major crises.

- There is so much at stake here and so many powerful international powers to evaluate and pass judgment on the event the possibilities that, regardless of the outcome it would not turn out well for the *Card,* the captain, the officers and the crew who doing their job.
- Regardless of the outcome Robert Mills and the Benchmark Consulting Group would probably never obtain another Navy contract, a vital element in the financial position of the firm.
- What other internal pressures was facing the captain and his executive crew?

3. Conduct an Analysis of the situation to determine the severity of the risk. (fact gathering)

Sometimes the executive has time to assemble sufficient facts to offer assistance in determining the best course of action. More often than not the time frame for fact gathering is limited to just a few hours or worse, a few minutes. When any crises event occurs or is looming on the horizon one must know the status of conditions.

Securing inside support

In assessing the conditions one must consider their own experience and training to calculate the conditions and the probability of success.

It may be impossible to know current conditions in all areas that are affected by the risk so having competent support staff who are on top of their assigned areas of responsibility is vital.

- Does the captain have support from the executive team?
- Does he have support from the management team (those first line and middle managers)?
- How do you know?

Fortunately in this case Mills had developed an open minded culture. From the time he came on board he had the executive staff analyzing the condition of their departments, taking action to upgrade, update and upscale, and most importantly in this circumstance he had them seek situations that would create turbulent times for their department and the ship. His subordinate executives were available to him and he was to them. In the Navy the captain is the chief executive officer and as such is responsible for the overall condition of the ship and its crew. The executive officer is the chief operations officer and handles most operations and administrative conditions so the officers have a daily relationship with that person.

The captain sought for and received wise council from his executive team. Council not decisions.
- Commander McCormick knew the Cuban's flank speed and the time it would take to catch up to the *Card* whose top speed was eight knots.
- CIC knew the exact location of the *Williams* and the time it would take to rendezvous with the *Card* and where the Cuban would be at that time.
- Grubaugh informed him that if the Cuban came within range of the guns and the torpedoes the *Card's* only defense would be the after guns and they were not as dependable as the forward gun and in light of limited ordnance their best chance was a head on engagement.
- CIC said the Cuban had the *Card's* trajectory and were firing for effect for the purpose of destroying the ship and its crew.
- ComResDesRon and ComResDesDiv informed him the air support would be sixty minutes away and to avoid engagement if at all possible but use his discretion - which means you make the call and if you are wrong we are not responsible it all falls on the shoulders of captain Mills.
- His own recollection of current facts told him sixty minutes would be too late.
- Captain Mills had a high level of confidence in his management team. They had been drilling for offensive and defensive events for six months and were in the proper mindset for dealing with critical life and death issues.

What other information was conveyed to the captain that he needed to consider before deciding to evade or engage?

Securing Outside support

When outside support is available and dependable do not hesitate to seek guidance from those outside experts. – guidance – not decisions.

In some cases that outside support is outside your executive staff but inside the organization. There may be lower level managers or hourly employees with the knowledge, and maturity to offer information about the condition or capability of equipment and other resources that could be brought to bear on the situation at hand.
- We received some dubious support from ComResDesRon and ComResDesDiv
- What other outside support is available to him if he thinks he needs it and why would he consider any other information?

Evaluate alternatives

For the *USS Card* the alternatives were few;
- Wait and see if the Cuban really intended to challenge the *Card* to combat.
- In spite of the differences in the speed of the *Card* compared to the Cuban they may have had enough of a head start to at least put them in range of the *Williams* or the Navy fighter planes before suffering any damage.

What other alternatives are available?

What seems to be the best practical solution?

- Pick one of the alternatives offered by the author and/or those offered by your team.
- Support your decision.

Take Action:

The next step is initiate the course of action that will engage the crises, implement strategies and tactics using the resources available, with competent personnel exercising authority to do what they are trained to do.

In this case, as in every case, where a critical situation existed it is the chief executive who is in charge because he/she is ultimately responsible for the activities and the outcome.

Risk Management Axioms

- Risk is a course of action taken under conditions of uncertainty, exposing one to possible loss in order to obtain some desired outcome.
- To ensure subordinates are on top of their area is to hold regularly scheduled briefings where they bring current conditions, problems
- The executive in charge must develop, maintain and test on open-minded culture.
- More often than not people (not just executives with organizational stability at risk) take risks under threat of a sure loss where the consequences of not taking some action would be difficult to overcome or devastating in other ways,
- "First lay plans that will ensure victory, and then lead your crew into battle; if you will not begin with stratagem but rely on brute strength alone, victory will no longer be assured" (SunTsu – The Art of War).
- "Danger has a bracing effect" (SunTsu – The Art of War).

Chapter 17 – When things go very, very, very wrong

Friday, 31 July 1970
USS Card
100 Miles off the Western Coast of Dominica, West Indies in the designated firing range

1445: "Bridge, Combat."

"Bridge Aye."

"The vessel is heading straight for us at 26 knots, it is gaining on us its fire control radar is still active and they are tracking us They are 15 degrees off the starboard beam."

"Miss Grubaugh have the live round from aft brought forward and prepare the forward gun and the forward torpedoes for action." Then to the entire bridge and those listening in on the intercom he said; "We can't take the chance that we can get them to the *Williams* before they catch up. It is a risky thing to do, but for the sake of the crew and the ship we will prepare to engage if that becomes necessary."

"Mister Gilliam bring her left to zero one five and maintain current speed"

"Aye, Aye captain zero one five. Helm come left zero one five."

The Captain leaned in and spoke directly into the intercom; "Radio, notify ComResDesDiv, ComResDesRon and Gitmo we are at GQ awaiting orders. Code in CincLantFlt." CIC keep the bridge and radio informed of the Cubans status. He turned to the duty Boatswain Mate. "Sound Battle Stations Not a Drill."

1351: The Duty Boatswain Mate pressed the General Quarters alarm setting off a loud clanging noise that was heard all over the ship. He shouted into the IMC; "Now General Quarters, General Quarters all hands man your battle stations, this is not a drill, this is not a drill, General Quarters, General Quarters, all hands man your battle stations, this is not a drill. Report when ready."

Lieutenant Grubaugh discarded her hat and donned the battle helmet with the built in voice powered radio.

The Captain replaced his hat with the battle helmet marked *Captain*. Mister Winthrop's helmet was marked *OPS*, Lieutenant Commander McCormick's helmet sported *XO*.

"Weapons manned and ready."

All stations reported in. They had performed this action literally hundreds of times in the past two weeks and they had it down to just a few minutes. This time there was a greater level of excitement. This may be the real thing.

Mister Goldsmith, Doctor Johnson and Mister Hooper came to the bridge.

The Captain keyed the Radio Central and CIC intercom. "Radio; send an enemy contact message to CincLantFlt, and Naval Base Gitmo informing them of the bogie's position. Inform them we have a damaged starboard engine and are capable of no more than eight knots."

He pressed the *off* button and moved away from the intercom for just a second, then back to it, keying the *talk* switch again; "And get me CincLantFlt on the horn. I want to talk to them personally . . . and link in GitmoNavBase, ComResDesDiv and ComResDesRon," the Captain ordered.

"Radio Aye," came the reply. "Would you like the Williams also?"

"Yes couple in the *Williams*." Radio brought up the proper frequency and transmitted the "ZULU" message.

1358: Bridge, Combat. This is Radio. GitmoNavBase and CincLantFlt (*Commander in Charge Atlantic Fleet*) acknowledged the message and orders not to engage unless fired upon. They request ZULU level updates."

Lieutenant Commander McCormick keyed the intercom. "Roger Radio, CIC give the bridge and radio ZULU level updates."

"CIC Roger."

The CIC complied. Every 15 seconds current bogie coordinates, course and speed were relayed to Radio Central and the Bridge.

"Did I see a Photographer's Mate on the manifest?" the Captain asked over his shoulder.

Mr. Goldsmith answered. "We got one from a reserve base in Montana . . . a First Class, I think. Ahh Charles Sandlin."

"Get him up here with a moving picture camera and a still shot camera."

"Aye Sir."

"Where is Williams?"

"The Yeoman, Captain?"

"Yeoman Williams. Yes."

"He is on the damage control team Sir," said Mister Goldsmith.

"I want him up here. He is pretty good with a camera I understand."

"Aye Sir."

The Captain keyed the intercom again. "Radio, where is my voice comm. with CincLant fleet?"

1407: "Getting it now Sir.""

"Radio, I want all combat communications recorded beginning now and until I say otherwise."

"Aye, Aye Captain."

The Radio crew was up to the task and in less than five minutes the two high commanders were on the radio telephone in touch with the *Card* and all communications over the phone patch and the combat communications systems was being recoded.

1412: Admiral Pulaski was first to speak; "Captain I understand you have damage to an engine and may not be able to outrun the bogie if he intends to attack, but I want you to use your discretion. But be advised the destroyer *Williams* has been dispatched to your area - ETA, one hour. The fighter planes at Gitmo are in-op for the day, but we scrambled two fighters from NAS Jax – ETA 52 minutes. We would rather you did not engage unless fired upon."

"Captain Mills, this is Captain Sorenson, I understand you have very limited ordinance."

"Our ordinance is limited but we do have firepower. I understand Sir, your desire that we not engage but it may very well be that we will be with Davy Jones before the fighters get here. The bogie is in attack mode. If he fires on us, we will engage." The Captain, knowing Radio Central was monitoring the broadcast, gave orders to his communication people: "Radio, put this phone patch into the combat communications system."

"Radio, Aye." The patch was made. The brass commanders stood by and listened to the events.

Williams and Schultz appeared on the bridge with photo and moving picture camera equipment.

"Williams, take the still shot camera, Schultz you're on the film. I want constant recordings of the events. We are going to need some evidence of this encounter."

Smiddy, the forward look out, stood on the catwalk in front of the pilot house. He lowered his binoculars and keyed his sound powered phone. "Bridge, boogie sighted dead ahead, coming on fast."

"Lieutenant Grubaugh, we have very limited ordinance," the Captain said. "So if we are forced to engage we must be careful to use them wisely. Load the forward gun with a dummy round and stand ready to fire a warning shot with dummy."

"Aye, Aye Sir." Though everyone in the GQ heard the orders Lieutenant Grubaugh repeated the order to the Gunner's Mates.

"Boats'n order all hands to put on life vests." The word was passed over the 1MC.

"Prepare the forward torpedo tubes with a live fish. If a shot across their bow doesn't stop them and they want trouble we will provide it."

1415: There were two instant flashes from the oncoming ship, followed by a vague frump, frump of gunfire off in the distance then the whine of shells heading for the *Card,* falling short and generating two columns of water sprouting up from where they entered the sea.

"What's he doing?" shouted the Weapons Officer, " He is way out of range. He signaled hostile intent way too early, surely they know that warning will allow us time to prepare retaliation!"

Commander McCormick took the challenge. "Either the pirates are driving the ship and don't know what they are doing, or a humiliated Cuban officer is driving it and knows exactly what he's doing."

"Torpedoes in the water!"

"We are out of range; they will die before they get here."

"I think you are right Mack," said the Captain. "That is a Cuban officer who would rather have us sink him than have the pirates take over his ship. Phelps on the forward gun is that right?"

"Yes Captain."

The Captain keyed the combat intercom system. "Lieutenant Grubaugh put a live round in the forward gun, we may only get one shot and it has to be dead on."

"Aye, Sir." She passed the order to the torpedo team and the forward gun mount.

"Tubes one and three ready."

PN3 Benson ejected the dummy round and inserted a live round. Phelps and Benson set the coordinates, the elevation and distance.

"What do you think Brennie?"

"I think we got him nailed Robbie."

"Bridge, forward gun mount is manned, loaded, enemy on target and ready."

The ships company suddenly became aware of the frailty of their ship as it came under the actual assault of flying bullets and torpedoes. This was not like the battles at Gitmo, this was real!

1418: Bridge this is CIC we are in range they will be in range in 30 seconds, They are hostile and are firing live rounds.

They have our trajectory, whether there is a Cuban officer that wants us to sink him, or whether it is a pirate on the guns, they may very well deliberately or on purpose put a shell down our forward gun mount," said Grubaugh.

" Agree Lieutenant," the captain said. "Fire torpedoes one and three."

"Fire torpedoes one and three," The Gunnery officer said into the combat communications system.

The fish sprang from their tubes and sped toward the enemy.

"Fire, forward gun Lieutenant."

"Fire the number one gun."

GM1 Phelps engaged the firing mechanism lighting up the forecastle with its powder blast and the big gun spat out its deadly projectile toward the renegade menace. Brennie turned and smiled at Robbie. They both looked back at the pirate ship. In a few seconds the sky was alight with a brilliance that painfully shocked the eyes of those peering through binoculars. They saw the enemy's forward gun mount explode followed with fire and smoke on the forecastle.

They turned again to each other her hands clutching his upper arms, his hands holding her waist. They were almost dancing, with big smiles of joy. They were proud of each other. Their eyes met. Suddenly there was no other world but the one in each other's eyes. They were in love and probably have been since they both heard the eight bells at their first meeting. It was as though they were suspended in a vacuum. The rest of the world was a blur. The only sound they could hear was;

"Marry me Brennie, Marry me. I'll convert. I will be a Gunnersmate."

"Yes Robbie, I will."

The sudden explosion threw a blinding red flash across the forecastle and up to the pilot house carrying with it a blistering hot shock wave and the stench of cordite, charred flesh and steel creating a blazing inferno that seemed to engulf the entire bow of the ship. The Cuban's last shell had hit its mark.

The force of the detonation changed the normal five pounds per square inch air pressure to about two thousand pounds per square inch. The pyrotechnics, concussion, heat and pressure of the eruption of the Corvette's shell was enough to instantly tear away muscle from bone and limbs from body; tearing up the steel deck plates and gun parts transforming them into shards of bent fragments with razor edges blowing out in all directions, tearing to small pieces everything in their path.

In their path were . . . Brennie . . . and Robbie.

The shrapnel and concussion ripped into the number two forward gun ripping into the bodies of those behind the bulwark of the gun mount inflicting serious injuries to the gun crew. Shrapnel and concussion swept forward to the pilot house behind and above the number two gun mount melting the paint and leaving a black char.

The flames and heat seared the faces of the bridge lookouts like a hot iron.

The *Card*'s number one torpedo hit the pirate ship at the water line on the port side a second before torpedo three hit it on the same side. Plumes of fire and smoke bellowed from the enemy ship.

Instinctively Damage Control assigned to the forward weather decks responded with firefighting equipment pumping large volumes of water from deck hoses desperately trying to stop the fire and black smoke billowing from the *Card's* gaping wound. They had practiced this many times but they did not think they would be doing this for real.

The casualty recovery team responded almost immediately and began to collect the dead. They rehearsed it so often they could have done this in their sleep. This was not in their sleep. This was not a dream. This was a nightmare they never expected to experience, not on this trip. They collected the remains of Phelps and

Benson and placed what was left of them both on the same stretcher and took the stretcher to the quarterdeck as they were instructed, during the drills.

Doctor Johnson and Corpsman Harris surveyed the scene. The number one gun mount was completely decimated. In its place was a gaping hole filled with billowing black smoke and leaping fire. There was clear evidence that the victims were killed instantly.

In his assessment, Harris peered aft. The number two forward gun mount was badly damaged and the two gunners were severely wounded.

Doctor Johnson joined casualty control unit 2 as they ascended on the number two gun mount and tended to the wounded. After stabilizing them, they were carried to the triage area on the quarterdeck as they had done in the simulation at Gitmo.

The damage to the bulkhead of the pilot house was bad but none of the debris had penetrated it. Harris spotted the forward lookout on the catwalk that runs the length of the Pilothouse. He was hanging on to the railing. "How ya doin' Smiddy?"

Smiddy stared blankly at the devastation that was once the forward gun mount. He was in shock. "I'll never forget it as long as I live," he said.

"I know," said Harris. "Stay where you are Smiddy, I am coming up there with you."

"It was terrible . . . "

Harris bolted up the ladder to the catwalk and placed his right arm around the look out. He pulled him in close and placed his left hand squarely on the man's chest. "You're in shock Smiddy boy. You must close your eyes and rest."

"I am very tired."

"Close your eyes and rest."

Smiddy let his head fall against Harris' chest, and closed his eyes, and slipped into eternal rest. What Harris had not told Smidlap, was there was nothing left of him from the waist down.

1428: The pirate ship stopped dead in the water. All guns and torpedoes ceased. The strange flag was lowered and a white shirt was hoisted in its place. "Cease fire," shouted Lieutenant Grubaugh.

1438: The Captain keyed the 1MC: "Security detail go below to the magazine and draw weapons - Side arms and rifles. Step lively now!"

The Anti-Aircraft Artillery unit amidships and the after guns were trained on the intruder. Damage control team two and three were still fighting the fire on the forward part of the ship and below in the chief's quarters.

1454: The *USS Card* moved in cautiously. Gun shots were heard coming from the Cuban vessel. An officer on the bridge shouted across to the *Card's* officers. In

English heavy with a Spanish accent he informed the *Card* of his vessels condition.

"We have struck! (*Ensign taken down indicating surrender*) We are a Cuban vessel high-jacked by south Caribbean pirates. Most of the pirates are dead; I have the leader of the pirates on the bridge with me. He is wounded but he is alive. He is my prisoner."

The captain leaned over the rampart of the flying bridge. "Who are you?" the Captain shouted back.

"I am the Executive Officer. My Chief Engineer, helmsman and several others from the Engine Room are here. The others who were on board at the time have been murdered and thrown over the side by the pirates."

The captain leaned over as far as he could on the rampart of the flying bridge so the Cuban would have no question as to who was addressing him. Why did you fire on my ship?"

"The pirates had control of the bridge, the engine room and the weapons," The Cuban officer shouted back. "Once they began firing on you we were able to overpower them."

"Your ship is sinking," said the *Card's* Captain.

"We will allow you to take us aboard your ship. But we refuse to be prisoners of the United States Navy."

"We will take you and your legitimate crew aboard and you will be treated with respect. But you will be our prisoner until we reach Guantanamo Bay. Your prisoners will be taken to the brig below."

"Very well, I will allow it."

The ten person security team assembled on the main deck, each with a rifle and a side arm. They stood by the railing facing the Cuban ship.

1500: Eight members of the *Restolf's* crew came out on the 0-1 level. Between them were two scrubby looking men who were tied together. They looked as though they had suffered a severe beating. The *Restolf's* Executive Officer and his Chief Engineer came down the ladder from the bridge to the 0-1 level quarterdeck manhandling another scruffy sailor tied with a line. He had no shirt. He suffered from massive contusions around the face and head, shoulders and chest.

Mister Hooper, Mister Gilliam, the Quarterdeck watch and another sailor wearing side arms came to the quarterdeck prepared to apprehend the Cubans as they came aboard.

"No one will fire on these men, without my personal order is that clear?" said the Captain

"Are there any others on board?" asked Mister McCormick.

"No. The other pirates were killed during your attack."

"How were they killed?"

"It's hard to tell. With all the confusion they may have shot themselves," the Cuban replied.

"That works for me," said Captain Mills in a voice too low for the Cuban to hear. He chose not to push it. "In similar circumstances, I may have shot the intruders myself."

1513: The *Card* came close enough to lay a gangplank and the men came across.

1518: The *Restolf's* XO saluted the Captain of the *Card* who peered down from the bridge.

"Permission to come aboard."

"Granted."

The sailors of the security team assisted the injured pirates aboard. Another contingent of security personnel took them below and locked them in the brig. The Cuban Executive Officer and his Chief Engineer were assisted aboard.

"You and your Chief Engineer will be sequestered in the wardroom under house arrest. The pirates will be locked in our brig. Your other eight sailors will be placed in the enlisted quarters under arrest conditions. You will be treated with respect."

"Aye, Aye Captain."

"Doctor Johnson, see to the wounds of the prisoners."

Doctor Johnson joined the arrest team as they took their prisoners below.

The *Card* backed away from the Cuban vessel. The ship sat motionless as oil seeped from its damaged hull It was as though she was bleeding to death. Grim faced seaman lined the *Card's* rails and watched as the bow slowly dipped into the sea. The stern rose up standing the ship on its bow under water, then it slowly slipped beneath the surface.

The Captain stood on the bridge as the *Card* turned away and headed toward Guantanamo Bay.

1526: Two fighter jets appeared over the horizon.

"Bridge this is Radio Central. Captain I am patching voice comm to the fighter jets. You have it now."

"*USS Card, USS Card* this Navy 103 do you copy? Over.

The captain pulled the mike from the holder by the intercom and drew it to his mouth.

"Navy 103 this is *USS Card* we read you over."

"This is Navy 103 do you require assistance?"

"This is *USS Card*, Negative, that is a negative. We have sunk the hostile ship and have taken the crew and their prisoners aboard. Over."

"This is Navy 103, do you need air cover? Over."

"This *is USS Card*, Negative, Navy 103 we have the situation under control."

"This is Navy 103. Good day sir."

"This is *USS Card*. Thank you Navy 103. Out."

The two fighter jets turned on the after burners and made a white streak in the sky as they speedily disappeared over the horizon.

"Well done Captain Mills," came the word from the Navy brass that had been privy to the action over the combat communication system. "Our congratulations to you and your crew. We share the horror of the loss of life and our best for the wounded."

The communication link with the brass was taken down. Final instructions were from ComResDesDiv5 to the Captain to belay the firing practice and head for Guantanamo Bay and make a full report upon arrival.

1730: Mister Hooper came to the bridge. "I have the damage report Captain."

"Report."

"We took one round, a direct hit on our forward gun, setting off a live round in the ready. The explosion took three casualties and four wounded. Two of the wounded are severe enough for the doctor to recommend hospitalization at Gitmo. Our number one forward gun was totally destroyed, and the number two gun is damaged beyond repair. Repairs are too major for a tender. There is pyrotechnic and smoke damage to the pilot house, the bulwark and the wind screen to the bridge. That damage is repairable on board. Damage below decks was to the forward Chief's quarters, and the women's quarters. The fire was out in less than two hours. That damage will require major work at a repair pier. The deck below the Chief's quarters was untouched and there was no compromise in the water tight integrity of the ship."

"Thank you for your report Mister Hooper. In your opinion, can we make it to our home port with this damage?"

"I conferred with Lieutenant Commander McCormick, Mister Winthrop and Chief Gruber. We all agree we are secure for the trip home with some minor repairs. We can do while at sea on the trip home."

The Captain laid a hand on Mister Hooper's shoulder. "My compliments to you, Mister Gilliam and Lieutenant Winchester and to your damage control team. This is a true testimony to your excellent training."

"Thank you Captain. I will pass that along."

"Please do, and I will thank them myself when I see them."

"May I say Sir it's a good thing we were at General Quarters. Otherwise we would have had casualties below decks."

"We will get home and let BuShips tell us what to do as far as repairs."

"I hate to say it Captain, but I doubt ComResDesRon will agree to repairs."

"I think you may be correct Mister Hooper."

"It's a shame too, after all the work we put into this ship."

"We all love this ship, Mister Hooper, but it may have finally served its purpose."

In less than an hour, all ships and US Naval facilities were notified of the *Card's* experience.

1800: The Captain prepared a radio message. He called the bridge messenger and instructed him to take it to Radio Central with instructions to transmit it to the Gitmo Naval Base, ComResDesDiv5, ComResDesRon34, CincLantFlt and BuShips (Bureau of Ships). The message described the battle, the sinking of the Cuban Warship, the prisoners and their status, the loss of life, the wounded and the damage to the *USS Card*. The report contained the details from the First Lieutenant's inspection. The Boatswain and the XO consider the *Card* sea-worthy for the trip to their home port. The message spoke of Captain Mills' intent to stop at Gitmo to prepare their dead and wounded for the trip home. The *Card's* dead would be taken to the home port by their shipmates and escorted to their final resting place by members of the ship's company. He informed them that he expected the starboard engine to be repaired within the hour and they could once again resume normal steaming with both propellers.

1800: The Destroyer *Williams* pulled alongside the *Card*. The Signalman asked if they needed to take on the *Card's* dead and wounded and the prisoners. The Captain informed them that all can remain until they get to Gitmo.

The *Williams* signaled they would follow the *Card* to Guantanamo. A few minutes later another signal was flashed; "A message to the officers and crew of the *Card*: Captain Pierce and the officers and crew of the *USS Williams* conveys compliments to Captain Mills and the officers and crew of the *USS Card*. Well done! And a salute to those gallant warriors and shipmates who fell in battle."

1920: The Engine Room reported the starboard engine was repaired and the ship could once again make full speed.

A pall wafted over the ship and the crew as they made their way back to the Cuban island. Fear, shock and fatigue left little room for any outward show of emotion. There was an air of oppression that affected all hands as they went about their duties at their assigned stations. No one on the crew had experienced anything like that in their lives. Everyone knew those who were killed and those who were wounded, some not as much as others, but they were shipmates and that made them family.

Captain Mills entered his cabin. He needed to be alone now. He slowly lowered himself into the wing-back lounge chair he had brought from his posh Benchmark office. He closed his eyes and leaned his head against the plush buttoned chair back. He breathed a long sigh. The weight of command lay heavily on him at this moment. He felt he should address the crew. He knew what unexpected events as horrendous as this can do to morale. When . . . Tomorrow? That would give them all time to come to grips with the events. No tomorrow is too late. They need to hear from their Captain. They need to hear some encouraging words that will help them to recover. What to say. "Perhaps just a few words from the heart would be the best." He stood up and walked to his desk. He opened the top drawer and pulled out his Bible. He opened the front cover. There on the inside cover his father had written;

To my son, a proud American Naval officer: When things are not going well remember; there are always restless and treacherous seas and stormy skies. Some are more frightening than others. Under any turbulent circumstances the one in command must stand resolute in the face of adversity and in the presence of those who report and take charge. This is no time to abandon ship.

Dad
August 31, 1954

1940: The Captain entered the bridge area. He held up his hand to indicate he did not want the Boatswain Mate of the Watch to announce his arrival. Instead he ordered him to call the crew's attention for an announcement.

The metallic crackle of the 1-MC again gave warning that another announcement was forth coming. "Now hear this! All hands stand down and give ear to the Captain."

"Ladies and Gentlemen this is your Captain. I feel I need to say something about what we all experienced a very short time ago. . . We were surprised by a hostile attack on our ship. We were forced to engage and we did. . . We sank the pirate ship, but I dare say none of us are moved by a sense of victory. I think we are just relieved to be done with it . . . We all discovered that fighting the enemy is not just an extension of drills. I know that every officer and enlisted among us are trying to come to grips with the events of the day, events we had trained for, but didn't expect to actually experience at this time. Let me remind you, this is a United States Navy Warship, and you are United States Navy warriors. You performed as you were trained to perform. You accomplished what you were trained to accomplish."

He had thought to end it here, but then, he thought a congratulations, from the Captain was in order.

"You have a reason to be proud of the actions you took today. You met a real enemy and faced that enemy under fire, and prevailed. But we lost dear shipmates . . . and sustained damage to the ship we have all come to love."

There was another long pause, but the crew could hear the metallic sound of the open mike, and waited to hear more.

"This cognitive dissonance you are experiencing comes from the fact that we are not at war, and yet we were forced to engage in a wartime action and we had no time to think about it . . . we had to act. Fortunately, we were prepared and we stepped up and did what we had to do. Let us grieve for our fallen shipmates, but let us carry on as we are expected to do. Down through the ages, US Navy ships have sustained loss of life and injuries. We owe it to our predecessors and to our fallen, and to ourselves to stand tall and carry on. I congratulate you all for your performance today."

The Captain stepped away from the microphone, and the duty Boatswain Mate stepped up pressed the talk button. "That is all, carry on."

The evening and night went by uneventfully. The pirate prisoners were stowed in the brig below decks. Mister Hooper placed armed guards to ensure their security and incarceration. They were allowed to shower and received fresh clothing. A good meal was delivered to them from the galley, they ate in their cell. The enlisted Cuban survivors were under armed guard in the after enlisted berthing area. They showered and were provided with clean clothing. They took their meals with the chiefs in the chief's mess. The Cuban Executive Officer and his Engineering Officer were incarcerated under house arrest in officer's country. They showered, were provided with clothing to replace the tattered clothing they wore when they came aboard. The Engineering officer ate evening meal with the officers in the wardroom.

The Cuban Executive Officer took the evening meal with Captain Mills in his stateroom. "We were embarrassingly surprised by the pirates during the night when two-thirds of our crew was ashore." The Cuban confessed. "They over powered the Quarter Deck Watch moved quickly through the ship capturing those of us they needed, and killing the others. Our radio operator sent a signal but we were not sure it was received by anyone. We knew the Americans were scheduled in the deep water firing range off Dominica. I managed to convince them it was a good spot learn how to use the ship's weapons. We were depending on an encounter with an American warship to allow us to get control of the situation."

"How many pirates were there?"

"There is no way on knowing for sure. But as far as our government is concerned it was over 100."

"I understand. No matter, they are in 800 fathoms of water."

"Your ship sank quickly. One of my officers thinks someone scuttled her."

"We were sunk by a US Naval warship, Captain. That is what my report will show."

"And mine as well Sir."

Being the captain of an organization is fraught with peril. You call on your experience and the experiences of your crew to identify as many possible contingencies as possible. You prepare your crew to handle those contingencies. There is never a guarantee situations will occur as you expect, but if your people are "in the game" they will step up and apply the knowledge and training they have and perform at the level necessary regardless of the actual event.

In spite of defeat, or dubious victories the work must go on. Sometimes things go wrong. Sometimes things go very, very wrong in the course of human and organizational existence. There will be losses sometimes even devastating losses that bring one to suffer or grieve. But in spite of these losses, or maybe sometimes, because of them, the work must continue.

Though emotional energy maybe siphoned off, the commander must renew the focus on the mission and get the crew back to work. Morale can withstand disasters and losses as long as the mission is not lost.

In the case of great loss, whether loss of life or loss of jobs or damage to the facility, or injuries from a tragic circumstance, the crew needs to hear from their captain. They need encouragement, direction, and refreshment. They need to hear that those in charge understand, and have compassion on the crew and not just the organization. They need to be informed about the severity of the situation and that management has taken steps to return to normalcy as soon as possible. Facing and overcoming the challenges of life, especially those unexpected challenges, strengthens us to face and handle the other challenges that will inevitably come.

Being the one in command is tough enough. Being the one in command during turbulent times and just after crises is a lonely phenomenon. All eyes are directed to the one in command. Everyone involved or interested in the events have their own thoughts regarding the events and how it was handled. They will think back, taking notice of the Captain's demeanor, facial expressions, and the tone of the skipper's voice. They will recall his deportment and behavior toward those involved. They will pay attention to those same behaviors in the wake of such events. They will draw conclusion and make judgment on the professionalism of the one in command. That conclusion will track that chief executive for the balance of that leader's career.

Everyone knew as near normal operations must continue but there was not the usual cheerfulness, or the vigor that is normally the case with competent seaman going about their business at a job they have come to appreciate.

Now there was sadness. The wind had been taken from their sails. But strangely there was also a stronger feeling of *shipmate camaraderie* among the crew, and a deeper appreciation for the *Card*. The watches changed on schedule, the business of the ship in the evening hours was handled with dispatch and correctness, food was available on the mess deck, but there was no movie, there were no games being played in the lounges.

In the life of every ship there will come a moment of decision that will affect her place in history, a decision that will honor or dishonor her and every sailor who ever sailed on her. That decision must be made by her Captain without hesitation and without consideration for personal gain or survival. It will be a decision that could seal the legacy of the ship forever. She will forever be the victor, whether still afloat or a grave in the deep, or just another ship that avoided it's time in the annals of greatness. The encounter with the Cuban Corvette was that time for the *USS Card*.

2200: "Now lights out. All hands turn into your racks and maintain silence about the deck. The smoking lamp is out in all berthing areas." Most of the sailors retired to their racks for the evening. The *Card* cruised toward Guantanamo at 12 knots.

Executive Assessment
When things go very, very, very wrong

On high stakes situations you cannot let the situation get you. You cannot lose your composure. You call on your experience and the experiences of your crew to identify as many possible contingencies as possible. You prepare your crew to handle those contingencies. There is never a guarantee situations will occur as you expect, but if your people are "in the game" they will step up and apply the knowledge and training they have and perform at the level necessary regardless of the actual event.

In spite of defeat, or dubious victories the work must go on. Sometimes things go wrong. Sometimes things go very, very wrong in the course of human and organizational existence there will be losses sometimes even devastating losses that bring one to suffer or grieve. But in spite of these losses, or maybe sometimes, because of them, the work must continue.

Though emotional energy maybe siphoned off, the commander must renew the focus on the mission and get the crew back to work. The crew of the USS Card bore truth to General Eisenhower's truism; *Morale is one and the same time the strongest and weakest of growths, it can withstand shocks and disasters on the battlefield, but can be totally destroyed by favoritism, neglect and injustice.*

In the case of great loss, whether loss of life or loss of jobs or damage to the facility, or injuries from a tragic circumstance, the crew needs to hear from their captain. They need encouragement, direction, and refreshment. They need to hear that those in charge understand, and have compassion on the crew and not just the organization. They need to be informed about the severity of the situation and that management has taken steps to return to normalcy as soon as possible. Facing and overcoming the challenges of life, especially those unexpected challenges, strengthens us to face and handle the other challenges that will inevitably come.

Captain Mills' dad said it best; *"Under any turbulent circumstances the one in command must stand resolute in the face of adversity and in the presence of those who report and take charge. This is no time to abandon ship.*

The Burden of the One in Command

Being the one in command is tough enough. Being the one in command during turbulent times and just after crises is a lonely phenomenon. All eyes are directed to the one in command. Everyone involved or interested in the events have their own thoughts regarding the events and how it was handled. They will think back at the demeanor of the captain, the facial expressions, and the tone of voice the skipper's deportment and behavior toward those involved. They will pay attention to those same behaviors in the wake of such events. They will draw conclusion

and make judgment on the professionalism of the one in command. That conclusion will track that chief executive for the balance of that leader's career.
The Cuban began firing before they were within range. Of course the Cuban Commander did this in order to cause the *Card* to advance and destroy.

Command Axiom:
- In circumstances where one begins in bluster, but afterwards takes fright at the enemy's numbers, shows a supreme lack of intelligence" (SunTsu – The Art of War).
- When things go wrong courage wins the day (George Patton)
- Courage is fear holding on one minute longer
- Morale can withstand disasters and losses as long as the mission is not lost.
- In a crises situation is not the time to share command. The CEO must shoulder the leadership – these are good times to have loyal competent staff to offer moral support as well as competence to accept and carry out delegated assignments.

Chapter 18 - The Aftermath - Recovery Management

Saturday, 01 August 1970
USS Card en Route to GTMO

0530: The shrill whistle of the boatswain's pipe again hurtfully interrupted the slumber and general ambiance of a moving ship at sea; "Now reveille, reveille all hands heave out and trice up."

0700: "Now breakfast is being served on the mess decks. Uniform of the day is working uniform."

0720: "Now on deck section Bravo, lifeboat crew of the watch to muster."

0750: "Now officer's call

0800: Mister Hooper assumed the Conn.

0815: "Now sick call. All hands having need report to sick bay."

1115: "Now sweepers man your brooms. Make a clean sweep down fore and aft. Clean all lower decks ladders and passageways, empty all trash cans. Now sweepers."

In spite of the damage and the sorrow of lost shipmates, routine must be maintained. Everyone knew they were expected to continue on doing what needed doing, countless tasks that were a necessary part of everyday shipboard activity. Routine must go on no matter what was happening elsewhere. The daily ship board business continued according to the plan of the day but something was different now. The business became even more important. A new attachment had been formed, an attachment each sailor knew was there just out of reach, and now it was all too real.

The captain stood on the bridge and looked down across the weather decks, at the sailors going about the business of the ship. As he glanced at the various groups assembled on the deck, he was reminded again of the isolation of command.

After the noon meal the order to turn to and commence ship's work was piped.

1600: The *Card* pulled into Gitmo Bay.

"This is the *U.S.S. Card*. Request berthing instructions. We have three dead, two wounded, we have eight Cuban prisoners. Two officers and three are enlisted from the Cuban Navy and three pirates. One is the Pirate leader."

The *Card* was instructed to moor on a pier near the navy base. Base police, a contingent of marines and civilians representing the State Department met them and took the prisoners. Two ambulances were dispatched to take the dead and wounded to the base hospital.

The remains of the bodies of the shipmates who had fallen in battle were transferred to the base morgue where they were prepared for their last journey home.

The wounded were taken to the base hospital where they were given medical treatment. At the insistence of each wounded sailor and the permission of the *Card's* captain and doctor they were permitted to return to the ship for the journey home.

1900: A radio messenger knocked on Captain Mills' stateroom door. He was wearing dress whites and the white guard belt of a radio messenger,

"Come in."

The messenger pushed the door open, and entered.

"A radio message from NavBase Mayport captain" he said as he extended his hand holding the message.

The captain retrieved the paper and read it as the messenger stood at attention and waited for further orders.

"Very Well. Send this message."

The messenger clicked the point of his ball point pen into service and prepared to write on a pad he had in his hand.

My dear Mrs. Benson, I will make the arrangements and God Bless You. Robert Mills Commander USNR-R *U.S.S. Card* commanding.

"Good Night Captain." He did an about face and exited the state room pulling the door closed behind him as silently as he could."

The destroyer escort commander read the message again. This time he took the time to ponder the significance of the words and the intention of the sender.

"My dear Captain Mills, My husband I received a letter from our son Robert Benson post marked Mayport Naval Ship yard. He informed me that he met a girl, Brenda Phelps, and that although he has only known her for a few hours he was going to marry her. He said she has no family and he was going to make her part of our family even though it meant he would have to go into the regular navy as a gunner's mate. I understand they were killed together. Would it be possible to have her remains placed in the same coffin as our son's remains and bury them both together? I understand there is not much of either of them after such a devastating blast. We want to honor Robbie's desire to make Brennie part of our family.

Sincerely and Respectfully

Mrs. Phillip Benson."

The Captain contacted the Navy Base Morgue and set up a meeting with the Medical Examiner.

2100: Captain Mills arrived at the morgue, found the Medical examiner, who was still processing the remains brought in from the *USS Card*. The captain asked him if he could place the remains of Phelps and Benson in the same casket.

"As you probably know commander, I am a stickler for by the book practices. It is highly unusual to grant such a request."

"I realize your predicament doctor, but I have heard that you are sympathetic of the families of fallen warriors." Phelps has no family and the Benson's want her remains to be buried with their son since they were engaged to be married."

"Highly unusual commander, but not prohibited. Consider it done. I will put the ID tags on the same box. There was not much to put in you know."

"I know. Thank you."

The *Card* rode the movement of the water generating a squeak of rubber fenders against the pier. It was if the ship was seeking a comfortable position to rest, and gather strength for the next action that will be required of her.

Executive Assessment
After action Assessment

In any organization there is never a question as to whether we should take risks. In order to grow and develop or in order to maintain our present position we must make decisions and take action to make some change that makes something happen. We cannot avoid risks. Avoiding risks is like not making a decision to handle some situation, the lack of a decision is a decision we have no control over. The same is true with risk taking. There are small risks, there are great risks and there are life or death risks.

As managers of managers who have responsibility for the health and stability of an organization and the people employed in it we have to know how to take reasonable risks. How the executive handles the risk affects one's career professional and personal growth.

Earlier in this series we explored the art and science of risk management. When a critical situation occurs, in spite of your risk management initiatives one is faced with the need to take some action that is riddled with risk with no clear assurance that any decision will be the right one.

The confrontation with the Cuban was not the only major risk the captain had to address in the course of his command of the *Card*. He took risks getting the organization to cooperate with getting the ship seaworthy and then combat ready.

He took a risk taking the ship out to sea knowing it would lose all power without foundering. He took a risk taking on the storm when top management and other commanders thought it was not necessary. He took a risk agreeing to take on the adversarial force in Guantanamo. And now he is faced with the greatest risk yet, the prospect of taking on a hostile warship from another sovereign nation bent on the destruction of his command and its crew.

Risk taking requires some responsible thinking. Depending on how much time one has in making the decision to go ahead with a risky action that thought process will take as long as your time allows. Sometimes it is months, weeks, days or hours. Sometimes, like this one, we have only a few seconds to consider:

Instruction:

Using the questions below let's assess our decision to take on the Cuban:

1. Assessing the situation
- What was the risk?
- What did we do about it?
- Why did we take that action?
- What were the outcome and the consequences?
- Did our action provide the results we wanted?
- What could we have done differently?
- What will we do to ensure there is not next time or that we will take the correct action next time?
- Who interfered with or obstructed the engagement because they failed to act?

2. Assess the risk:
- Did we assess the risk correctly in our last assignment?
- Based on our assessment did we do the right thing taking on the Cuban?
- Did we accurately identify and examine the external and internal pressures?
- Recognizing the short time span for assessing the situation and the consequences did we accurately consider the outside and inside support in making our decision?
- It appeared as though ComResDesRon, ComResDive, Gtmo navbase, CincLantFlt, were not comfortable with the *Card* taking on the Cuban. Did the fact that the *Card* prevailed relieve Mills from the consequences of the encounter?
- The Cuban Executive Officer said there were 100 pirates and they did not scuttle the ship. The Captain did not believe him. One may think there is an ethical problem here. One may ask is it ever good policy to support

another's after action report when it contains some errors even if the information was of no consequence. The answer lies in the questions; will this information hurt someone if it is discovered? To what extent does this information create a harmful circumstance that could be avoided?

3. The captain asked for information from his officers, he did not ask for advice or a decision. The captain was sure the information he received was factual and honest, His people did not withhold vital information even though it was bad news deciding to tell the captain they thought he wanted to hear. One may wall ask; what were the conditions that afforded that level of honesty? The captain had set a climate for dealing with reality not fantasy as they had before he came on board and that attention to the real facts that had to be realistically addressed brought with it trust that the messenger of bad news would be rewarded not shot.

Evaluate alternatives
- In some cases alternative assessments must be made quickly and one chosen before it is too late. In cases where major incidents have been anticipated and alternative actions have been pre-decided one can resort to training and conditioning for those evaluations.
- Sometimes the situation strikes so suddenly there are no other alternatives visible. This is the time when opportunity and preparation meet.
- There were other alternatives besides the ones Captain Mills and his staff recognized and Mills will need to explain those alternatives in an official inquiry. But he must be able to explain why the other alternatives would not suffice and he would need to effectively defend his decision.

Evaluate Progress
- The executive in charge of the turbulent conditions must have methods for keeping track of the progress toward resolving the issues of the crises. Feedback agencies (systems) are in place to provide instant update information of changing conditions and recommendations if progress is not satisfactory.
- The manager in charge of leading in the turbulence must continuously evaluate the progress. There needs to be milestones that indicate whether actions taken are accomplishing the mission. Adjustments must be made the moment situations change or the plan appears to be failing to secure the target outcome.
- In a difficult operation and especially in a crises the one in command must have competent subordinates available provide accurate information in which the commander can determine progress and make adjustments.
- If those subordinates skilled enough to offer recommendations for courses of action so much the better. Of course the one in command of the

situation has the ultimate responsibility for the outcome and thus is the one to select the action they deem appropriate whether their own assessment of another.

4. Dealing with outcomes

Once the crises have been engaged and the consequences of the engagement have materialized one must have a plan to handle those consequences whether negative or positive.

- What do you suppose will be the consequences of the engagement?
- What should be the captain's plan in dealing with the consequences?

In the meeting with the Cuban Officer there is some reason to suspect the Cuban's report was not exactly accurate. There was some question about the number of pirates and the swift sinking of his ship to name two. Apparently the captain's evaluation of his adversary's exaggerated report was in the best interest of the ship's crew, the officer's career and the reputation of the lost ship. Some would say the captain should report what he and his officers suspected, that any official report should not contain self-serving purposes. The question that needs to be considered is; *in what way would questioning the veracity of such a report as this benefit anyone?* When only hurt can be achieved by questioning a course of action and there is nothing to gain by this hurt, perhaps a prudent silence is called for.

The Benson family asked for a favor that was way out of line with the established order. But Captain Mills and the base Medical Examiner realized there will be times when the established order is not in order. When it is in the power of the decision makers to do good or withhold good the Steward Commander will never withhold good.

After Action review

At the closure of the crises or at a place where the turbulence is under control an after action review is necessary for lessons learned and provision for preventing a reoccurrence or provision for handling the next occurrence or a similar occurrence.

An After Action Report, or AAR for short, is a document detailing and evaluating the actions previously taken by a group or individual as part of a goal-oriented exercise or series of exercises. Organizations often compile and review such reports to determine how they can maximize the success of its operations. To ensure that your After Action Report helps the organization in question improve its performance, familiarize yourself with the correct format for such a report. One of the first and best examples of an AAR is Julius Caesar's "Commentaries on the Gallic War".

Chapter 19 Weathering the Consequences

After Action Learning
Sunday, 02 August 1970
US Naval Station Guantanamo Bay, Cuba

1000: It was ten hundred when captain Mills made his summoned appearance at Admin HQ in his dress whites. He carried a brief case with a detailed written account of the events exactly as he had written it in the Ship's log. He also carried film and still pictures of the entire event. He had a duplicate copy on board ship in his stateroom. He was going to avoid telling anyone about that set.

Commander Mills asked the duty petty officer if there were Audio Visual systems in the meeting room as he had some film, slides and still photos to display at the meeting. He gave the materials to the petty officer who set about preparing for the AV presentation in the rear projection room.

The *Card*'s captain was escorted into the large conference room. At the meeting were the naval Base Commander, Captain Morris, ComResDesRon Captain Buck Sorenson, and ComResDesDiv Admiral Pulaski.

As he entered the room Admiral Pulaski remained seated, but he smiled broadly and said "Good Morning captain Mills." ComResDesRon stood up and grabbing the Commander's hand, pumped it. "Good to see you Bob." He indicated a place at the conference room table where he was to sit.

After he was settled in his chair at the end of the table, Buck Sorenson took a seat on the right side of the table near captain Mills. He leaned forward toward the DE's commander and in his usual forward and loud tone he said; "You know Bob, it didn't take long before everyone in the Navy knew you were in conflict with that pirate ship. But I'll bet you there were only three people in the entire Navy who believed you would survive."

Captain Mills felt a sense of dread as to what was coming next but he maintained his composure. "Only three?"

"Me, Commander Garrett and . . . Captain Amber Jack Westaway. You see we were the only ones in the Navy that had ever had the pleasure of experiencing you in action."

"No commander succeeds without a competent crew dedicated to the mission" Said Mills.

"Well said Captain but competent personnel are developed and directed into effectiveness by competent leadership and management, so don't start handing your credit over to someone else."

The door opened and two men in dark suits entered each carrying a cordovan leather brief case.

They did not look in the direction of either officer, but set their briefcases on the table and popped open the gold plated locks, removed some papers and sat down. "I am Bernard Riggins from the state department. This is my associate, Richard Mikulski."

"I am Captain Sorenson, Commander Reserve Destroyer Squadron thirty four." This is Admiral Pulaski Commander Reserve Destroyer Division Five. You know Captain Morris and this, pointing to Commander Mills, Is the Captain of the *USS Card*, Commander Mills."

Good morning Mister Riggins." the ComResDesDiv Admiral said reaching out his hand offering him a business card. He seemed so insistent, Riggins took the card and without looking at it placed it in the small pocket inside his suit jacket. He withdrew one of his business cards and hurriedly moved it in the direction of the Admiral. The Admiral snatched the card and hid it in his shirt pocket under his Admirals uniform jacket.

The two suits did not acknowledge the introductions. Without making eye contact, the one who appeared to be the leader of the two began the transaction. "Let's get down to business shall we? Now Commander tell us what went on out there. How did you encounter this Cuban ship and why did you engage when ordered not to?"

Captain Mills spoke up. "I brought a copy of the report I entered in the ship's log. I also brought the film, audio from the combat communications system and some still pictures that should answer most of your questions.

"The Cubans are demanding reparations for the loss of their warship. They have accused the U. S. of an act of aggression against a sovereign nation's warship. They are telling the United Nations your ship attacked them and sank them without provocation and that you and your crew should be handed over to them to face murder and piracy charges. "

"Just how did the Cubans find out about the incident so quickly?"

"They were informed by the state department, of course. A situation such as this has international repercussions. They needed to know."

"What did the state department tell them?" Asked Sorenson

"Your report Commander." Demanded Riggins, ignoring the admiral's question.

"If the film is ready let's run it," said Mills as he opened the satchel and handed the still photos to his boss, captain Sorenson. He opened the packet and leafed through them as the film began. He passed the photos to his boss Admiral Pulaski. The Admiral leafed through them then turned his attention to the film. The lights dimmed and the black and white silent pictures showed up on the screen. The suits clicked their ball point pens into action and took notes on the yellow note pads they brought with them.

When the film had concluded, and lights were back on, the suits said nothing, but continued to write on their note pads.

Sensing the tension by the silence of the suits, Captain Sorenson spoke up. "Good report Captain, very thorough, very objective, not one self-serving piece."

Riggins reached across the table and snatched the packet of still photos from in front of the Admiral. "I will need to take the copies of your report and the film and photos back to Washington. Do you have any other copies of this material Commander?"

"I ordered my photographer's mate to make only one master and no copies. This is one of those situations that need to be scrutinized by top brass before it is released. We would not want copies floating around unescorted now do we?" said Mills.

"OK then. That is all commander. You may be called to Washington to testify." Mister Riggins stood up and began collecting the papers and pictures and stuffing them into his brief case. Mikulski closed his briefcase and headed for the door. "I'll retrieve the film" he said.

"To what committee will you be recommending he be called to testify?' asked Admiral Polanski

"I'm not sure yet. But for starters The State Department is concerned that Commander Mills, a reserve officer, may be guilty of hazarding the lives and safety of those under his command, and risking the destruction of a US Navy warship." To that add firing on and sinking a warship of a sovereign nation. I am sure there will be further charges once the investigation is complete.

"He was given permission to fire if fired upon" said the Admiral.

"He was told to use his discretion. That means everyone involved is clear of any wrong doing if the captain's decision goes wrong, everyone of course except the commander himself. Apparently it went wrong."

"What is the status of the Cuban officers and enlisted men I rescued?" asked Mills.

"The Cuban government claims you shanghaied them. But the Cubans you picked up are asking for political asylum. They claim they can't go back to Cuba after losing their ship." Riggins answered.

"It is exactly as I wrote it in the shop's log."

Mister Riggins walked to the door.

"Let's hope the world stage believes you," said Mister Riggins. As he swung open the door he turned to look at the *Card's* Captain. "The secretary of state is very concerned about this affair."

"I would think the president and the Joint Chiefs would also be interested" said Captain Morris.

"I don't work for them Captain." With that he exited and closed the door behind him.

"What just happened here?" asked the base commander with a look of surprise and disgust. "Was this an inquiry or an inquisition? Was this a witch hunt? Did I miss something? Did the Captain of the *Card* do something that would engage such an attitude, for this guy Riggins or his boss?"

"I hadn't intended to start an international incident", said Robert Mills, as he placed his papers into his brief case and pressed the locks closed. His tone was somber as he breathed out heavily, "I was just concerned for the safety of my ship and the crew."

"By your leave Admiral I will see that those two are escorted to their plane and find out what I can about their real mission here."

"Certainly, Captain Morris, I will see you tonight."

"Good day gentlemen."

The Admiral, leaned back in his chair, removed his pipe and a packet of tobacco from his brief case. "There will always be decisions made under conditions of uncertainty, he said. We make decisions or best guesses using what information we have available at the time with all the intelligence and discernment at our disposal and hope for the best."

He filled his pipe from the tobacco pouch. There will be consequences if you act. There are consequences if you don't act. There will be consequences regardless of the decision you make, but you accept the consequences and make adjustments as necessary to make the best use of those consequences."

The admiral paused as he struck a match and lit his pipe. He looked around for an ash tray to discard his match, and in so doing he noticed the "No Smoking" sign on the wall over the doorway. He pointed to the sign, shook the match until the flame went out. With one hand he held his pipe, with the other still holding the extinguished match, pulled an ashtray from his brief case and deposited the match into it.

"What indecisive executives fail to realize, he continued, is that incomplete knowledge is not the same as ignorance. Informed judgments can still be made, indeed they must be made and more often than not they are made in turbulent situations with precious little time to rely on nothing more than one's own intellectual and experiential judgment."

He paused again and took a long pull on his pipe, looking every bit the mature sage of the maritime service. Both the squadron captain and the commander were captivated by his casual demeanor and his apparent lack of concern over the events that just transpired, or the trouble Riggins and his silent partner were insinuating. The *Card's* captain and his boss were intrigued by the advisory path the Admiral was taking.

"Too often doing the right thing takes more courage that doing the wrong thing, or doing nothing."

The admiral took another long pull on his pipe and let the smoke out slowly. He examined his pipe as he finished his thought.

"You did what you had to do Commander Mills. It was the right thing. But the cold hard facts of life is that no one expected the *U.S.S. Card* to perform so well, not in the Gitmo exercises and certainly not in the face of aggressive hostile action. Effective commanders will have enemies, especially when that commander is proving his critics wrong. Too often when the critics think they are losing, they resort to personal attacks on their enemy's honor or character."

He turned his attention to the Commander of ResDesRon and the Captain of the *Card*. "That is the problem we are involved with here. Only it is not with your unexpected success, it is between the President and the Secretary of State. It is no secret there is no love or respect between Secretary of State and the President ever since they battled it out in the presidential election. The President only hired him to keep him out of the country and in a subordinate position. Little good it does," said Admiral Pulaski.

Captain Sorenson took up the trail. "He would like nothing better than to bring down the President. They have been looking for something to do it and they will play this. Riggins is the Secretary's hit man. Men like him have no scruples and no conscience. They have one goal and that is to pick up power points to enhance their career. . . Dangerous people."

"Dangerous people, Admiral Pulaski repeated. This guy Riggins was not sent here to investigate, he came here to find, or manufacture evidence that this encounter was the Navy's blunder. The President, being a Naval Academy graduate provides more fuel for his fire. He has flushed many a good officer and statesman down the drain in order to feather his own nest."

The admiral pointed his pipe at Commander Mills. "I hope you kept a copy for your own protection."

"I told the Photographer's mate not to make a copy."

"I understand your Mister Goldsmith's Yeoman Williams is a clever lad," said the ResDesRon commander.

"That he is sir. And you will be pleased to know he holds you in high esteem."

"Is that right?"

"As a matter of fact he sent a gift over to your stateroom on the *Lancing* just about an hour ago."

'"Captain Sorenson and I will be flying back to Washington and take this up with some powerful forces of our own Commander." said the Admiral.

"After I stop by my stateroom and pick up some personal items. Captain Sorenson interjected. The Admiral and I will be checking in on this guy Riggins to see how he is representing your story."

If we see he is performing as predicted, he will have some explaining to do to his boss and maybe the president," said Admiral Pulaski.

The Admiral leaned back in his chair and with a smug said "They will want to know, since he had the only copy, how it ended up on the desk of Joe Franklin of CBS news with his business card attached," he said holding up Riggins' card. "with a note saying *compliments of the state department."*

The two captains smiled at each other, when they realized why the Admiral insisted on getting Riggins' business card.

Captain Mills turned again to Captain Sorenson. "I want to take our dead and wounded back to our home port on the *Card*, and arrange for transfer there at that time. The families will want to meet us there to travel with their fallen kin."

"I think that is a good idea. Granted."

The Admiral stood up, retrieved his hat from the table. Placing his hand on Mills' shoulder he said. "I want you to come ashore with Captain Sorenson and me this evening. The base commander is entertaining some people at his house on base."

"Thank you Admiral. . . I . . ."

"Consider it an order Captain Mills. Twenty-hundred. I will have my driver pick you up."

1700: The officers were assembled around the supper table. All were present. Mister Faulk was the OOD but took his scheduled meal time. BM1 Furman was the duty petty officer and "held down the fort" until Mister Faulk returned. Furman had been given leave to eat earlier. The meal had just begun when Commander McCormick spoke up.

"Are you permitted to tell us what happened in the meeting with the state department representative and ComResDesDiv?"

"It was not a pretty sight, commander. It seems this guy named Riggins from the State Department claims the Cubans want reparations for the ship we sunk. They claim our actions were an act of piracy and we shanghaied their crew. Admiral

Pulaski seems to think the Secretary of State plans to use this event to embarrass the President. A revolting development all around to say the least."

The officers were instantly and visibility angered by the notion that an act of defense was to be used for political gain, by both the Cubans and a disgruntled loser of the last presidential race.

"It wasn't the Cubans we defeated, said Lieutenant Grubaugh; it was a band of renegade pirates."

Doctor Johnson placed his cup in the saucer in a deliberate manner. The officers could tell he had a pithy thought on his mind and they were anxious to hear it. "Abraham Lincoln was in a situation similar to this at one time. He told a story about a shepherd who was tending his sheep when a wolf came in looking for evening meal. The shepherd drove the wolf away. The sheep called him a hero, a liberator, while the wolf denounced him as a destroyer and one who takes food out of the mouths of the needy."

Mister Winthrop wiped his mouth with his napkin, and while replacing it in his lap, taking care it was properly place said; "And I would add there are plenty of wolves in positions of influence who have the audacity and the means to convince the sheep the shepherd was not to be trusted, using this very incident as their evidence."

"Hear, here" the officers said in unison.

"Are we letting them get away with it?" asked Mister Faulk.

"Fortunately, as you know I wrote a complete report of the incident and we recorded the entire affair on film and still pictures, with audio sound. That will either deliver us or indict us" said the captain.

"All the mucky-mucks in fleet command over heard the entire bloody affair" said Goldsmith.

"And this . . . Mister Riggins took the evidence with him?" asked Commander McCormick.

"He did. He thinks he has the only copy."

"You ordered the photographer not to make any copies that only the original was to be handed over" said Mister Hooper.

Mister Goldsmith entered the discussion; "He did, but he did not give those same orders to me or Williams. Who knows how many copies he made! He took one copy to captain Sorenson on the *Lancing*. I dare say if Mister Riggins wants to claim no such evidence exists, or he edits any of it for his own desires, he will be in for a shock when he finds there are other copies. Smart move I would say."
"Still I don't trust those birds," said Mister Faulk.

"Interesting situation . . . We will see how it plays out", the captain added.

1800: The meal completed the officers went about their business. The captain decided to go to the bridge. He had left a magazine there, and an unfinished article was demanding his attention. Mister Winthrop had hoped to see the captain alone, and did not want to intrude on his quiet time in his cabin, so when he saw him going to the bridge he followed him. As the captain was leafing through the magazine mister Winthrop came through the doorway onto the bridge.

"I had hoped to see you alone captain," he said as he stood near the doorway. "I did not want to say this in front of the other officers, as it would sound a bit self-serving. Apparently Mister Riggins and the Secretary of State are unaware of the naval Winthrop's profound interest in the *Card,* its crew and particularly its captain, whom they feel they owe a great debt, for saving their wayward offspring's career."

"Thank you Mister Winthrop, that is very encouraging."

"Sir," he said, as he backed through the doorway and down the hatch. He had delivered the message and felt it inappropriate to continue any further communication with the captain on this subject.

The captain managed a smile. "Cast your bread upon the waters and it will return to you in due time, Ecclesiastes 11:1", he thought.

2000: Captain Mills sat alone in the back seat of the Navy car that took him to the Base Commander's house.

Captain Morris greeted Captain Mills and introduced to the other guests. He greeted his boss and the Admiral. He felt as though he were having an out of body experience as his mind steered steadily on events of the past hours. He barely noticed the items of the five course meal.

After the meal Captain Morris and his guests enjoyed port and cigars in a large, well-appointed parlor and the adjoining lounge that opened up through large French doors. The commanding officer of the *USS Card* forced himself to pretend to enjoy the company of visiting congressmen and some of the other senior officers. Some, who were assigned to the Gitmo system and others who were visiting from ships having business there. But the events of the last two days took up permanent residence in his conscious mind.

Captain Jack Westaway, Amberjack Westaway, spotted Captain Mills standing alone in the lounge area. He quickly snagged two bottles of Heineken and walked swiftly through the French doors. As he drew near to his combat exercise opponent he announced; "The beer you won Captain Mills." He handed one of the bottles to the *Card's* commanding officer. "It is a rare thing to lose a bet on the combat exercises, he said, but clearly I underestimated you and your ASW team."
"You are a formidable opponent Cap'n Jack, and a gracious runner up."

"You mean a gracious loser."

"You are no loser captain. Runner up maybe, but only this time. I dare say this is not likely to happen again."

"It seems I was not the only one who underestimated you and your crew," The sub commander began, "and now it seems you have another opponent and this one is not so easily defeated by gallantry and skill. I of course speak of this bird Riggins and his boss. The Navy will clear you, of course, but your career in the Navy will be stalled for some time, and the state department having political goals to meet, will take advantage of this incident. It's a good thing you are competent, Bob, and have friends in influential places. You're going to need them."

"A revolting development to say the least."

The sub Commander smiled. "Groucho Marx once said; "Politics is the art of looking for trouble, finding it everywhere, diagnosing it incorrectly, and applying the wrong remedies."

"Groucho Marx was insightful man, as well as a great comic."

Amber Jack raised his bottle and pointed it at Captain Mills. "Well here's to your remarkable showing in the war games, and in the real thing. You beat us both fair and square. I hope to see you again in the fleet. Or maybe I'll have another go at you next year."

Admiral Pulaski appeared through the French doors and approached the two commandeers. They assumed an attention stance and directed their attention to the ResDesDiv Commander. He set his smile on Captain Jack, and with a nod acknowledged his presence; "Captain Westaway."

"Sir."

He turned his attention to Robert Mills. "Captain Mills, Captain Sorenson and I want to be there when your dead crew members are brought to your ship. What time will that be?"

"Zero eight hundred Sir."

We will stand on the pier and render the salute when they are removed from the car. Don't afford us any special attention. We will be there until the honors are completed then we will leave. Does that meet with your approval?"

"It does Sir, thank you. And it will be appreciated by the crew."

"How soon after the service will you weigh and proceed to your home port?"

"As soon as we can complete the preparations for getting underway. I hope we can shove off by Eleven-hundred."

"Excellent! Please feel free to stay and enjoy the evening, or to take your leave and return to your ship."

"Thank you Admiral, I would prefer to return to my ship."

"My driver will take you. Good evening Captain, and don't concern yourself with Mister Riggins or whatever schemes The State Department may have up their sleeve. We have our own methods, and, from what I just learned, we have the Winthrops, and no one ever underestimates that bunch."

Executive Assessment
After Action Learning-1

The cold hard facts of command: If you are correct someone else will get the credit. If you are wrong there is no doubt where the blame will land. But any process worth going through will almost always get tougher before it gets easier. One engaged in any worthwhile process must have the will to overcome and persevere.

Command is one thing, but responsibility, the duty to those who depend on you, is the greater burden. It is a burden that only a captain can bare, a burden that must be felt not just dealt with. A burden one must take personally.

There will always be decisions made under conditions of uncertainty, We make decisions or best guesses using what information we have available at the time with all the intelligence and discernment at our disposal and hope for the best.

There will be consequences if you act. There are consequences if you don't act. There will be consequences regardless of the decision you make, but you accept the consequences and make adjustments as necessary to make the best use of those consequences."

What indecisive executives fail to realize is that incomplete knowledge is not the same as ignorance. Informed judgments can still be made, indeed they must be made and more often than not they are made in turbulent situations with precious little time to rely on nothing more than one's own intellectual and experiential judgment."

Too often doing the right thing takes more courage than doing the wrong thing, or doing nothing.

Whether the crises are industry-wide, National or just your ship, there will be some politicians who cannot stand by and watch good crises go to waste. There will be those who will find fault or try to manufacture fault with your activities in order to promote their own agenda. It is times like this where a long term investment in good public relations and networking pays off. If the community is familiar with your operation, and the employees like working there, fault finders will have a hard time making a case against you. It pays to be competent and to have a reputation for being very good at what you do. In turbulent times it pays to have influential friends you can count on.

Command Axioms

- Being the captain of an organization is fraught with peril. You call on your experience and the experiences of your crew to identify as many possible contingencies as possible.

- You prepare your crew to handle those contingencies. There is never a guarantee situations will occur as you expect, but if your people are "in the game" they will step up and apply the knowledge and training they have and perform at the level necessary regardless of the actual event.

- In spite of defeat, or dubious victories the work must go on. Sometimes things go wrong.

- Sometimes things go very, very wrong but spite of the losses, or maybe sometimes, because of them, the work must continue.

- Though morale maybe siphoned off, the commander must renew the focus on the mission and get the crew back to work.

- In times of great distress the crew needs encouragement, direction, and refreshment. They need to be informed of the severity of he situation and to hear that those in charge understand, and have compassion on the crew and not just the organization

- "Sometimes you must fight the battle twice before you win." (*Margret Thatcher*)

- There are those who are prone to spread untrue embellishments about the good works of others. No matter how thin they slice it, it is still baloney.

Chapter 20 The return voyage home

Sunday 02 August 1970
US Naval Station Guantanamo Bay, Cuba

2100: The *Card* pulled away from the nest to allow the other ships to move out. She spent the night anchored in the bay.

Monday, 03 August 1970
US Naval Station Guantanamo Bay, Cuba

0400: Reveille was piped. All hands, except those coming off the 0400 watch hopped out of their racks and began taking care of the early morning personal preparations. Mister Winthrop assumed the OOD duties on the quarterdeck.

0415: The ship board intercom came to life; "Now turn to, scrub down weather decks, sweep down all compartments, empty all trashcans, now sweepers."

0545: The Boatswain keyed the 1-MC (ship-wide address system) and made an announcement that sent chills up the spine of the entire ship's company. They had heard it before, but this time was different.

"Now all hands make preparation for getting underway. The ship will shift from shore power to ship power in five minutes."

At the end of the five minute time period the quartermaster counted down the seconds. The shift was made without a glitch.

0600: "Now . . . set the special sea and anchor detail. The maneuvering watch will lay to the bridge."

0640: "Now . . . The Officer of the Day has shifted the watch from the quarterdeck to the flying bridge."

0655: The final getting underway order was given.

"Now . . . hoist the anchor."

The anchor was raised, and cleared the water.

"Anchors aweigh sir," came the report from the quartermaster.

"Very well," Mister Winthrop acknowledged.

"Mister Winthrop." The captain's voice was low and there was hint melancholy.

Mister Winthrop turned to face the captain. "Yes captain."

The captain breathed out slowly. There was a pause. Then in the same low voice he said;

"Take us home."

"Aye, aye Captain" he responded in a similar tone.

The captain and the OOD expressed what every sailor on board was thinking and in the same frame of mind. Glad to be going home with a cognitive dissonance of, on the one hand, mission accomplished, and on the other sadness at the loss of shipmates and gaping wound in the ship they come to love.

The anchor was properly secured by the deck hands on the *Card*. The Boatswain Mate of the Watch blew a long whistle blast and passed the word to shift colors. The jack and ensign were hauled down smartly and the *steaming* ensign was hoisted on the gaff and the ship's call sign was hoisted.

Now the ship was settled in typical gentle Caribbean swells, gently swaying and moving forward with its usual metallic sounds and vibrations as if nothing had happened.

Robert Mills peered down from the bridge over the damaged windscreen on to the forecastle area. Moving his gaze along the ruptured number two gun mount and the ragged edges of the gaping hole that was once the Card's prize number one gun mount. He was feeling her pain as his own. She was hurt, but not crippled. Poor girl, she doesn't deserve this. She was showing signs of wear and survival, like those who served on her. Every member of the *Card's* family, felt as if she was glad to leave all this behind and go home. He turned his attention aft to the ensign that fluttered from the gaff; she was still flaunting her colors. He recalled what he told the Coast guard Admiral just few months ago; "She was a fine old bucket in her day, and she needs go out in style, into a red sunset [*red sky at night a sailor's delight*] with her ensign flying, her crew standing in pride." Well, he thought, she made a good showing, and she may be relieved from service when we get home, but she is going home wearing the scars of battle, and carrying a victorious crew riding her home with pride.

The captain could not get the sight of the Cuban vessel out his mind. He played the memory again and again, the ragged pieces of steel the black smoke, the way it stood on end and slid quietly into the ocean. She was once a vital, living creature, a way of life for the sailors who manned her, now a place of permanent rest to those who slept in her damaged hull beneath the sea.

The scene on his own ship constantly invaded his mind, the sight of a lethal shell heading for his ship, hitting the forward gun mount and ripping apart two of his crew, not just any two, but a special two, who found a greater reason for their attachment to the *USS Card*. He witnessed another shipmate being killed and others suffering horrendous injuries.

Killed in action! It was a difficult thing to consider . . . three of your own. Smiddy was a good lad. Benson and Phelps was not just two seamen who were killed in a battle that should never have happened, they were Robbie and Brennie two young people who were just going through life, until they found each other on board this ship. It seemed like a waste. It was a sacrifice of three lives, and for what purpose? And yet, he thought, in times of defense against the forces of evil, no sacrifice is in vain. No matter how great or small. He recalled something he read: "It matters not when a man dies or where but that it is at a post of duty and honor."

His mind dwelled on his crew. This crew was different somehow, toughened, more confident perhaps, a feeling of camaraderie and oneness, now held together by their trade, their recent experiences, their loyalty to the ship and to each other. Time and distance, hours and days spent in every sort of condition had all left their mark on the crew. They had come a long way from where they were when the captain came on board just six months ago.

When this voyage is over he will be replaced by another commander, his job completed. He had received his orders in January, a six month temporary assignment to the *USS Card*. Beginning in February, he had six months to bring the *Card* up to combat readiness and join the squadron for combat readiness exercises in Guantanamo Bay Cuba in July.

He had worked on many temporary assignments as an organizational consultant with private industry and in his capacity as a reserve officer in the organizational development division of the Navy department. He knew going in this would be a different and more difficult assignment. He had never had command of a ship and while he assisted in helping sick organizations get well, he could walk away when the assignment was over. He could walk away from this one as well . . . but . . . this time it was different. This time it was personal.

He had talked about shipmates and organizational cohesiveness and he understood what that meant, but this time it was different, this time it was personal. This was not just another organization, not just another ship that needed his investigative prowess and his organizational development skills. Captain Sorenson realized this ship and this crew did not need a consultant, they did not need an executive, they did not need a manager, they did not need a leader. They needed a captain.

They needed someone who could invest himself into this operation, someone who could understand this was a living breathing organization in need of a steward and could be, not just the one in charge, but the one who is personally responsible, personally involved, the one in command. And involved he was. This was his ship. This was his crew, his shipmates, his problem, his family, his responsibility, his command.

Command is one thing, but responsibility, the duty to those who depend on you, is the greater burden. It is a burden that only a captain can bare, a burden that must be felt not just dealt with. A burden one must take personally.

The Captain made a tour of the ship. He began his trip in the engine room, then up to the next level, walking forward on one deck and aft on the other, looking into every compartment making eye contact with every sailor he saw, saying nothing just nodding with a smile of approval to each one. No one spoke but smiled and nodded in return.

His tour completed the captain informed the bridge he would be in his cabin. It was not going to be an easy task, and it was one he had not had to do before; write letters to the families of those warriors who had fallen in battle. Before writing the letters he thought it would be best to catch up the ship's log regarding the encounter with the pirates. Perhaps this would help him find the words to put in the letters. That done he was still unable to face the next of kin he turned his attention to the report to Cinclantfleet and ComResDesRon. He had been at it for over an hour when he heard the announcement over the 1-MC. "Captain Mills your presence is respectfully requested on the fantail."

The Bridge knew he was in his cabin, why announce it ship wide instead of using the intercom?

He leaned back in his chair, squeezed his eyes with his thumb and fore finger, gave a sigh. He stood up, placed his hat on his head and exited the cabin door, past radio central and through the door leading to a ladder that would take him to the main level. Once through the door he had a clear view of the 02 level. Behind the stack the ship's company and those sailors permanently assigned to the *Card* were peering down on the fantail.

He took the ladder to the main level and walked along the outer weather deck to the fantail. All the sailors who had come on board in Norfolk and Mayport were standing to quarters in dress whites. There was a pathway between the ranks. At the end of pathway standing with his back to the ensign was the ship's doctor. As captain Mills approached the doctor he saluted. Captain Mills returned the salute.

"What is this all about doctor?"

"Sir, the reserves that came on board in Norfolk and Mayport request permission to stay with the ship to the home port rather than to be put off where they came aboard. We want to be there when our shipmates that died in battle are delivered home. We realize, as reserves that are only here for a two week training cruise and are not considered part of the crew but in view of all we have faced together with the *Card*'s ship's company we feel kinship to this crew and the ship and to those who were killed in action."

"Doctor Johnson", he began. Then he paused and turned his attention to the reserves that had come aboard in Norfolk and Mayport. He took in their starched white uniforms, their looks of resolve. These sailors were serious. He turned to look at the *Card*'s reserve and regular ships company standing around on the 0-2 level.

"All you reserves that came aboard in Norfolk and Mayport. And you, the reserves and regulars of the *Card's* ships company. This goes for all of you. There is saying in the maritime service that is as old as Solomon. *You cannot be considered part of the ship's crew until you are part of the ship.* It is clear to me that every sailor here is a part of this ship, and the ship has become a part of you."

He paused as he gathered his thoughts. The only sound was the steady drone of the ship's engines and the bubbling of the sea in the wake of the screws that propelled the *Card* toward its journey home. The Captain cleared his throat and continued.

"The community that exists on board a maritime vessel is a close knit community. Shipmates are a community unto itself more than any you will find ashore. And it is doubly true on board a naval warship where lives depend on each other. It comes about when those on board respect certain customs, traditions, rules of conduct and responsibilities. That coupled with mutual trust among the crew . . . that comes when each person is committed to performing their duties for the good of the ship and their shipmates."

There was another pause as the captain took a deep breath then once again facing his crew he continued.

"The events of the past two weeks we have faced together. We are all shipmates."

He turned and faced the doctor. "Your request is granted doctor. You all have earned it."

A rousing cheer was raised by every sailor on board.

The Captain did an about face and walked briskly forward, up the ladder to the oh-two level and back to his cabin.

"That's our skipper, said one of the regular Navy sailors standing on the 0-2, He is a man, not just an officer."

He had stated aloud what every sailor was thinking. This captain would lead them anywhere. Look where we are with all odds against us. We were the *Carp*, the *Tuna*, the chicken of the sea. Now look what we have become. Captain Mills had us make plans then work those plans. Not just plans for dealing with the expected, or the war games, but he had us make plans for the unexpected.

We survived the storm of the century, a storm that sank a ship with regular navy crew.

We faced difficult fleet wide drills, and had qualified right along with regular navy ships. We had faced an actual enemy bent on our destruction. We engaged and prevailed. Command, leadership, authority they were not mere words. The person who carried them had to embody these traits, had to earn the right to employ them through a personal commitment, not just to the mission but to the people assigned to that mission.

The *Card* and its crew had not only faced the adversaries of opponents attacking them in a realistic battle scenario, and the unleashing of Mother Nature in one of the most horrendous storms in this century. They faced the unbelievable horror of facing a real enemy bent on your destruction. The Card had yet another onslaught to face.

Just off the coast of South Carolina a great storm surrounded them, with dark clouds, lightning and thunder, heavy rain like a giant fire hose with full force churning and thrashing the sea that threatened with a vengeance. The ship's crew watched this fearsome storm as it encircled the craft. What an awesome, frightening, yet wonderful and immaculate vision to behold. But where the ship sailed there was peace and calm, and a bright sun sent streams of light like a rainbow down on them. It was if the Eternal Master Himself was holding back the evil forces of fate. This deluge circled without touching them or disturbing the ship or the water in which it moved. Suddenly it ran off over the horizon and disappeared.

The Dark Before the Dawn

Monday, 03 August 1970
CBS News Room
New York, New York

0700: "This is Joe Franklin, CBS Morning News. The Cuban Ambassador to the United Nations has filed an official protest against the United States over, what they call an act of aggression against the Cuban government when on Friday the thirty first of July a US Navy destroyer attacked and sank a Russian made Cuban Navy Corvette in the Caribbean Sea 100 miles west of Dominica. "The Cubans are demanding reparations for the loss of their warship claiming they were attacked without provocation. They are also demanding the arrest of the Captain of the *USS Card* and handed over to face murder and piracy charges. The Cuban Ambassador claims he has film and audio evidence of the attack. The American ship came from the Navy Base at Guantanamo Bay, Cuba. We will continue to follow this story."

Tuesday, 04 August 1970
White House, Office of the President

1300: The President's secretary entered the oval office with a stack of files, each one displaying the seal of the Federal Bureau of Investigation. "Here are the files you requested Mister President."

"Thank you, Barbara."

"Sir, the Secretary of State is waiting outside."

"Send him in please."

The president remained sitting behind his desk. The Secretary of State stood near the desk for a few minutes, waiting for the President to invite him to be seated. His face and general posture clearly communicated his total disdain of the man at the desk and the fact that he was summoned to the office, no doubt to seek his help in getting out of this mess with the Cubans. And now the Russians are getting involved.

"Don't bother sitting down, Bill. This won't take long. I have here FBI files, and Navy CSI files. Did you know that Captain Mills had audio and film recordings of the entire event?"

The secretary's demeanor did not change. "Yes, Mister President, Bernard Riggins took them into custody. There was only one copy, and Mister Riggins has analyzed them."

"And he shared them with the Cuban Ambassador?"

"I understand he did, yes."

"Did you know the entire event was overheard on the radio by the Commanders of Reserve Destroyer 34, and Reserve Division 5, the Chief of the Atlantic Fleet and their immediate staff?"

The secretary began to show some anxiety, but said nothing.

"Bill you campaigned against the Navy Base in Gitmo. It was your feature point in the campaign. You accused the navy of violating the peace in the Caribbean and harassing the Cubans. Did you think this incident would embarrass me and convince the American people you were right and I was wrong? Don't bother to answer that. Here is a question you will answer."

The secretary shifted his weight and his expression became more defiant. He was not going to help the president out of this one. This incident will give him the leverage he needs for the next presidential race.

"Bill, did you know Bernard Riggins gave the Cubans an edited film and audio tape, showing only the *Card* sinking the Cuban ship and taking the crew?"

The secretary's demeanor changed. Fear overtook him. He had not counted on this. He knew Riggins had fudged documents before, in order to secure the results he wanted to favor his boss but he could not believe he would go this far.

"Ah, no Mister President. I had no idea."

"Did you know the Cuban ship was under the command of pirates?"

"That was not confirmed, Mister President."

"Perhaps you and your Mister Riggins counted on there being only one set of pictures and films. I have a copy of the un-edited version." The President pressed a button under his desk and three very large Secret Service agents entered the Oval Office.

"Bernard Riggins has been arrested. He will stand trial and I am sure he will spend a great deal of time in prison. His associate, Richard Mikulski, has turned state's evidence against Mister Riggins."

The secretary nervously glanced at the Secret Service Agents, then back to the President.

"I will be holding a press conference in two hours. At that time I will tell the citizens of the United States what really happened out there. I will tell them I have released, to all the news networks, the film and audio recordings of the incident. Malcolm Breckenridge (US Ambassador to UN) has handed over copies of the film, still pictures and the Captain's report to the Cuban and Russian Ambassadors.

"Mister President, I had no idea . . . I suppose you want my resignation."

"No Bill. At the news conference I will announce that I have fired you for your part in this mess."

"Mister President, surely a person in my position, should be allowed to resign with some dignity. I will simply say I want to spend more time with my family."

"A person of your position, who has done what you did, should be arrested and prosecuted. If I had undisputable proof you knew what Riggins was up to I would have you arrested. You have betrayed your President, you have betrayed your office, and even more egregious, you betrayed the citizens of the United States."

"Mister President, You . . . you can't be serious. I have given my life to public service. You can't let a superlative career end this way!"

We will not argue whether your career has been superlative or not. Or, whether you served the public or if the public served you. But, yes, your career will end this way and it will end now!"

"I had nothing to do with misleading the Cubans. It was Riggins. I sent him down there to gather information. He had no orders to fabricate a story that would embarrass the United States."

"Gentlemen, escort this man to his office. Stand by while he cleans out his desk. And make sure he leaves the building,"

Executive Assessment
When Sabotage Caused the Turbulence

If the turbulence was the fault of someone in the organization, whether it was done for personal gain or malevolence they need to be publically exposed and prosecuted. The public needs to be informed of the action they take in order to restore the public's faith and protect the integrity of its management and its future associations.

The perpetrator should not be allowed to resign. They must be fired, prosecuted and sued to recover any assets they stole or destroyed.

I worked with a manufacturing company in the late 1970's who chose this course of action with several of its management personnel. The company was finding it difficult to recruit good people. What management discovered was that the third shift had become a den of iniquity, with gambling, promiscuous sexual activities and drugs. To be sure, the president hired an undercover detective to work the shift and gather information as to what was going on and who was responsible. He discovered several hourly employees were orchestrating the activities, with the full knowledge of several supervisors and the shift superintendent, who also played no small part in the goings on. When sufficient evidence had been acquired, the company president authorized the police to enter the plant and arrest all those who were guilty. The raid was conducted under the watchful eye of one of the local television news camera crews.

The President issued a public statement, and the organization's reputation was once again restored.

- The higher the position, the greater the stewardship obligation.
- The higher the position, the greater the accountability.
- The higher the position the greater the faith others give.
- The higher the position the greater the damage when unfaithfulness is discovered.

After Action learning -2

- There are always restless seas in one's life. Everyone will encounter stormy seas. Some are more frightening than others. In troubled times, in one's professional and personal life, security is being effected by evil outside forces of heathen competition or decisions of government. Under any turbulent circumstances the one in command must stand resolute in the face of adversity and in the presence of those who report and take charge. This is no time to abandon ship.

Chapter 21 They sailed out with shame they returned with fame

Wednesday 05 August
Off the Coast of Virginia

1300 As a result of a radio message from NavBase in Norfolk the captain ordered all personnel except the below decks crew to shift into dress whites and be prepared to stand to quarters as the *Card* passed in the waters off the coast of Virginia near the Norfolk naval Ship Yard.

The quartermaster on the bridge sounded the word for all hands not actually on watch and those that could be spared to stand to quarters around the weather decks port and starboard, fore and aft to receive honors.

1500 A destroyer that was patrolling off the coast of Virginia anchored at a spot that intersected with the *Card's* trajectory and waited for it to pass by.

As the *Card* neared the position a submarine surfaced and waited in stand-by as both vessels assembled an honor guard on the main deck. The *383* passed between them at ten knots. As the *Card* came abreast of the honor guard those standing to quarters presented a right hand salute as the quartermaster dipped the ensign. The crew of the *Card* did not return the hand salute, but the ensign was dipped in response. Each ship also sounded their horn in passing. A fitful show of respect for a ship and crew that had endured so much, a strange event to be sure for an organization who just six months earlier was the laughing stock of warships everywhere.

1600 The captain appeared on the bridge. He looked alert, clean shaven and dressed in fresh starched whites. His cap tilted back slightly on his head, the officer's crest was polished to bright sheen. There was no trace of the agony he must be enduring. He placed his hands on the railing. He wanted to feel the vibration of the engines in his hands.

1800 Lieutenant Winthrop walked across the tilting deck and rested his hands against the rail, feeling the ship moving beneath him like a living creature. His thoughts were visiting the recent past. The time before Captain Mills came on board.

1813 Lieutenant Commander McCormick passed though the hatch that lead from officer country to the 01 weather deck. He clasped his hands behind him and slowly walked along the rough non skid coating on the steel deck letting the sun and wind play with his shirt and hat. He glanced up to the 0-2 level where Mister Winthrop was looking down.

The far-away look in Mister Winthrop's eyes gave evidence he was oblivious to the officer below. Mister McCormick climbed the ladder and joined the navigator.

Several seconds went by before Mister Winthrop realized he had company. "Oh sorry Mike, I was adrift there for a minute. I was thinking about the day the captain plastered the ship's motto on the bulkhead of the mess decks and in the wardroom. Who would have thought at that time we would be standing here, now having not only made it to Gitmo, and qualified, but defeated the *Amberjack,* sank the *Red Fin*, and engaged in enemy combat and prevailed?"

They both were unaware of the pitch of the ship with its forward and aft, up and down rocking motion spraying white foam from forward wedge of the stem.

"We were caught in a mindset that had trapped us," Mister McCormick added. Then along came Commander Mills. He had a manner that at first seemed easy going, even casual. It took us a while as we all doubted his ability. We mistook his easy going manner as weakness. But one thing we could not dismiss was his tenacity, his fogbank forcefulness. He set in motion mechanisms that made us take actions that exposed not only our mental set but our competence."

Staring off into the distance, as if looking into the past, Mister Winthrop continued. "I have had plenty of time to think about the events that occurred over the past six months, Mike, and I have learned more in these six months about management and executive leadership than the entire time I was in the academy.

You know the most difficult aspect of his style in turning this ship around was to turn us around.

But unlike the other skippers he is not one of those guys who leads by example. He made in possible for us to be our own example. He did not make us do it his way, he made us do it our way, but he made us do it. He set a clear course. He gave us a chart and rules for performance."

Mister McCormick interrupted; "He not only gave us a plan he implemented the reporting procedures that not only established accountability but allowed us to see our progress, and gave us evidence of our accomplishments."

"And his relentless pressure for performance reporting, continued Winthrop, it required us to come to terms with what we had to do. He made it possible for us to do things, but do them our way, not his way. He realized the problem we were experiencing was not incompetence."

"I agree John, The problem was not that we were incapable of using our own management and leadership skills to bring the ship on station, it was our mind set. He made us do it our way. Every member of this crew, officer and enlisted, brought us to this point It was our way that brought us to this point.

Pounding, and bounding over the main steadily due north her wake churning up a white and cream colored astern. Every hour put the past few days behind them, every turn of the screws carried them nearer to home. They felt a closer kindred to the ship than they had ever felt before. They felt her pain. She was showing signs of a difficult few days, there were visible signs of wear and survival, like those who served on her. Every member of the *Card's* family, felt as if she was glad to leave all this behind and go home.

**Thursday, 06 August 1970
Early Morning
USS Card
Entering the Chesapeake Bay**

As the *USS Card* entered the Chesapeake Bay all hands realized this was not the same ship and crew that began this journey when Robert Mills took command. They were all different now.

0800: The *Card* and her crew were nearing the channel that led them into Curtis Bay and home. Mister Winthrop studied his charts and provided Lieutenant Grubaugh with the coordinates she would need to guide them in. He felt a cause of satisfaction for the *Card's* performance, and a sense of pride he once thought he would never experience aboard this ship. The sun beat down on the little vessel, the sky was clear and pale blue as the ship glided softly on the gentle current.

Every sailor who could be spared was topside to see the pier that had been their home port for so long. They would have a clear view of it when they rounded the bend. A rousing cheer went up from every soul when the pier came in sight. There was a shudder from the ship itself as if she too were cheering with her crew. The cheering grew louder when they realized what awaited them at the spot they were to moor.

"Bridge, Engine Room. This is Mister Faulk. What is going on up there?"

Mister Winthrop keyed the toggle to the Engine Room and simultaneously the ship-wide intercom. "This is Mister Winthrop. There is a crowd of people standing on the pier. They stretch from the pier into the parking lot. They are holding banners, and cheering! All personnel who are not absolutely essential to the docking of this ship are permitted on deck." Realizing he had not received permission from the Captain, he turned to see if approval would be granted retroactively from the *Old Man*. A smile, nod of the head and wink provided the answer.

To those who served recently on other ships, this would not normally be a big deal. There was usually a reception committee waiting for ships of the line to return home. But this was not the gallant ship of the line the others were. This was a reserve ship stationed at a Coast Guard Base. This was the *Card*. This was not normal. But then again, nothing that happened to the *Card* in the past eight months was normal for this much maligned little can.

As the ship moved in closer one could recognize their family members smiling and holding banners that displayed; *Way to go Card, Our heroes of the USS Card, Welcome Home USS Card*. And another large banner that said: *Seek, Strike, Prevail*.

There were banners heralding the Heroism of the dead and wounded. Many banners displayed the names of those who suffered death and injuries.

There was Candy Gilliam and the boys standing with Mrs. Sharon Alexander to be. There was Rex Sterling all smiles standing head and shoulders above everyone else. There were the wives and children and mothers and fathers of the other sailors. There were news vans and reporters from the newspapers, radio and television. There were Mister and Mrs. Benson. There were two flag draped hearses. There were two ambulances. There were the Smidlaps accompanied by Uncle Billy Ledbetter. They would not need the hearse designated for Orville. Uncle Billie insisted he take his nephew home in his truck.

There were high ranking naval officers standing near the line handlers. The Naval Academy had sent their choir and the Academy Band. All around people were embracing each other, kissing, laughing and shouting.

Many of the crew remembered Mister Gilliam's prophetic words uttered during the drill weekend in March; *"I am proud to have the opportunity to serve on the Card. Can I be proud to serve with her crew? I can tell you ladies and gentlemen, I will give this ole girl my best efforts in an attempt to give her a proud reputation. If you will do the same, we may go to Gitmo in disgrace, but we will return in Glory."*

Command Axiom:

- It is in turbulent times when personal integrity and commitment to vows of loyalty are tested. It is through turbulent times that relationships are cemented or destroyed, whether in life, in marriage or in organizational experience.

- Let us not be weary in well doing; for in due season we shall reap if we faint not." (Galatians 6:9)

The Captain

'Only a seaman realizes to what great extent an entire ship reflects the personality and ability of one individual, her Commanding Officer. To a landsman this is not understandable and sometimes it is even difficult for us to understand. But it is so!

A ship at sea is a distinct world in herself and in consideration of the protracted and distant operations of fleet units the Navy must place great power, responsibility and trust in the hands of those leaders chosen for command.

In each ship there is one man who, in the hour of emergency or peril at sea, can turn to no other man. There is one who ultimately is responsible for the safe navigation, engineering performance, accurate gunfire, and morale of his ship. He is the Commanding Officer. He is the ship.

This is the most difficult and demanding assignment in the Navy. There is not an instant during his tour as Commanding Officer that he can escape the grasp of command responsibility. His privileges in view of his obligations are almost ludicrously small; nevertheless Command is the spur that has given the Navy its great leaders.

It is a duty that most richly deserves the highest, time-honored title of the seafaring world ... CAPTAIN.'

Joseph Conrad

Glossary of Naval Terms

Aft	Near the stern
After	That which is furtherest aft
Admiral two stars	Naval officer rank O-8 equal to Major General in Army
Admiral three stars	Naval officer rank O-9 equal to Lieutenant General in Army
All Hands	All ship's company no exceptions
Astern	Directly behind the ship
Aweigh	Anchor is clear of the bottom and the ship is underway
Aye, Aye	Reply to a command or order, to acknowledge understanding of the meaning
AWOL Bag	Overnight bag sailors take with them on liberty
Belay	Disregard, discontinue, or stop current action
Between the Devil and the Deep	In wooden ships, the "devil" was the longest seam in the hull of the ship. It ran from the bow to the stern. When at sea and the "devil" had to be caulked, the sailor sat in a bo'sun's chair to do so. He was suspended between the "devil" and the sea — the "deep" — a very precarious position, especially when the ship was underway.
Boatswain (boat – son)	Officer, usually a warrant officer in charge of the deck.
Boatswain's mate	Enlisted person responsible for various duties pertaining to the deck
Bridge	Area of the superstructure from which the ship is operated (Conn)
Bulkhead	Vertical partition in a ship (wall but never called a wall)
BuPers	Bureau of Personnel. Naval Human Resources and assignments
BuShips	Bureau of Ships
Cabin	Living compartment for the ship's commanding officer

Captain	The chief executive officer plenipotentiary on board a sea going vessel. Also Naval officer Rank O-6 equal to Colonel in the Army
Carry on	Order to resume previous activity after interruption
Chain of Command	The succession from superior to subordinate through which command is exercised.
Chart	Nautical counterpart of a road map, showing land configurations, water depths and aids to navigation
Colors	The national ensign; the ceremony of raising and lowering the ensign
ComDesDiv	Commander Destroyer Division
ComDesRon	Commander Destroyer Squadron
Commander	Naval officer rank O-5 equal to Lt. Colonel in Army
Companionway	Opening in the deck giving access to a ladder for going up or down
ComResDesDiv	Commander Reserve Destroyer Division
ComResDesRon	Commander Reserve Destroyer Squadron
Conn	In charge of or controlling the ships seagoing operations while underway
Course	The ship's desired direction of travel, not to be confused with heading
Coxswain	(kock-son) Enlisted person in charge of a boat usually acts as a helmsman.
Crow's Nest	The raven, or crow, was an essential part of the Vikings' navigation equipment. These land-lubbing birds were carried on aboard to help the ship's navigator determine where the closest land lay when weather prevented sighting the shore. In cases of poor visibility, a crow was released and the navigator plotted a course corresponding to the bird's flight path because the crow invariably headed towards land. The Norsemen carried the birds in a cage secured to the top of the mast. Later on, as ships grew and the lookout stood his watch in a tub located high on the main mast, the name "crow's nest" was given to this tub. While today's Navy still uses lookouts in addition to radars, etc., the crow's nest is a thing of the past.
Dead ahead	Directly ahead; relative bearing of 000 degrees

Dead astern	Directly behind the ship 180 degrees relative
Dead in the water	Complete loss of all power resulting in no propulsion and no steering. Adrift, vulnerable to the elements and the sea.
Deck	Horizontal planking or plating that divides a ship into layers (floors - but never called floors)
DD	Destroyer – Ships before 1970 were small ships with two stacks
DE	Destroyer Escort – Small ships with one stack usually 310-306 feet long anti-submarine warfare responsibilities.
DER	Destroyer Escort with sophisticated radar systems mounted on the mast for ASW & AA defense.
Dock	Space alongside a pier where ships are tied
Dogwatch	A dogwatch at sea is the period between 4 and 6 p.m., the first dogwatch, or the period between 6 and 8 p.m., the second dogwatch. The dogwatches are only two hours each so the same Sailors aren't always on duty at the same time each afternoon. Some experts say dogwatch is a corruption of dodge watch and others associate dogwatch with the fitful sleep of Sailors called dog sleep, because it is a stressful watch. But no one really knows the origin of this term, which was in use at least back to the 1700s.
Eight Bells	Aboard Navy ships, bells are struck to designate the hours of being on watch. Each watch is four hours in length. One bell is struck after the first half-hour has passed, two bells after one hour has passed, three bells after an hour and a half, four bells after two hours, and so forth up to eight bells are struck at the completion of the four hours. Completing a watch with no incidents to report was "Eight bells and all is well." The practice of using bells stems from the days of the sailing ships. Sailors couldn't afford to have their own time pieces and relied on the ship's bells to tell time. The ship's boy kept time by using a half-hour glass. Each time the sand ran out, he would turn the glass over and ring the appropriate number of bells.
Eight O'clock reports	Reports received by the executive officer from departmental heads shortly before 2000 (twenty hundred 8 PM).
Ensign	The national flag or the lower grade of a naval commissioned officer equal to a second lieutenant in the Army.
Executive Officer	Second officer in Command. Chief Operating Officer.
Fantail	The after end of the main deck
Fathom	Unit of depth equal to 6 feet.

Flank Speed	Top Speed.
Fleet	An organization of ships, aircraft, marine forces, and shore-based fleet activities, all under one commander, for conducting major operations.
Fore and Aft	The entire length of the ship.
Forecastle – (fok-sul)	Forward section of the main deck, generally extending from the stem aft to just about the anchor windlass.
Galley	Space where food is prepared (kitchen, but not called kitchen).
GQ	General Quarters – A condition of full readiness for battle.
GQ alarm	An alarm that sends all hands to their designated battle stations.
Heading	The direction toward which the ship's bow is pointing at any instant.
Heave to	To stop or reduce headway just enough to maintain steerageway.
Helm	Mechanical device used to turn the rudder (usually a wheel aboard ship, a lever in boats).
Helmsman	A person who steers the ship by turning her helm (also called steersman).
Knot	Nautical miles per hour. Knot = 6,076.10 ft. per hour or 1.5 miles per hour.
Ladder	Shipboard flight of stairs.
Lee	An area sheltered from the wind, downwind, the side of the ship not receiving sea or wind
Lieutenant	Officer Rank O-3 equal to Captain in Army.
Lieutenant Commander	Naval Officer Rank O-4 equal to Major in the Army.
Lieutenant Junior Grade	Officer Rank 0-2 Equal to a First lieutenant in the Army.
Log	A complete daily record, by watches in which is described every circumstance or occurrence of importance or interest hour by hour

Main Deck	The upper most complete deck.
Mate	Another sailor.
Mustang	An officer promoted from enlisted ranks and received a commission
NavBase	Naval Base. The actual command that houses several operational departments and naval stations.
NavSta	Naval Station.
NROTC	Naval Reserve Officer Training Command - a college program that trains college students to be officers in the Navy. They receive a commission at graduation.
Overhead	Underside of a deck which forms the overhead of a compartment (ceiling but never called a ceiling).
Passageway	A corridor used for interior horizontal movement aboard ship.
Petty Officer	Non Commissioned Officer E-4 to E-9 equal to Corporal to sergeant status in the army.
Pier	Structure extending from land into the water to provide a mooring for vessels
Pipe	To sound a particular call on a boatswain's pipe.
Plan of the Day	Schedule of a day's routine and events ordered by the executive officer and published daily aboard ship or at a shore activity.
Port	To the left of the centerline of the ship when facing forward.
Quarterdeck	Deck designated by the commanding officer as the place to carry out official functions; station of the officer of the deck while the ship is in port.
Quartermaster	Naval rating charged with navigation-related duties.
Running lights	Navigational lights shown at night by a vessel under way.
Sea Anchor	A device for holding it end-on to the sea.
Seamanship	Skill in the use of deck equipment, in boat handling.

Secure	To make "fast" to stop or cease from an activity, to make an area off limits for general use
Shake down	A rigorous series of events designed to train crew for some activity and/or to discover problems with the ship in order make corrections.
Ship's Company	All hands permanently assigned to a ship or station.
Sound	To determine the depth of water.
Sound Powered Phones	Phone system powered by voice of user.
Special Sea and Anchor Detail	Crew assigned special duties when leaving or entering port.
Squadron	Two or more divisions of ships or aircraft.
Square	To make things right, to ensure a proper relationship.
Square away	To make shipshape, to put in proper order.
Stack	Shipboard chimney.
Stanchion	Vertical posts for supporting decks, smaller, similar posts for supporting lifelines or awnings.
Starboard	Direction to the right of the centerline as one faces forward.
State Room	A living compartment for an officer or officers.
Stem	Extreme forward line of the bow.
Stern	The aftermost part of the vessel.
Superstructure	The structure above a ship's main deck
Swab	Mop (slang for enlisted sailor).
Wardroom	Officers messing and meeting compartment.
Watch	One of the periods, usually 4 hours, into which a day is divided.

Weather deck	Any deck exposed to the elements (weather).
Windward	In the direction of the wind – The side of the ship being hit by wind, weather, and sea.
X-Ray	Damage control material condition – Personnel remain at general Quarters until condition is secured.
Zebra	Damage Control material condition (a grave battle condition).

A US Navy ship in commission, including ready reserves can never be left unattended. At minimum of one-third of the assigned crew must be on board at all times. The auxiliary equipment must be *fired* up at all times, especially the electricity and water supplies. Of course it is axiomatic that all vital equipment on board must be under guard. Shipboard routine, whether in port or at sea, is a 24 hour seven days a week operation. Work duties are divided into watches of four hours at a time, except the dog watches which are two hours.

000-0400	Mid Watch
0400-0800	Morning Watch
0800-1200	Forenoon Watch
1200-1600	Afternoon Watch
1600-1800	First Dog Watch (two hours)
1800-2000	Second Dog Watch (two Hours)
2000-2359	First Watch

Ships Bells are struck from reveille to taps except during divine services, or when the ship is darkened, for security reasons or when the fog signal is being sounded. The bell informs watch standers the time of watch.

Hours of watch		Bells	Rings (Strikes)
0030	First half-hour bell	One	*
0100	First hour	Two	**
0130	First hour and half	Three	** *
0200	Second hour	Four	** **
0230	Second hour and half	Five	** ** *
0300	Third hour	Six	** ** **
0330	Third hour and half	Seven	** ** ** *
0400	Fourth hour	Eight	** ** ** **

Psalms 107: 123-128

They that go down to the sea in ships, that do business in great waters;

These see the works of the Lord, and his wonders in the deep.
For He commands, and raises the stormy wind, which lifted up the waves.

They mount up to the heaven, they go down again to the depths; their soul is melted because of trouble.

They reel to and fro, and stagger like a drunken man, at their wit's end.

Then they cry unto the Lord in their trouble, and he brings them out of their distresses.

The Navy Hymn

Eternal Father, strong to save, whose arm hath bound the restless wave, Who bids the mighty ocean deep Its own appointed limits keep;

Oh, hear us when we cry to Thee, for those in peril on the sea!

O Christ! Whose voice the waters heard and hushed their raging at Thy word, who walked on the foaming deep, And calm amidst its rage didst sleep;

Oh, hear us when we cry to Thee, for those in peril on the sea!

Most Holy Spirit! Who didst brood upon the chaos dark and rude and bid its angry tumult cease, and give, for wild confusion, peace;

Oh, hear us when we cry to Thee, for those in peril on the sea!

O Master of love and power! Our brethren shield in danger's hour; From rock and tempest, fire and foe, protect them wheresoe'er they go;

Thus evermore shall rise to Thee Glad hymns of praise from land and sea.

Anchors Aweigh
(1906 version) Taken from the Naval History & Heritage Command website

Stand Navy out to sea, Fight our Battle Cry; We'll never change our course, So vicious foe steer shy-y-y-y.
Roll out the TNT, Anchors Aweigh.
Sail on to Victory
And sink their bones to Davy Jones, Hooray!
Anchors Away, my boys, Anchors Aweigh.
Farewell to foreign shores, We sail at break of day-ay-ay-ay. Through our last night on shore, Drink to the foam,
Until we meet once more. Here's wishing you a happy voyage home.
Blue of the Mighty Deep; Gold of God's Sun
Let these colors be till all of time be done, done, done,
On seven seas we learn Navy's stern call:
Faith, Courage, Service true, with Honor, Over Honor, Over All.

Naval Academy Version
Stand, Navy, out to sea, Fight our battle cry;
We'll never change our course, So vicious foe steer shy-y-y-y;
Roll out the TNT, Anchors Aweigh;
Sail on to victory, and sink their bones to Davy Jones, hooray!
Anchors Aweigh, my boys, Anchors Aweigh!
Farewell to college joys, we sail at break of day-ay-ay-ay;
Through our last night on shore, drink to the foam,
Until we meet once more, here's wishing you a happy voyage home!
Stand Navy down the field; Sails set to the sky;
We'll never change our course, So Army you steer shy-y-y-y;
Roll up the score, Navy, Anchors Aweigh;
Sail Navy down the field, And sink the Army, sink the Army Grey!
Get underway, Navy, Decks cleared for the fray;
We'll hoist true Navy Blue ,So Army down your Grey-y-y-y;
Full speed ahead, Navy; Army heave to;
Furl Black and Grey and Gold, And hoist the Navy, hoist the Navy Blue!
Blue of the Seven Seas, Gold of God's great sun;
Let these our colors be Till, All of time be done-n-n-ne;
By Severn shore we learn, Navy's stern call:
Faith, courage, service true, With honor over, honor over all!

"**Anchors Aweigh**" is the fight song of the United States Naval Academy, and as a result, the song is strongly associated with the United States Navy. It was composed in 1906 by Charles A. Zimmerman with lyrics by Alfred Hart Miles

If you enjoyed this book, you will like the first book in the Stewardship of Management Series:

THE STEWARDSHIP OF EXECUTIVE MANAGEMENT: FOR THE MANAGER WHO MANAGES MANAGERS

ISBN 1-4196-9577-0   ISBN 9781419695773

This book is the beginning of the story of the USS Card.

Both books have been combined into a novel. Look for:

USS CARD

ISBN 13:978-1466314429 and ISBN 10: 1466314427

Made in the USA
Columbia, SC
27 March 2020